CONTEMPORARY ANTHROPOLOGY OF RELIGION

*A series published with the Society for the
Anthropology of Religion*

Laurel Kendall, Series Editor
Curator, Division of Anthropology, America Museum
of Natural History

Published by Palgrave Macmillan:

Body/Meaning/Healing
By Thomas J. Csordas

*The Weight of the Past: Living with History in Mahajanga,
Madagascar*
By Michael Lambek

*After the Rescue: Jewish Identity and Community in
Contemporary Denmark*
By Andrew Buckser

Empowering the Past, Confronting the Future
By Andrew Strathern and Pamela J. Stewart

Islam Obscured: The Rhetoric of Anthropological Representation
By Daniel Martin Varisco

*Islam, Memory, and Morality in Yemen: Ruling
Families in Transition*
By Gabrielle Vom Bruck

*A Peaceful Jihad: Negotiating Identity and Modernity
in Muslim Java*
By Ronald Lukens-Bull

The Road to Clarity: Seventh-Day Adventism in Madagascar
By Eva Keller

Yoruba in Diaspora: An African Church in London
By Hermione Harris

*Islamic Narrative and Authority in Southeast Asia: From the
16th to the 21st Century*
By Thomas Gibson

Evangelicalism and Conflict in Northern Ireland
By Gladys Ganiel

*Christianity in the Local Context: Southern Baptists
in the Philippines*
By Brian M. Howell

The Christianity of Culture

Conversion, Ethnic Citizenship, and the Matter of Religion in Malaysian Borneo

Liana Chua

palgrave
macmillan

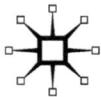

Parts of Chapter 4 were previously published in "Fixity and Flux: Bidayuh (Dis)engagements with the Malaysian Ethnic System." *Ethnos* 72 (2): 262–288. Reprinted by permission of the publisher (Taylor & Francis Ltd, http://www.tandf.co.uk/journals).

First published in 2012 by
PALGRAVE MACMILLAN®
in the United States—a division of St. Martin's Press LLC,
175 Fifth Avenue, New York, NY 10010.

Where this book is distributed in the UK, Europe and the rest of the world, this is by Palgrave Macmillan, a division of Macmillan Publishers Limited, registered in England, company number 785998, of Houndmills, Basingstoke, Hampshire RG21 6XS.

Palgrave Macmillan is the global academic imprint of the above companies and has companies and representatives throughout the world.

Palgrave® and Macmillan® are registered trademarks in the United States, the United Kingdom, Europe and other countries.

ISBN: 978–0–230–12046–4

Library of Congress Cataloging-in-Publication Data

Chua, Liana.
    The Christianity of culture : conversion, ethnic citizenship, and the matter of religion in Malaysian Borneo / Liana Chua.
        p. cm.
    ISBN 978–0–230–12046–4 (alk. paper)
        1. Dayak (Indonesian people)—Borneo—Religion. 2. Dayak (Indonesian people)—Borneo—Rites and ceremonies. 3. Dayak (Indonesian people)—Borneo—Ethnic relations. 4. Anthropology of religion—Borneo. 5. Christianity and culture—Borneo. 6. Borneo—Religious life and customs. 7. Borneo—Ethnic relations. 8. Borneo—Politics and government. I. Title.

DS597.367.D93C56 2011
275.95'40089992256—dc23   2011025385

A catalogue record of the book is available from the British Library.

Design by Newgen Imaging Systems (P) Ltd., Chennai, India.

First edition: January 2012

10 9 8 7 6 5 4 3 2 1

Printed in the United States of America.

For Geoff Moggridge and Juliana Lim

Contents

Illustrations

Figures

Map

Acknowledgments

Rather like the histories of conversion described herein, this book has followed an erratic but rewarding trajectory over the last few years. I am grateful to Laurel Kendall for helping to kick-start that process and for her persistence and encouragement as I groped my way through it. A four-year Research Fellowship at Gonville and Caius College, Cambridge, provided the time, freedom, and resources to bring the project to fruition, and I owe a huge debt of gratitude to the Master, Fellows, and staff for giving me this almost decadently supportive start to my academic career.

Some of this book started out as part of my doctoral dissertation, which I completed on a William Wyse Studentship at the Department of Social Anthropology, University of Cambridge, in 2007. Big thanks are due here to Amiria Salmond, my supervisor, and to my examiners, Marilyn Strathern and Janet Carsten, who also provided valuable suggestions for taking things forward. Over the years I've also benefited from exchanges—both lengthy and brief—with Poline Bala, Julius Bautista, Susan Bayly, Ludek Broz, Jacob Copeman, Greg Delaplace, Kelvin Egay, Joseph Goh, Dave Henkel, Hew Cheng Sim, Casey High, Holly High, Mette High, Martin Holbraad, Leo Howe, Richard Irvine, James Laidlaw, Jayl Langub, Monica Janowski, Chris Kaplonski, Webb Keane, Martin Laverty, David Leitner, Jon Mair, John Postill, Susanna Rostas, Katharina Schneider, Sara Shneiderman, Mark Turin, Soumhya Venkatesan, Sunny Sanderson, Peter Varney, Piers Vitebsky, Lee Wilson, and many others.

For early guidance on Bidayuh matters, I am grateful to Fiona Harris, Robert Winzeler, and Pamela Lindell, whose writings provide important contextual and comparative information in the ethnography that follows. I am also indebted to the participants of several academic fora at which I aired various bits of the book: these include research seminars and/or conferences at Cambridge, University College London, the University of Aberdeen, Goldsmiths College, the Sainsbury Research Unit (University of East Anglia), the Forum on Religion (LSE), Universiti Malaysia Sarawak, the Asia Research Institute in Singapore, and the Institute of Social Sciences, University of Lisbon. Finally, two anonymous readers provided thoughtful, critical, and detailed comments on an earlier draft on this monograph, all of which were instrumental in improving the final product.

Much of the fieldwork on which this book is based took place during my doctoral fieldwork (2004–2005), and has since been supplemented by once- or twice-yearly stints between 2006 and 2010. These trips were funded by the William Wyse Fund, the Evans Fund, the Smuts Memorial Fund, and Bartle-Frere Memorial Fund at the University of Cambridge, a RAI/Sutasoma Award from the Royal Anthropological Institute, and later, a postdoctoral British Academy Small Grant (which covered a different but relevant fieldwork project). Prefieldwork and writing-up support was also provided by Fitzwilliam College and the Ling Roth Fund in Cambridge. Finally, the Cambridge University Museum of Archaeology and Anthropology awarded me a Crowther-Beynon grant to amass a new Bidayuh collection, which much abetted my research. My fieldwork in Sarawak was carried out with the permission of the Sarawak State Planning Unit, and supported by the Majlis Adat Istiadat and Sarawak Museum. I am grateful to Sanib Said, who was then Director of the Sarawak Museum, and to Jonas Noeb of the Majlis Adat Istiadat for village jaunts in his jeep, stimulating conversations, and part-time *babai* duties. The Institute of East Asian Studies and later, the Faculty of Social Sciences at Universiti Malaysia Sarawak (UNIMAS) served as vital academic bases during my time in the field, and I've greatly appreciated their support and intellectual stimulation.

My greatest debts, however, are to the people with whom I have lived and worked in Sarawak—and above all to the inhabitants of Kampung Benuk, who welcomed me into their lives with such generosity and good humor. My adoptive parents, Midah anak Jub and Nipi Ahlian anak Segar, took a bit of a gamble in letting a foreign (and, as it turned out, quite inept) young woman into their home, and I must register my deep gratitude to them, their children, and their many relatives for being so impossibly good to me since 2004. My first village contact was the late Paka anak Otor, whose idiosyncratic mini-museum—a feat of personal dedication—drew me to Benuk in the first place. Although our acquaintance was sadly cut short by his death, his family—especially his wife, Sumuk Meroi (Sajir anak Sepen)—has continued to be a vital source of knowledge, friendship, and support.

During my time in Benuk, I worked with two village heads, the formidable (late) Nija anak Radak Majud and his successor Bundu anak Suwap, as well as the Penghulu, the late Henry Jehom, and various members of the village committee (JKKK). For a multitude of reasons, the following people also deserve particular thanks: Bai Toyan, Sumuk Nyangǔ, and the remaining *nyamba gawai*; James Sakas, Denis Sembus, and the leaders and members of all three village churches; Sumuk Renon, Sama Rhating, Ndǔ Rhating, Sama Jererd, Ndǔ Jererd, Sama Steven, the late Ndǔ Steven, and their families at Sumur; the late Sumuk Mieh and family; Jinun anak Wisen for basket-collecting and *arak*-drinking; Albert Tajomiva and Lloyd Huffman for their help with research and translation; Carlos and Bai Boi for teaching me Bidayuh in their own unique ways; Sumuk Pang and Bai Arit for jungle trips, WWF videos, and *tandak*; the late Bai Gaut for lessons in the old ways; John Gotot; Gian, Tori, and their family; Cathy; Ndǔ Jem; Porin Bohoi and family; Sumuk Chichi (Puan Zaiton); Diyong Siye and his wife; Tabut Siyor; Isabel Julau anak Mejat, and many, many others whose names must be omitted on account of space. *Begǔ terima kasih yǔn sopǔrǔg; aku raru jebǔng di bara angan!*

Beyond Benuk lies a network of people whose help, support, and friendship made my fieldwork almost unduly enjoyable. Vincent Eddy, Jessie, and their family were the first Bidayuhs I met (through Cecilia Shin), and they were unstintingly generous in helping me settle into Sarawak and always providing a haven of food and conviviality. In 2007, I began working in four other Bidayuh villages—Taba Sait, Pain Bojong, Semban Teleg, and Rejoi—on a different project. These experiences nevertheless provided many further insights into conversion, Christianity, and other facets of Bidayuh life, and I especially thank Simo anak Sekam and family, Pauh and his wife, Bai Evelyn and Sumuk Evelyn, Josephine and family, Jahil and family, and Tone and family. In Kuching, I've found ready company and support with Poline Bala, Esther Bala and all their family, Simson Pitu, Narong Daun, Donald and Marina Tan, Ramsay Ong, Bibiana Foong, Nelson Tan, Aloysius Lau, Johannes Ridu, Jacob and Garnette Ridu, Eric and Annie at the Fairview, and Fedrick John anak George. I am also grateful for the support and insights provided by various priests, notably Fathers James Meehan, Joseph Lee, Arul Sagayaraj Mariadass, and the other friars at St Ann's.

Finally, for keeping me from succumbing to "Permanent head Damage" (as friends in UNIMAS so charmingly put it) in the course of research and writing, I am grateful to Geoff Moggridge and our respective families. My thanks to all of them for their unflinching support, their slightly perplexed interest in my work, and always being there while heroically managing not to question the wisdom of what I've been doing.

A Note on Orthography

The inhabitants of Kampung Benuk speak a variation of Biatah, one of four broad Bidayuhic dialects officially recognized in Sarawak—although they often describe themselves as simply "speaking Benuk." Since the late-nineteenth century, Bidayuh languages have been romanized in various ways, notably through the long-standing vernacularization projects of the Anglican and Catholic churches. In the 2000s, the Summer Institute of Linguistics (now SIL International) established the Bidayuh Language Development Project that sought to record and revitalize the different dialects, to lay the groundwork for their use in educational resources, and to create a unified Bidayuh orthography (see Rensch et al. 2006: 23–27). While this project—which is now supported by UNESCO and various Bidayuh organizations—has made important strides in this direction, the new orthography has not been widely adopted by rural villagers, many of whom draw on a combination of Christian material and a healthy degree of improvisation (some of which is taking place through new platforms, such as Facebook!) when writing their language.

In view of this, I have opted—for the moment, at least—to largely align my spelling with that of William Nais' 1983 *Bidayuh-English Dictionary* (1988). While not without flaws, it remains the most comprehensive Biatah resource to date and best reflects the orthographic system with which many literate Bidayuhs in my fieldsite will currently be familiar. As the new orthography gains ground through educational material and other efforts, however, this may well change. Consequently, my decision here is more a pragmatic one than a concerted attempt to prescribe a "correct" orthographic approach to Bidayuh.

Introduction

[A]n anthropologist is someone who uses the word "culture" with hope—or even with faith. Wagner (1981: 2)

It was early October 2004—barely a month after I had started fieldwork in Kampung Benuk—and any faith I had had in "culture" was rapidly disintegrating. My most important informant, Paka anak Otor, had died quite suddenly, and I was now committed to attending the nightly Catholic prayer sessions that would take place at his home over the next week. These were inevitably raucous, overcrowded, and bizarrely jolly affairs, involving massive communal meals, all-night drinking and gambling sessions, and endless socializing, all thickly pervaded by the smell of incense. At times, it felt as if the entire village had crammed into a single wooden house, which in retrospect made death the perfect occasion on which to begin my new life in the village. At the time, however, I felt only sickly bewilderment as I tried in vain to keep up with the rapid-fire conversations around me, and croaked vague platitudes in Malay, the Bornean lingua franca I had recently learned.

I had arrived in Sarawak with the intention of studying Bidayuh cultural identity, and with the precise aim of working with Paka, owner and custodian of a private "mini-museum" in which he displayed old ritual objects and other antiques.[1] Unlike the anthropologist of Wagner's imagination, my interest was not a holistic "culture of the Bidayuh" but how Bidayuhs themselves construed and constructed the concept of "culture" through sites such as Paka's museum. In that respect, "culture"—*budaya*, my Malay dictionary informed me—became something of a verbal talisman that I constantly introduced to conversations in the hope of eliciting immediate recognition. Despite my best efforts, however, I was often disappointed, and apart from Paka, who had garnered a reputation within Sarawak as an expert on Bidayuh culture (Chua 2006a: 5), few villagers seemed interested in discussing "*budaya* Bidayuh." Now with Paka no longer around, I began wondering whether I was looking for the wrong thing: whether, unlike their political leaders (Chapter 1), people in the village simply weren't interested in "the Bidayuh culture."

On the day of the funeral, I wandered downstairs to the mini-museum, which had been turned into a gambling den for the mourning period, and was hailed by several middle-aged men seated among empty beer cans and peanut shells. Amid the banter, I tried taking advantage of our location and asked whether they knew much about the ritual objects on display. Heads shook all round. One man explained that these were from earlier times and that only some aged people in the village now knew about the old rituals, *adat gawai*. When they died, he mused nonchalantly, *adat gawai* would be lost, since everybody else was now Christian. Recalling how the same objects had been incarnated as emblems of Bidayuh culture in tourist brochures, coffee table books, and official publications on Sarawak, I asked them whether there would still be "*budaya* Bidayuh" after *adat gawai*'s demise. At this, my interlocutors looked puzzled, until the same man recalled that *budaya* was what I had earlier claimed to be studying. "Well, all this is *budaya*," he began, gesturing at the objects around us. "But soon the old ways will be gone. If you come back in two or three years, there'll be no more *gawai*.[2] You'll just find us like this: people sitting around, eating, drinking."

If my faith in the usefulness of "culture" had been flickering, this incident momentarily extinguished it. Following Paka's death, I decided to scale back my original plan to look for "culture" and "Bidayuh identity," inferring from conversations such as this that my informants were either uninterested in constructing a cultural identity for themselves or, worse, had simply absorbed the statist rhetoric that publicly defined, and indeed valorized, "Bidayuh culture" as a collection of *adat gawai*-based paraphernalia. These, together with heirlooms, architecture, and handmade artifacts, appeared in my brief experience to have been swept up in a multiculturalist framework shaped and manipulated by the Malaysian government. Consequently, I decided that focusing on *budaya* would lead to an ethnographic dead end filled with reifications, misapprehensions, and political constructs that had little to do with the reality of village life. Instead, I began to turn my attention to Bidayuh conversion to Christianity over the last few decades, hoping to find in it something more dynamic and less stilted than essentialized notions of "culture."

In retrospect, the shift in focus was fortuitous, as it was along this religion-oriented path that *budaya* later came hurtling back in my direction. In the process of studying the old ways, *adat gawai*, I found myself increasingly drawn to the question of what *budaya* might be. As I discovered through attendance at Christian services and the few remaining *gawai* ceremonies, at which camera-toting villagers and visitors jostled for views of the proceedings, it was impossible to study religion in a contemporary Bidayuh village without notions of "culture" entering the frame. The people with whom I lived, as it turned out, *were* interested in "culture," but in ways that I had not fully anticipated. Far from being a purely political conceit, their version of it was also indelibly religious: a product not only of the national multiculturalist milieu but also of their engagements with Christianity over the last half-century. To understand what was going on, I would have to study both the culture of Christianity in the village and the Christianity of "culture." Their close, and not always unproblematic, enmeshment is the theme around which this book revolves.

Christianity, Culture, and the *Adat Gawai* Question

The Bidayuh are indigenous inhabitants of the Southeast Asian island of Borneo, comprising 1 of almost 30 officially recognized ethnic groups of the Malaysian state of Sarawak. Most of their 160,000-odd population lives in villages in the mountainous southwestern corner of Sarawak, around the state capital Kuching. Up to about the 1960s, these were relatively self-sufficient, rice-planting communities, practicing shifting cultivation on the vertiginous slopes and jungles in their surroundings and supplementing their livelihood by trading jungle products and cash crops with Malays and Chinese at riverine bazaars in exchange for cloths, metals, weapons, beads, and Chinese ceramics (Map 1).

For most of the twentieth century, this predominantly agricultural system—as well as the rituals that revolved around it—remained intact, cocooned by the broadly paternalistic policies of a succession of British rulers (Chapter 1). In 1963, however, Sarawak gained independence as part of the new Federation of Malaysia, with far-reaching consequences for its rural communities. Almost overnight, Bidayuhs became enrolled in an intensive, state-led program of development and modernization, which greatly expanded rural infrastructure and medical and educational facilities and facilitated the migration of young adults to cities and towns throughout Malaysia for schooling and employment. At roughly the same time, Bidayuhs began

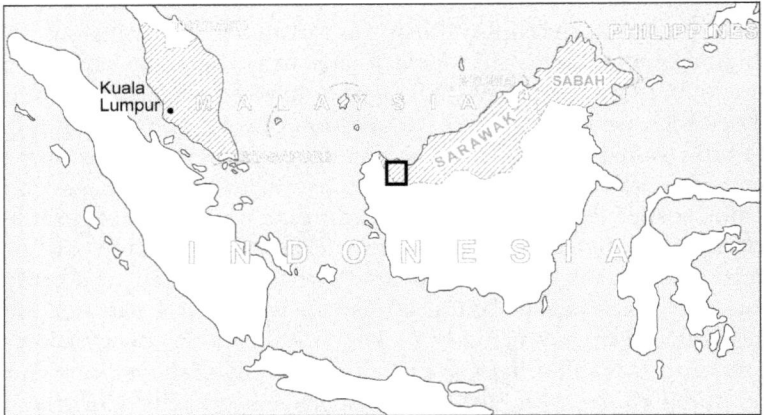

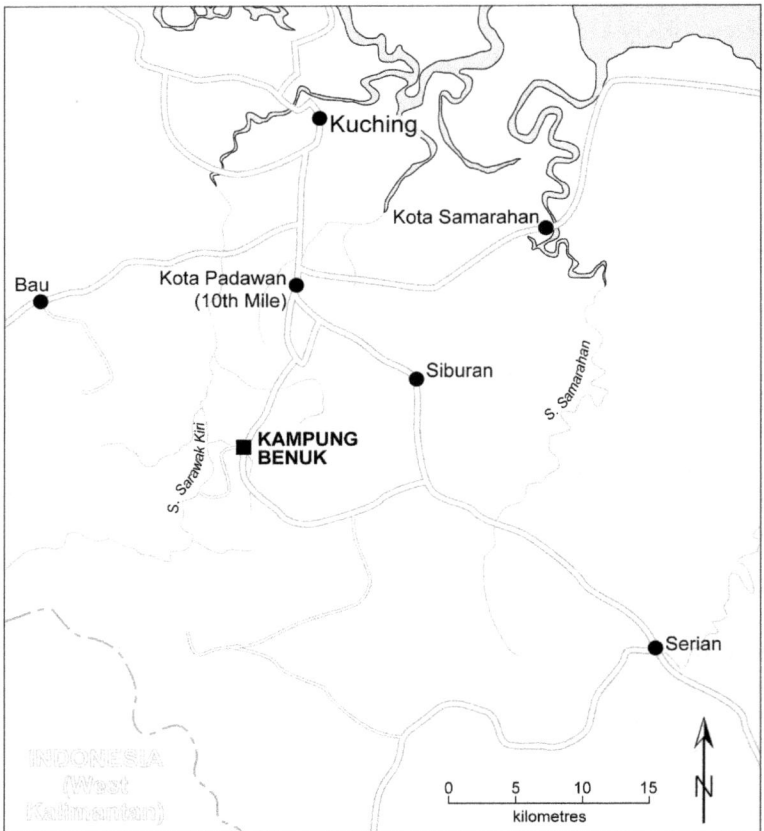

Map 1 Map of Malaysia, showing Sarawak and Kampung Benuk. Map reproduced by the Cartographic Unit, Department of Geography, Cambridge University.

converting in large numbers to various strains of Christianity, resulting in the gradual but extensive abandonment of the old rituals, *adat gawai*. By the time I began fieldwork in 2004, the vast majority of Bidayuhs had become Christian, leaving behind small handfuls of elderly *gawai* practitioners in a number of villages, including my adoptive village. Today, most Bidayuhs are self-consciously *moden* (modern) Christians who see themselves as having a real stake in Malaysia's social, political, and economic milieu.

The intertwined trajectories of Malaysianization, urbanization, and conversion to Christianity form the historical backdrop to the present study, and more specifically, to the conundrum that runs through this book: what should we make of the continued existence of *adat gawai* in the Christian present? As we shall later see, this is not merely an analytical challenge for the anthropologist but a very real social, moral, and religious quandary for Bidayuhs themselves. More than addressing the fate of the old rituals in the contemporary world, it raises challenging questions for both parties about the nature and location of conversion, the interplay between continuity and change, the extents and limits of relatedness, and indeed the very matter of religion.

At the ethnographic crux of this investigation lies what I shall describe as the *adat gawai* "question": a curious, apparent paradox that characterizes many Christian Bidayuhs' engagements with the old ways. As the episode at the mini-museum revealed, *adat gawai* occupies an ambiguous niche in Kampung Benuk, acting and being recognized as both a ritual complex and "Bidayuh culture." Like the men at Paka's wake, most people agree with almost cheerful indifference that the rituals are on the verge of dying out with their practitioners; this village is now Christian and *moden*, they say, and the old ways are no use to us. Moreover, almost all Christians, young and old, concur that Christianity liberated Bidayuhs from a dark, fearful, *gawai*-following past, musing that life today is now "free" (*bebas/biya*). Taken at face value, these assertions seem to indicate that Bidayuhs are really quite relieved to have made that break from *adat gawai* and that they have acquired the "sense of social discontinuity after the adoption of Christianity" (Bialecki, Haynes, and Robbins 2008: 1143), which, as I explain below, certain anthropologists have recently identified as so central to conversion.

The situation, however, is complicated by another prominent set of discourses and practices that, far from advocating rupture from the old rituals, actively maintain and even forge new connections with them. This is clearly demonstrated on the few occasions during the year that *gawai* rituals are undertaken by the elderly practitioners. Mostly held at the longhouse in the center of the village, these are colorful, noisy, and very public affairs that unfailingly attract large audiences of Christians. Many of them contribute food, drink, and cash to the events, help with the preparations and proceedings, and generally add to the boisterous, crowd-filled atmosphere so crucial to their success. In fact, without their help, *adat gawai* in Kampung Benuk would probably have died out years ago, for the elderly practitioners now lack the numbers and physical capacity to carry out the rituals on their own.

This is a point about which my acquaintances are strongly aware—not least because it throws the community's much-cherished sense of Christian unity into question. Unlike most other villages, which contain one or two Christian denominations, Benuk has three congregations: Anglican, Catholic, and a small branch of the evangelical Sidang Injil Borneo (SIB, or Borneo Evangelical Church). While the differences between these churches make no odds in daily life, *adat gawai* is one of the few topics that regularly generate tensions and disagreements between them. For the 25 or so households that are part of the SIB, the old rituals are the work of the devil and thus need to be steered well clear of. This stance, however, sets them in opposition to the Anglican and Catholic majority, who, in addition to supporting *adat gawai*, often depict it as being the same as, similar to, or generally commensurate with Christianity. Put differently, apart from the vocal repudiations of the past by a small minority, the bulk of Christians in Kampung Benuk appear to be crafting a relationship of continuity and contiguity between *adat gawai* and Christianity. And the idiom through which they do so is that of *budaya*—"culture."

What should we make of this muddy ethnographic situation? And how do we reconcile my Anglican and Catholic acquaintances' claims to being free from the past with their efforts to sustain connections with it? In the chapters that follow, I shall address these concerns by embedding the *adat gawai* question in the complex social, moral, religious, and political nexus in which rural Bidayuhs live. I suggest that despite their conflicting attitudes toward *adat gawai*, Anglicans, Catholics, and SIBs are in fact grappling with similar concerns, expectations, and experiences—all of which shed important light on the complex trajectories and manifestations of conversion to Christianity. My argument, in brief, is that the majority of Bidayuhs' desire to maintain continuity and contiguity with the old ways—as well as the minority's refusal to do so—stems not only from their (dis)engagements with the ethnic, religious, and cultural politics of contemporary Malaysia but also, crucially, from the processes of Christianization that they have undergone in recent decades. This relationship is emblematized by the notion of *adat gawai*-as-"culture," which I use here as the ethnographic springboard for an exploration of conversion, Christianity, and experiences of Malaysian citizenship in Bidayuhs' lives.

At base, this book is (to play on a much-cited phrase that I shall later examine) about continuity *speaking*: about the diverse ways in which Christian Bidayuhs seek to forge, articulate, and enact connections with the past, the old rituals, and the elderly *gawai* practitioners. In this respect, it may be seen as a friendly, and hopefully constructive, rejoinder to recent developments in the anthropology of Christianity—a relatively new comparative project that has greatly complicated and enriched the study of religion and conversion. In the past decade, contributors to this nascent subfield have made great strides in refocusing anthropological attention onto the distinctive theological, sociotemporal, and cultural features of Christianity itself—particularly in demonstrating how conversion is often characterized by experiences of discontinuity and rupture. Yet, in the midst of all this, rather less attention has been paid to continuity—the notion of which, I suggest below, has received an analytical battering in recent years. The thrust of my argument, however, is that continuity does matter and that taking seriously its ethnographic and discursive manifestations in our fieldsites not only augments our understandings of discontinuity but also makes for a more nuanced appreciation of multifarious forms that conversion and Christianity can take.

By approaching the *adat gawai* question from this angle, my study seeks to put the themes and concerns of the anthropology of Christianity in dialogue with those of a different, long-standing field of inquiry: the study of cultural consciousness. As the next section reveals, insights from the burgeoning anthropological literature on this topic can be gainfully applied in some ways to the Bidayuh situation. However, I shall also suggest that the dominant scholarly response to such diverse ethnographic occurrences is limited by its tendency to "explain [them] away" (Henare, Holbraad, and Wastell 2007: 1) through primarily political idioms and frameworks. While acknowledging the importance of politics to the *adat gawai* question, then, my aim is to push things even further by simultaneously exploring its ritual, religious, moral, and material dimensions. In this respect, as I shall later explain, my interest is in exploring both the politics and the poetics of Christianity, "culture," and conversion in contemporary Bidayuh life.

"The Nice Thing About Culture is that Everyone Has It"[3]? Antiessentialism and the Study of Cultural Consciousness

In the last few decades, the concept of "culture" has, as Marcus Banks said of ethnicity, "escaped from the academy and into the field" (1996: 18) as a "ubiquitous descriptive" (Strathern 1995: 156) through which to assert distinctiveness at every level of human organization. Yet, faced with the unsettling realization that, beyond the academy, the concept has been "fetishized...in ways that put [it]...beyond the reach of critical analysis—and thus of anthropology" (Turner 1993: 412), scholarly responses to these developments have often been cagey at best, and caustic at worst. "[T]he fact that culture is now such a popular concept, reaching well beyond anthropology," writes Lila Abu-Lughod, "should be cause for suspicion, not self-congratulation for anthropologists" (1999: xviii).

A comprehensive survey of the vast scholarship on "culturalism" (Sahlins 1999: 401) is beyond the scope of this book. Broadly speaking, however, most anthropological analyses have gravitated toward two poles, which we might loosely term the "invention of tradition" (Hobsbawm and Ranger 1983) and "imagined communities" approaches in recognition of their most influential proponents (Anderson 1991). The first posits that while a certain authentic version of culture, society, or tradition—variously defined as "custom," "convention," or "routine" (Hobsbawm 1983)—exists, many so-called traditions are really relatively recent "responses to novel situations which take the form of reference to old situations" (ibid.: 2). The second, conversely, elides the question of authenticity by "naturaliz[ing] the artifice of invention" (Thomas 1992: 213) and insisting that people are constantly engaged in constructing and reconstructing social realities. These positions stand at opposite ends of a single spectrum, encompassing between them various opinions. What unites them all, however, is a deconstructionist impulse that refuses to take notions such as "culture," "tradition," and "nationhood" at face value and seeks to trace how they have been forged, contested, and propagated over time. Their "analytic task," in other words, "is not to strip away the invented portions of culture as inauthentic, but to understand the process by which they acquire authenticity" (Hanson 1989: 898) and "emotional legitimacy" (Anderson 1991: 4).

Such approaches have come to dominate the anthropological study of cultural consciousness (Sahlins 1999; Tobin 1994), revealing how "culture" and other essentializations have been used to "mobilize...group[s] of people for political change" (Otto and Pedersen

2005: 37; see also, e.g., Babadzan 2000; Brosius and Polit 2011; Kahn 1998; Keesing 1989, 1996; Lindstrom 1982; Steedly 1999), to participate in a global, neoliberal mode of commodification (Comaroff and Comaroff 2009; Linnekin 1997), and to generate a sense of common identity, purpose, and belonging through various forms of "imagined community" (e.g., Adams 1997, 1998; Barnard 2004; Handler 1984, 1988; Hanson 1989; Kahn 1993; Kipp 1993; Linnekin 1983, 1991, 1992; Pemberton 1994; Schiller 1997). By highlighting the ways in which such models and discourses are shaped, manipulated, and challenged, these writings thus shift the analytical focus from their content to their political, social, and economic embeddedness. Accordingly, in his trenchant critiques of "contemporary movements and ideologies of cultural identity" in the Pacific, Roger Keesing (1989: 20, 1996), for example, argued that local elites, "separated by gulfs of life experience and education from village communities where they have never lived" (Keesing 1989: 31), had absorbed and reproduced "Western fantasies" (ibid.: 32) of native culture as part of their political machinations.

In a similar vein, Richard Handler has written several influential pieces on "the continual 'objectification' [by nationalists] of what is imagined to be Québécois culture" (1988: 11). Wandering around fairs, festivals, and folklore exhibitions, he notices how "culture and traditions [have] become objects to be scrutinized, identified, revitalized, and consumed" (ibid.: 12) in the form of dances, artifacts, music, and other putative fragments of heritage. Yet, he insists, the timelessness and changelessness imputed to these entities are merely illusory:

> Neither nationalists nor anthropologists can document authentic culture, culture understood as the thing itself, for the thing itself is the attempt to capture it. Each new attempt creates an object which is inherently inauthentic. (Handler 1984: 64)

For Handler, discourses about Québécois culture must be understood as deriving from international "identity politics," whereby "[g]roups seeking enhanced political status" seek to "prove that they [are] indeed groups with a past and, hence, [have] the right to a future" (2011: 40–41). Such "misleading" ideas, he argues, are propagated "throughout the modern world of nation-states and ethnic groups" (1984: 61). Consequently, rather than search for a red herring, anthropologists should engage in what, following Sapir, he calls "destructive analysis" of the notions of "discrete, neatly bounded cultures" shared by nationalists, culture claimants, and mainstream anthropology (1985: 171).

In some ways, this impulse toward "denaturalizing any group of ideas and any grouping of people" (Tobin 1994: 130) offers a useful means of apprehending the *adat gawai* question. Looked at from a distance—or indeed after a month of fieldwork—the transformation of *adat gawai* into "Bidayuh culture" may appear to be a classic case of invention, imagination, or "ethno-commodification" (Comaroff and Comaroff 2009), motivated by and enacted within the context of official Malaysian multiculturalism. As Chapter 1 reveals, my informants have worked out that "looking like a culture" (Hirsch 2007) is a productive mechanism for accruing political, financial, and other benefits in this milieu. Consequently, one could plausibly argue that most Bidayuhs' attitudes toward the old ways have been forged within a distinctly *moden*, Malaysian political framework, and must thus be analyzed in those terms. Indeed, an argument to this effect has already been made by Robert Winzeler (1997), who describes the transformation of the *baruk* ("head-house") into a Bidayuh ethnic emblem as a process of "cultural objectification," and a means by which Bidayuhs have been able to deploy concepts such as "culture" to political ends.

The implications and limitations of Winzeler's argument will be examined in Chapter 7. My point here, however, is that while there are many political dimensions to the *adat gawai* question (chapters 1 and 4), focusing primarily on them reveals only part of the story. By deconstructing and historicizing reifications such as "culture," the dominant "denaturalizing" framework demystifies them and opens them up to comparative analysis, while also underscoring "autochthonous creativity and agency" (Brosius and Polit 2011: 7). Yet, this strategy also risks flattening diverse ethnographic occurrences into offshoots of primarily political or neoliberal processes, while glossing over concerns of genuine moral, social, affective, and material significance for the people involved in them. In so doing, they open up an implicit but powerful cleavage between anthropological analysis and native exegesis (Henare, Holbraad, and Wastell 2007; Viveiros de Castro 2003).

Within this framework, it is often only the analyst who can see, and thus critique, how objectifications and essentializations are created. Here, the study of different societies' engagements with "culture" and other global concepts all too easily becomes the study of "their" reifications and misapprehensions—"their" failure to understand the processual, dynamic, contingent nature of social reality (Sahlins

1999; Tobin 1994). Yet, an important question that this book asks is: What if we approached the study of cultural consciousness through a different lens, one shaped not by encompassing political considerations, but by native exegesis and experience? More specifically, what if we took seriously the religious, moral, and affective dimensions of the *adat gawai* question, and situated the politics of "Bidayuh culture" within the tangled nexus of conversion and Christianity? The next section broaches this question by introducing a body of literature that will form an important theoretical and thematic backdrop to the explorations in this book: the anthropology of Christianity.

On Anthropologizing Christianity

Beyond its political dimensions, the *adat gawai* question elicits complex anthropological concerns about the nature and extent of conversion, religious change, and cultural transformation. What, for a start, does conversion entail—a shift in "inner" states and propositional understandings, a change in habitus, organization, and affiliation, or combinations of all these factors? Can "world religions" maintain their shape and distinctiveness in diverse local conditions? Does conversion always mandate breaking with the past? And what happens to those bits of the past that persist, resurface, or evolve in the present?

Such questions have been lobbed between different schools of thought since at least the 1970s. In recent years, however, they have been given new vitality and urgency by scholars working on the self-styled anthropology of Christianity. In the mid-2000s, when its theoretical and analytical concerns were being delineated and debated in Euro-American academic circles, I was in Sarawak conducting fieldwork, heedless of their existence. Yet, I was not entirely removed from them, for many parallel debates were taking place among my Bidayuh acquaintances, for whom questions about the nature, manifestations, and extent of Christianity, the fate and relevance of *adat gawai*, and the connection between the old ways and the new were never far away. In the following pages, I shall address a number of overlapping concerns that apply to both the anthropology of Christianity and the present ethnography: the matter and location of religion, the forms that Christianity takes, and the place and significance of (dis)continuity in conversion. These will culminate with the question of how we might approach an ethnographic situation of denominational pluralism and incomplete conversion by drawing together, rather than holding apart, anthropological analysis and native exegesis.

Politics and Poetics: On Locating Religiosity

Although anthropology has a long history of studying Christianity and Christian societies (e.g., Barker 1992; Christian 1989; Douglas 2002; Jenkins 1999; Leach 2001; Leach and Aycock 1983; Rafael 1993; Sahlins 1996; Turner and Turner 1978), efforts to create a self-conscious, comparative body of work unified by its interest in Christianity took off only in the early to mid-2000s (e.g., Bialecki, Haynes, and Robbins 2008; Cannell 2005, 2006; Engelke 2007; Engelke and Tomlinson 2006; Howell 2008; Lampe 2010; Robbins 2003, 2007; Schwarz and Dussart 2010; Tomlinson 2009; but cf. Hann 2007). Spearheaded by Joel Robbins (e.g., 2003, 2004, 2007), this movement has also co-opted various ethnographies that while not always written specifically as contributions to the field have nonetheless become prominent representatives of it (e.g., Cannell 1999; Coleman 2000; Harding 1991; Keane 2007; Keller 2005; Meyer 1999; Scott 2005).

According to its proponents, Christianity has remained an "occluded object" within anthropology (Cannell 2006: 11): a consequence of what they allege (perhaps a little too sweepingly[4]) is a general lack of ethnographic interest in Christian societies (Bialecki, Haynes, and Robbins 2008: 1140; Cannell 2006: 8–14) and a reluctance to take its distinctive forms and content seriously (Cannell 2005; Coleman 2010; Robbins 2007). In this respect, the new subfield's main claim to analytical and theoretical novelty is its commitment to concertedly engaging with Christianity's theologies, models, and ideals as objects of interest in their own right. Such an approach thus pushes scholars to apprehend Christianity as a distinctive phenomenon that maintains its own "cultural logic" (Tomlinson and Engelke 2006: 18) and "monolithic characteristics" (Whitehouse 2006: 296) even while crossing historical, cultural, and regional boundaries.

In advancing their arguments, anthropologists of Christianity often contrast their work against a large and diverse body of late-twentieth-century studies of conversion, many of which stem from the same antiessentialist milieu as the literature on cultural consciousness. These studies, which we might loosely term "cultural particularist,"[5] tend to emphasize the fragmentation, incorporation, and transformation of world religions within specific contexts—most often those of non-Western, "modernizing" communities—not infrequently concluding that conversion "has less to do with Christianity itself than with...traditional religion" or other quintessentially local factors (Kammerer 1990: 277). Like scholars of cultural consciousness, these writers eschew putative wholes and essences, such as religious doctrine and theology, focusing instead on the social, political, economic, and moral circumstances in which they are received and transformed.

According to Robbins and other recent commentators, the chief flaw of such approaches—which remain influential in studies of conversion—is that they do not take the content of Christianity sufficiently seriously. They thus have the "object-dissolving" (Robbins 2003: 193) effect of subtracting everything Christian from Christian conversion, including the fact that it can "impose some radically new sociocultural models on [its adherents]...in ways that are broadly comparable cross-culturally" (Whitehouse 2006: 296). To redress this perceived imbalance, Robbins advocates a return to theologies, meanings, ideal models, and structures—in short, to Christianity as a culture and "a meaningful system in its own right" (Robbins 2004: 3), which is able to "hold its shape as its travels" (Robbins 2001a: 7–8). This ideational focus is shared by many other advocates of the anthropology of Christianity, which has thus far revolved around such themes as the production and limits of meaning (Engelke and Tomlinson 2006), conceptions of freedom, moral responsibility, and personhood (Keane 2007; Robbins 2004), and the relationship between anthropology and theology (Cannell 2005; Robbins and Engelke 2010).

At this stage, some readers may detect a whiff of déjà vu—and for good reason. The "cultural particularist" scholarship against which the anthropology of Christianity often sets itself did not exist in a vacuum but was in many ways a reaction to another earlier scholarly tradition: a Weberian (1956) tendency to privilege orthodoxies, beliefs, and other "intellectualist" features (Horton 1971) of world religions, which ran through a vast spectrum of twentieth-century scholarship (e.g., Bellah 1964; Frazer 1922; Geertz 1993b; Tylor 1913). Critical of such approaches for propagating a "myth of the Christian monolith" (Hefner 1993a: 5), "cultural particularists" of the 1980s and 1990s turned instead to "how in Christianity as in Islam or Buddhism, the powerful thrust of orthodoxy interacts with, and is changed by, local religious belief and action [and other factors]" (Schneider and Lindenbaum 1987: 2). The result was a proliferation of ethnographies that reveled in the patchy, contingent, and resolutely local variations of world religions, each deemed as legitimate as the next.

Viewed in this light, current trends in the anthropology of Christianity may be seen as yet another installment in a long-running analytical struggle to define the very matter and location of "religion."

If "cultural particularists" sought to introduce politics—gritty, relational, real-world factors—to the study of conversion, their successors have tipped the analytical seesaw back toward its poetics—its orthodoxies, beliefs, and models.[6] In this regard, it is instructive that recent criticisms of Robbins's and his colleagues' work have often been couched in equally broad terms, highlighting their overarching analytical (and polemical) tendencies rather than their ethnographic specificities. In an apposite replay of earlier "cultural particularist" critiques, for example, Hann depicts recent contributions to the anthropology of Christianity as suffering from a "deep-seated problem of idealism" that leaves them with "little to say about economic and political contexts" (2007: 402), while Harri Englund has argued that the "concept of Christian culture" on which Robbins's work hinges "seems unable to attend to the situated nature of Christianity and other religions, lived and pursued as they are within contexts in which social relationships are rarely confined to persons who share one's own religious outlook" (2007: 482). These and similar responses (e.g., Barker 2008; Hann and Goltz 2010; McDougall 2009; Pelkmans 2009) suggest that even now the analytical seesaw continues to tilt back and forth between what we might loosely term political and ideational approaches to conversion and religion.

What hangs in the balance in this ongoing debate, however, is not only an understanding of religious change but also an understanding of the identity of Christianity itself. Having proliferated in so many settings around the world, can Christianity still be treated as a definitive, monolithic culture? Or do claims of its coherence dissolve in the face of local politics and cultural particularity? Should we, for that matter, be talking about Christianit*ies* rather than a single Christianity? For Robbins and his colleagues, the first suggestion is, unsurprisingly, the most compelling. Yet, in many ways, this reflects the fact that most (though not all) contributors to this subfield work with small, relatively bounded, Protestant "convert cultures" defined by their adherence to a single branch or sect of Christianity.[7] In such settings, the methodological temptation to treat Christianity *as* culture (Robbins 2004) and vice versa is undoubtedly high (see also Englund 2007: 482–483; Hann 2007: 405). And despite acknowledging that alternative forms of Christianity exist (Bialecki, Haynes, and Robbins 2008: 1152; Engelke 2010: 196; Howell 2003; Robbins 2003: 198, 2007: 17; Tomlinson and Engelke 2006: 19), these scholars have had a propensity to use the ideal, rupture-oriented Protestant model employed by Robbins (2007: 11, n. 7) as "a synecdoche for Christianity as a whole" (Coleman 2010: 799).[8]

I raise this point not to bleat about the lack of coverage of "my" particular experience of Christianity but to highlight the fact that the anthropology of Christianity as it currently stands is somewhat imbalanced—skewed in thematic and analytical favor of the ideal Protestant models that encouraged its demarcation as a distinctive "cultural" field in the first place (Englund 2007: 482; Scott 2005: 104). Yet, as the works of Fenella Cannell (1999, 2005, 2006), Holger Jebens (2011), Michael Scott (2005, 2007), and others reminds us, there are many other forms and experiences of Christianity out there, not all of whose adherents speak the same language of rupture and discontinuity. One way of dealing with their absence is, of course, to challenge the necessity and desirability of delineating an anthropology of Christianity, as Hann has done (2007: 406). Another is to wade in anyway, as I shall shortly do, in the hope of introducing further complexity and subtlety into what remain ethnographically, theoretically, and methodologically significant questions.

My aim here is not to tip the analytical seesaw in one or the other direction but to strike a balance between antiessentialism and cultural analysis (Scott 2005: 101), between dealing with the socioeconomic and political circumstances of rural Bidayuhs' lives on the one hand and taking seriously the doctrinal, moral, and cultural influence of Christianity on the other. To do this, I shall think and write through several features of my acquaintances' lives—their ethnotheological understandings and actions, affective and moral experiences, day-to-day relations, and material engagements—which are neither purely ideational nor purely economic or political but are often irreducible combinations of all these features. Lingering, for example, on the dietary and praxiological demands of marrying a Malay (Chapter 4), the implications of being anointed with the customary *gawai* blessing (Chapter 5), the lived dilemmas of loving one's neighbor (Chapter 6), and the shifting fate of ritual objects in Bidayuhs' relations with the Malaysian state (Chapter 7), this book highlights the multifaceted, expansive nature of religiosity: the fact that it is at once poetic and political, doctrinal and praxiological, intimate and public, and deeply imaginative and profoundly tangible.

Consequently, while my earlier injunction to avoid reducing the "culturalization" of *adat gawai* to a political affair still stands, the reverse is equally true, for it cannot be bracketed off from its wider context and treated as a purely religious or cultural matter. By treading this middle line, I hope to move beyond the essentialist/antiessentialist impasse into which debates over religion and cultural consciousness can sometimes lead, toward a peculiarly Bidayuh understanding of conversion, Christianity, and "culture." The theme that serves as an analytical and ethnographic backbone to these explorations is that of (dis)continuity, which, as the following section will explain, is also an important feature of the anthropology of Christianity.

Thinking—and Speaking—of (Dis)continuity

The last decade has seen a growing interest in theorizing Christian conversion as rupture as both an analytical concept and as part of the discourses and experiences of those who undergo it. The foremost advocate of this approach—indeed, the person who has turned (dis)continuity into an explicit theoretical issue for anthropologists—is Robbins, whose influential 2007 article, "Continuity Thinking and the Problem of Christian Culture," is worth briefly encapsulating here.

Robbins's rupture-oriented model of conversion powerfully exemplifies how Christianity can be treated as a cultural entity rather than as "an empty container that different peoples proceeding from dissimilar principles have from time to time filled up with their own infusions" (Wood 1993: 306–307). In his article, Robbins posits that most ethnographies of conversion in non-Western societies are constrained by a deep-seated inclination to seek "some enduring cultural structure that persists underneath all the surface changes" (2007: 10). Assuming that "people cannot but perceive the new in terms of their received cultural categories" (ibid.), such scholars thus treat Christianity as nothing more than "a thin [content-less] veneer overlying deeply meaningful traditional beliefs" (ibid.: 6). Guided by this analytical conjecture, Robbins argues that anthropologists remain cynical about the "claims that that previously non-Christian converts make about their [new] lives" and beliefs (ibid.: 10). In my reading, this generates a disjuncture between analysis and native exegesis, for

> [i]n pursuing their doubts about what converts say on these matters, anthropologists often come to suspect that those who make these claims are not Christians at all or at least that they fail to live up to their own self-professed Christian ideals concerning discontinuity and change. (ibid.)

The problem of "continuity thinking" as Robbins defines it is thus two-pronged, consisting of both an analytical problem—anthropology's reluctance to take the content and culture of Christianity seriously—and a methodological one, namely, anthropologists' unwillingness to take their Christian informants seriously. As I suggested earlier, the extent to which this is a reasonable assessment of the field is in fact debatable. But what I wish to highlight here is Robbins's response to this apparent deficit, which is to draw on his own research among millenarian Urapmin Christians in Papua New Guinea. His ethnography reveals with especial clarity how Christianity contains its own models and discourses of discontinuity, which provide "for the possibility, indeed the salvational necessity, of the creation of ruptures between the past, the present, and the future" (ibid.: 11). This awareness, Robbins argues, "remains at the forefront of its followers' minds" (ibid.), such that converts often "represent the process of becoming Christian as...an event, a rupture in the time line of a person's life that cleaves it into a before and after" (ibid.).

Robbins asserts that such discourses of change and discontinuity must be properly addressed rather than dismissed as "suspect" (ibid.: 13) or atypical. Correspondingly, he proposes that anthropologists should develop analytical "models of cultural discontinuity" (ibid.: 17) through which to approach Christianity and conversion. He thus presents a solution to the shortcomings of continuity thinking by engaging with *dis*continuity as both a local trope and the basis of his analysis. In this sense, I suggest, Robbins moves toward aligning anthropological analysis with native exegesis, by situating what his Christian informants say and do within a theoretical framework adequately equipped to deal with them. Here, it is significant that he uses his *ethnographic* material—millenarian Christianity in Papua New Guinea—as a corrective to what he sees as anthropology's long-standing *analytical* failure to address the nature of religious change. Put simply, his message is that we should start taking discontinuity seriously because our Christian informants do.

Robbins's article clearly foregrounds the link between Christianity's inherent discontinuities and their manifestations in converts' discourses and experiences. While not the first to theorize or interrogate conversion as rupture (e.g., Engelke 2004; Meyer 1998), it arguably provides the most ambitious and compelling articulation of it, turning it into an explicit theoretical and ethnographic subject for anthropologists of religion. The logic behind this analytical move is, of course, fundamentally sound: if anthropology's aim is to "grasp the native's point of view, his relation to life...*his* vision of *his* world" (Malinowski 1972: 25; italics in original), then it makes sense to seek a good fit between anthropological analysis and native exegesis, or at least to ensure that they don't completely contradict each other. If the

Christians with whom we work are talking constantly about discontinuity and rupture, who are we to tell them that they are wrong? Yet, juxtaposed against the ethnographic situation I have just described, the limits of this focus should become apparent.

As I mentioned earlier, Christians in Kampung Benuk largely concur that conversion has entailed breaking away from the past and *adat gawai*. Yet, that sense of discontinuity is simultaneously tempered—and in many cases, overridden—by a strong and pervasive sense of *continuity* with the old ways and their practitioners. Here, connections and invocations of similarity are as much in evidence as breakages and discourses of rupture. With the exception of the SIBs (who, as Chapter 5 reveals, are not as removed from such ruminations as they may seem), most of my village acquaintances do not subscribe to the rupture-oriented discourses that Robbins and others identify as so central to Christian doctrine and experience, but are active *thinkers and speakers of continuity*. Faced with such ethnographic occurrences, what should the anthropological analyst do?

My aim here is not to come down on either side of the argument, and thus incorporate Bidayuhs' discourses into an overarching argument for or against continuity. Instead, I shall approach this question sideways by developing the methodological impulse that, as I suggested earlier, underlies Robbins's approach and is one of its key strengths: to align anthropological analysis with native exegesis. My contention is that if this impulse is to be followed through, then we must also take seriously what I have been dealing with in my fieldsite: those instances in which native exegesis and practice center on *continuity*. Doing so does not entail replicating the *analytical* sins of "continuity thinking"—as later chapters will reveal, this is not an argument that fundamentally nothing has changed—but it does ensure that we do not dismiss ethnographic manifestations of continuity thinking and speaking as figments of a misguided anthropological imagination. In the recent anthropological rush to theorize and identify discontinuity in Christianity and conversion, we have perhaps risked throwing out the ethnographic baby (continuity speaking) with the analytical bathwater (continuity thinking). One of my aims here, then, is to ensure that the former is not dismissed as irrelevant to the debate.

My other aim, however, is to take things further by complicating and interrogating discourses and experiences of continuity[9] in the same way that anthropologists of Christianity have recently complicated and interrogated rupture (Engelke 2004, 2010; Harris 2006; Meyer 1998; Robbins 2001b; Schwarz and Dussart 2010). As will later become clear, far from being "in no need of explanation"

(Robbins 2007: 31), the relationship between continuity and discontinuity in the context of Bidayuh conversion is often uneven, complicated, and even contradictory. The (temporal, historical) past, conceptions of the past, *adat gawai*, and *adat gawai* practitioners are not the same thing, even if they are often spoken of in the same breath; and it is important for both analyst and informant to distinguish between them. Moreover, the motivations, sources, and scopes of "continuity" can vary significantly: attitudes toward the past that are structured by Christianity (Chapter 5), for example, are not the same as worries about "returning" to one's earlier lifestyle after conversion (Chapter 4), or dilemmas over one's neighborly relations with *adat gawai* practitioners (Chapter 6). In this respect, an important objective of my book is to use the *adat gawai* question to explore the different shades, degrees, and articulations of *both* continuity and rupture in my acquaintances' lives. By thinking through them, I seek to reveal not only how Bidayuh conversion has been a simultaneously social, political, material, and moral process but also how Christianity itself can take multiple and sometimes unexpected forms while still retaining distinctive cultural and theological characteristics.

Bidayuh Matters: People, Places, and Fieldwork

This book is not a comprehensive survey of "the Bidayuh" but a particular portrait of a Bidayuh community at a particular point in time. Before outlining its content, however, I would like to linger on a few features of Bidayuh life and my fieldwork that will lend shape, color, and analytical salience to the chapters that follow. The ethnography is based largely on my research in Kampung Benuk (figure I.1), a Bidayuh village of nearly 500 households nestled amid limestone hills in the Penrissen area south of Kuching.[10] My doctoral fieldwork took place over 14 months from 2004 to 2005 and has since been supplemented by once- or twice-yearly visits of between two weeks to three months from 2006 to 2010, as well as regular trips to the Singai region (2003–2010) and more recent work (2007–2010) in four villages in the Padawan area: Taba Sait, Pain Bojong, Semban Teleg, and Rejoi. Although moving between these different regions has left me acutely conscious of the differences—and sense of difference—between Bidayuh communities, it has also revealed the many historical, demographic, and social similarities between them.

Like its neighbors, Benuk has undergone many demographic and socioeconomic changes over the last few decades. Once famed for its large longhouse—a sprawling wood and bamboo structure—the

Figure I.1   Kampung Benuk, 2007.

village now consists mainly of individual cement dwellings, often with satellite dishes perched on their colorful zinc roofs. These are linked by networks of narrow, tarred roads and dusty paths—some with road signs, introduced in 2006—which are crisscrossed overhead by electric wires. Motorcycles, cars, and vans are found everywhere, as are refrigerators, electric fans, sofas, display cabinets, and coffee tables. Noises from the ubiquitous television sets, radios and—since rural telecommunications masts were installed nearby in 2007—mobile telephones are as much a part of the village soundscape as those of the chickens, cats, and dogs roaming about in it. Perhaps the only "modern" amenity that the village presently lacks is piped water, although this is likely to be introduced by the government in the not-too-distant future.

Having reaped the benefits of expanding rural educational systems and increasing urbanization, most—though not all—working-age adults have eschewed their parents' and grandparents' swidden farming lifestyle and see *moden* employment in Kuching and other urban areas as the way forward. Although illiteracy and joblessness remain common in rural areas,[11] virtually every household will have at least one wage-earning member on whom they rely heavily. While a significant minority of rural Bidayuhs have become teachers, civil servants, office workers, and other white-collar professionals, most of them work in relatively low-paid jobs as cleaners, drivers, factory workers, domestic helpers, construction workers, and caretakers. Because of the village's relative proximity to nearby towns and cities—the road journey time to Kuching was cut to just over an hour with the tarring of a large arterial road in the late-1990s—these people have effectively become either daily or weekend commuters, shuttling between town and city on a regular basis.

The upshot of such constant movement is that nobody can really describe themselves as purely village oriented, or isolated from the urban centers in which governmental policy is shaped, wages are earned, children are educated, and consumer goods are obtained. Instead, there exists a pervasive awareness of the constant traffic of persons, things, and ideas between village and urban areas. In many ways, Kuching and its environs are as much a part of village life as the mountains, fruit trees, and rice farms surrounding it. While there are thus undeniable tensions that stem from the growing socioeconomic disparities between those who have done well in the *moden* world and others who struggle within it, these are largely superseded by the fact that in a village where pretty much everyone is related, it is—for the moment, at least—difficult to define clear groups of haves and have-nots, urbanites and rural poor.

Apropos of this, people's construals of communal life are often underpinned by a vague ethos of horizontal parity and interdependence—a theme to which we shall return in Chapter 6. Such self-depictions and practices were arguably what led Leach to describe Land Dayaks (as Bidayuhs were then known) and Ibans as being strongly "egalitarian" in outlook and organization (1950: 75–78; see also Freeman 1970; Geddes 1954) in contrast to the "stratified" societies of the Kayan, Kenyah, and other groups in central Borneo. This is still in evidence, for example, in the realms of household membership and village leadership, whereby rights and positions cannot be inherited but must constantly be achieved and recognized by others (Chua 2009b). Now, as in the past, moreover, a rhetorical ideal of equality—or more specifically, of not standing out from the crowd—exercises a strong hold on village interactions. I heard several times during fieldwork, for instance, that individuals should never flaunt their success, because this would inevitably attract jealousy, malice, or misfortune. Indeed, the consequences of such behavior were made embarrassingly clear several times, when individuals who did show off their wealth or status were swiftly brought down a peg by a combination of gossip, ridicule, conspicuous indifference, and sheer intransigence. In this way, the community as a whole continued to invoke a vague notion of group parity and sameness.

On an average weekday, then, Kampung Benuk can only be described as quiet: following a large morning exodus of students and workers, a scorching silence usually settles on the village, as the remaining residents—mainly elderly people, housewives, and young children—get on with their day's tasks. By contrast, weekends bring with them a rush of life, noise, and color. Every Friday evening, Benuk's population begins to surge with returnees who have been working and living in town all week. This is the time when families gather for large meals—often spending all afternoon cooking, chatting, watching television, and snoozing—and carry out work on their houses, farms, and gardens. It is also when events of any consequence, such as weddings, birthdays, church fetes, and discos featuring "band boys" singing the latest Bidayuh, Iban, and Malay hits, are held. Sunday mornings, meanwhile, see the community's three churches come alive as nodes of weekly sociality, with people dressed in their good clothes thronging the roads on their way to and from services.

Most of my weekends during fieldwork would thus pass in an exhausting haze of barbequed pork, karaoke, Christian prayers, alcohol, and ceaseless socializing. Such oscillation between different village states did not go unnoticed by my informants, who often commented that I must get really bored during the week, when nothing *rami* (fun-filled, raucous, crowded) took place. There was, however, also a distinctively *moden* feel to such *rami*-ness, for weekends were not only the time when family and friends returned from the city with gifts, food, and gossip but also when contraptions such as VCD players, satellite television, and new cars could be exploited and displayed. At the same time, the difference between the "old" and the "new" worlds should not be overstated. The elderly women with whom I spent many weekdays, for example, were also self-consciously *moden*; and when we were not hunched over pepper vines or winnowing rice, we might be watching the news or Filipino and Korean soap operas on television. Similarly, many city workers thought nothing of donning their hats and rubber boots and hefting large rattan baskets on their back as they headed off, machetes in hand, to clear their vegetable plots at weekends. While acknowledging, and in many ways objectifying, the difference between "old" and *moden* worlds (Chapter 1), then, my acquaintances nevertheless saw themselves as having a foot in both. And as later chapters will show, this awareness of their simultaneous inclusion in two spheres can sometimes give rise to their own dilemmas.

This brings us to an important methodological and analytical point. In the following chapters, the village will crop up constantly as a conceptual and descriptive unit. By using it thus, I do not mean to reify Kampung Benuk as that artificially bounded, homogeneous Village of classical ethnography, but to mirror my acquaintances' own tendency to talk about it as a distinctive place and their key unit of corporate identity and belonging. During fieldwork, I was struck by their manifest keenness to assert how different Bidayuh communities were from each other—and, by implication, how much better Benuk was than anywhere else. Within days of arriving, for example, I was swiftly disabused of the assumption that I was learning Biatah—the Bidayuhic dialect that Benuk is officially classed as using—and told that here, people used *tong Benuk*, the Benuk way of speaking.[12] In fact, my acquaintances continued, every village had its own *tong*, none of which were as easy to follow as Benuk's. If I met Bidayuhs from Serian, I wouldn't understand what they said; and if I went to Bau it was even worse, because they not only spoke differently but also extremely fast, like birds. Consequently, they concluded with satisfaction as I scribbled frantically in my makeshift dictionary, I had a lot to learn because even they couldn't understand what Bidayuhs from elsewhere said.

This last point was only partially true, because as I also discovered, my acquaintances were actually rather good at picking up and switching between different Bidayuh dialects[13]—a reflection of the general impulse toward "translatability" that I examine in Chapter 4. What remained strong, however, was the rhetoric of difference: the conviction that each village's language, like its other characteristics, was unique to it. Indeed, the importance of village-based distinctiveness was made clear during a conversation that I had with a young man at one of Benuk's many community events about my doctoral research. "Of course we're Bidayuh in Benuk," he reflected as we sipped cool beers in the warm night air, "but it's no use you *telling* people [in my dissertation] we're Bidayuh, because how will they know which *rais* [village/place of residence] we're from? *Rais* Sarawak is OK, *rais* Benuk is OK, but *rais* Bidayuh doesn't mean anything."

As these anecdotes suggest, many of my acquaintances use the village—their village—as a key reference point and means of locating themselves within the world. While not diminishing their awareness of its porousness and elasticity (Chapter 4), this tendency lends it a conceptual consistency as a singular, distinctive entity toward which their sense of belonging and affiliation is strongest. In this book, then, I use "the village" as an analytical unit in the way that my informants use it as a conceptual and praxiological unit: as a necessarily partial, but nonetheless discernible, thing through which to get on with life and ethnography. In other words, I use the village as what Matei Candea calls an "arbitrary location" (2007): one that is bounded for the purpose of anthropological (and native) analysis but that simultaneously implies a wider world through its "incompleteness and contingency" (ibid.: 180). At the end of the day, I suggest that for all the internal differences within it, there still exists a particular *village perspective* through which most of Benuk's residents conceive of and deal with their lives in contemporary Malaysia. And it is this perspective—rural, urban, religious, and political all at once—that I shall attempt to capture in the chapters that follow.

My initial forays into Sarawak took place through Christianity—or rather, through a series of Catholic connections. The first Bidayuh I met was Vincent Eddy, an English-speaking schoolteacher and highly respected church leader from Singai, whom I had got to know through a regional lay Franciscan network of which my aunt in Singapore was part. Through Vincent, I became acquainted with the Franciscan friars at St Ann's Catholic Church in Kota Padawan, the nearest town to Benuk—one of whom eventually introduced me to the woman who became my adoptive mother, Midah anak Jub, who was then chairperson of the St Ann's Ladies Guild. Ndŭ Pin ("mother of Crispin"),[14] as she is known in Benuk, was a dynamic woman who worked as a civil servant in Kuching and spoke good English. She and her husband, Nipi Ahlian anak Segar, who at the time worked for the Sarawak Forestry Department, had three children—two daughters at university in Peninsular Malaysia and a son still in secondary school. During the week, they stayed in their house in Kota Padawan, returning to the village only at weekends to see their families and tend their small gardens and farms.[15] Having been told of my intentions—to spend a year living in the village in order to study its culture and traditions—Ndŭ Pin agreed to let me stay as her adoptive daughter in her home in Benuk.

While often on my own in the family's two-story wood and concrete village house, I was never starved for company. Neighbors, relatives, and other acquaintances often popped by for chats, to inform me of the latest news or gossip, to summon me to church services and *adat gawai* rituals, or to sell cakes, fruits, and vegetables. The rest of the time, I would be walking around the village, meeting people and trailing them about the place, and frequently being invited into other houses. Being identified as the adoptive child of Ndŭ Pin gave me an instant route into village networks, determining which church I should regularly attend, on whose rice farms I should help, which houses I could ask for water when mine ran out, and so on. Indeed, as I explain in Chapter 4, my adopted status had already set me on the path toward incorporation into village life, as its inhabitants did to me what ought to be done to all newcomers: teach me to speak, eat, act, and generally "become" Dayak, as they call themselves.[16]

Armed with a shaky grasp of Malay and a cheerful capacity for humiliation, I began to acquaint myself with Kampung Benuk through daily walks, visits to Paka's mini-museum, church attendance, various rice-related activities, and fictive kin connections. It was through these activities, as well as the kindnesses of various residents who had picked up English and even Mandarin at work or school, that I gradually learned to speak the local dialect. As a young, unmarried woman I spent a significant amount of time with housewives and mothers as well as grandmothers, many of whom took it upon themselves to show me how to be a good village girl through rice-planting and processing, washing clothes in the river, basket weaving, and cooking, among other things. At the same time, my status as an outsider with "big schooling" and government connections also gave me a certain liberty to mix with groups of men, who would often congregate after meals to drink alcohol and smoke cigarettes while the women cleared up at the back.[17] At official functions, moreover, I was often invited to sit with or meet the (usually male) VIPs in attendance by the village head, who, after several months, took great pleasure in informing them that I was a student from Cambridge University who had now become a child of Benuk.

The useful ambiguity of my position was further complicated by various expectations, obligations, and (mis)understandings. The fact that I was a Singaporean Chinese automatically placed me in a wealthy, well-connected bracket, which meant that I was occasionally expected to display my largesse by doling out presents from the city, or even helping so-and-so's second cousin's son-in-law find a job. These hopes were usually tempered by the concurrent realization that I was a student without an income, but it took a while before I settled into a vague equilibrium of reciprocity with my informants. Second, the widespread knowledge that I would eventually write some sort of *buk* (book) about the village gave rise to oft-repeated admonitions that I should portray its inhabitants in a strongly positive light, as well as occasional attempts to get me to record in writing individual perspectives on contentious issues. And, as is almost inevitable in fieldwork,

I sometimes found myself caught up in gut-clenchingly awkward social tangles and rivalries, not all of which I handled competently. By and large, however, Benuk and I got along quite well, and my time there has been genuinely productive in all sorts of ways.

Outline of the Book

In essence, this is a story about Christianization and its social, political, moral, and religious consequences, all of which are embedded in a wider framework of Malaysianization and multiculturalism. Part I is an ethnographic prelude to the analytical explorations of Part II, providing a description of the world in which rural Bidayuhs live and the processes by which they have become Christians with "culture." Chapter 1 examines the *moden* Malaysian milieu of which Bidayuhs have been part since 1963, looking particularly at how Sarawakian multiculturalism has given rural communities an opportunity to alleviate their deeply felt sense of political and socioeconomic marginality. Their efforts, however, cannot be fully understood without reference to the two sets of religious practices that have been so central to their lives over the last century: *adat gawai* and Christianity. While Chapter 2 outlines some of *adat gawai*'s basic features and shows how they have shifted over the last few decades, Chapter 3 takes the partial form of a historical narrative that details how conversion to Christianity occurred gradually and patchily over many decades, until it eventually became the prevalent religion in Bidayuh areas.

Having set this ethnographic scene, the book then moves into more analytical territory, examining how continuity and discontinuity have been discerned, constructed, enacted, and debated in various different ways. To this end, the four chapters in Part II build on each other in exploring the culture of Christianity and the Christianity of "culture." Chapter 4 situates contemporary Bidayuh Christianity within the national scaffold of ethnic and religious politics, one largely constructed and defined in relation to a specific notion of Malay-Muslim exceptionalism. Beginning with the question of why many Bidayuhs possess an abiding suspicion of Malays, it paints a picture of my acquaintances as self-consciously "translatable figures" (Siegel 1986: 297), able to "become" different things as circumstances demand, while retaining their capacity to "return" to earlier identities and ways of life. The chapter shows how, with such flux becoming increasingly difficult to maintain, Christianity plays a vital role not only as a defensive buffer against Muslim hegemony but also as a means of participating fully in Malaysian *moden*-ity.

Chapters 5 and 6 extend this argument by examining how Christianity, as both an institutional force and an "ethnotheology" (Scott 2005, 2007), has shaped Bidayuhs' relations with and attitudes toward the old ways. Through an examination of both "inculturation" practices from the 1970s and the transformative influence of Christian models, concepts, and practices on Bidayuhs' lives, they trace how most villagers have developed a strong sense of continuity and contiguity between *adat gawai* and Christianity, the past and the present, and *gawai* practitioners and Christians. Yet, such discourses and experiences should not give rise to a simplistic *analytical* assertion that some underlying sociocultural structures and concepts have simply persisted in the present. Instead, the chapters demonstrate the complex interplay of both continuity and discontinuity in the conversion process—many of which are thrown into uncomfortable relief in relation to the *adat gawai* question. In this regard, the differences between Anglican and Catholic and SIBs' responses to the old rituals can offer useful insights into the complicated realities and dilemmas of Christian conversion. Cumulatively, they also reveal that missionaries and churches are not the only "change agents" (Barker 1992: 153) at work but that Bidayuhs are themselves active participants and actors in these processes.

Chapter 7 brings the exploration full circle by returning to the question with which this Introduction opened: what do we make of the transformation of *adat gawai* into "Bidayuh culture"? If the preceding chapters argue that the fate of the old rituals has been shaped by both Malaysianization and Christianization, this chapter reminds us of the need to also take *adat gawai* on its own terms and to examine how its very materiality and mechanisms also influence its place in Bidayuh villages today. Working through the examples of a "cultural dance" performance and the objects of Paka's mini-museum, I outline an alternative model of constitutive agency and transformation to those commonly deployed by scholars of cultural consciousness, arguing that *adat gawai*'s status as "culture" may not only be a case of ritual politicized but also one of politics ritualized.

Toward Exegetical Congruence

Like most anthropological writing, this book is ultimately an ethnographic fiction (Strathern 1987: 256; Wagner 1981)—a narrative that momentarily holds together scholarly and native exegesis for the purpose of description and analysis. In the following pages, academic concepts such as "religion," "conversion," and "culture" will comingle with Bidayuh ideas about *adat* (way of life), *agama* (religion), *budaya* (culture), and *jadi* (becoming), with each set being given the same analytical berth. By doing this, my agenda is not to depict a radically different Bidayuh ontology in which the familiar is entirely defamiliarized. Instead, my aim is to use both Bidayuh and anthropological concepts as I used them during fieldwork: as means of thinking *through* specific ethnographic phenomena, *with* the people with whom I lived. The relationship between them, then, is one of analogy rather than encompassment (Strathern 2008): here, each serves to challenge, illuminate, and expand, rather than subsume, the other.

In this way, I hope to extend the inescapable "coevalness" of fieldwork into the realm of anthropological writing and analysis (Fabian 1983). To this end, I shall pursue a methodological strategy that I call exegetical congruence—that is, the alignment, rather than the amalgamation or disassociation, of anthropological analysis and native exegesis. By this, I am not professing a slavish adherence to the romantic but untenable assumption that the "native" is always right, for merely rehashing what my informants say (which is plenty) would defeat the purpose of writing an anthropological monograph. Instead, this strategy reflects a fundamental commitment to ethnographic complexity and "thickness" (Ortner 1995: 174): to tracing the many, sometimes contradictory, projects of explanation, contemplation, and action that exist in my fieldsite, and using those projects as the basis of my analysis. The congruence that I seek is thus not linguistic or analytical but *exegetical*, which is to say that my acquaintances should at least recognize the concerns, etiological principles, relations, and effects described in this book, whether or not they couch them in the same words.

The impulse underlying this project is not far removed, I suggest, from the methodological approach adopted by Robbins in his article on continuity thinking (2007). There are, however, two important qualifications to be made. First, by "native exegesis" I refer not only to discursive or ideational forms but also to artifacts, actions, and modes of being in the world. As we shall see, words and concepts are not the only things through which Bidayuhs think, act, and account for what goes on in their lives. This is particularly true in the case of both *adat gawai* and Christianity, which, as chapters 2, 3, and 7 reveal, are characterized as much by their materiality and "orthopraxy" (Geertz 1993c: 117) as they are by their propositional and semantic content. If anything, then, this book seeks to enlarge the scope of native exegesis—and indeed the notions of "religion" and "the social"—by treating them as irreducibly embodied, practiced, and "thingy" phenomena.

Second, it is vital not to impute an artificial homogeneity to native exegesis—a tendency that sometimes rears its head in ethnographies of small-scale, bounded, self-consciously Christian "cultures." My aim here is not to imply that all Bidayuhs speak with one voice; quite the contrary, as the following chapters will reveal. However, I nevertheless argue that there *are* certain ontological and epistemological principles, mechanisms, concerns, and experiences that are shared (or at least recognized) by the majority of my acquaintances, even if they enunciate and respond to them in different ways. As Part II will reveal, such shared strands are not necessarily "old" ones—continuities from a persistent cultural past—but have also been developed and are constantly being reconfigured by both Christianity and the Malaysian milieu. By identifying and gathering them under the heading of "native exegesis," my aim is not to reify them but to work and think through them—just as my Bidayuh acquaintances do.

This brings me to a final point. In the places that we study, anthropologists are not the only theorists and philosophers around. A central aim of my ethnography is to trace the way my informants themselves not only act in the world but also contemplate, speculate about, and debate various notions about which anthropologists are also concerned—such as "culture," "religion," "(dis)continuity," and "Christianity." In this respect, far from remaining "outside the object of study," I am "arguing *within* the same world" as many Bidayuhs (Spencer 1990: 288, 290; italics in original). Rather than trying to hold "my" theoretical conceptions of "culture" at bay from "theirs," then, this book situates both anthropological and Bidayuh notions within a single analytical framework.

Such a project is not, of course, unproblematic. Aside from the inevitable gaps and contradictions in native exegesis (Chua 2009b), ethnographic fieldwork is fraught with indeterminacy and knowledge politics; "the ethnographer is not free from the epistemologist's quandary of having to explain how he knows what he knows" (Pina-Cabral 2009: 170). In this respect, I do not pretend that my writings and analysis are anything but personal translations, analogies, and interpretations, produced from a specific vantage point within that framework. Ethnography is not, and can never be, an indexical account of life as it is but will always remain the product of the relationship between anthropologist and subject (Wagner 1981). Yet, this recognition should not pitch us into what Peter Metcalf calls "an especial anthropological version of nihilism, the assertion that it is fundamentally impossible to know anything or say anything about another culture" (2002: 10). After all, there is still anthropology to be getting on with (ibid.). And on this note, let us now look more closely at the ethnographic context in which the *adat gawai* question will be played out.

Part I

Chapter 1

Looking Like a Culture: *Moden*-ity and Multiculturalism in a Malaysian Village

One Saturday during the dry season, I took my adoptive cousins to play at our favorite riverine haunt—a low-running creek on the outskirts of the village. Cars zoomed past on the main road as we splashed about in the sun-dappled water, picking up pebbles, foliage, plastic snack packets, and—as six-year-old Davina was thrilled to discover—some long, leafy stems of bamboo that had fallen from the bank. Extracting a pole twice her height from the water, she stuck it upright in the riverbed, and circled it in a youthful parody of the offertory dance performed around the "altar" at *adat gawai* rituals, shrieking gleefully, "I'm following *gawai!*" Minutes later, she and another girl were standing to attention before the same bamboo stem—now transformed into a flagpole—belting out *Negara Ku,* the Malaysian national anthem.

In its own inventive way, this sequence encapsulated many Bidayuhs' sense of living in a world in transition: of emerging from an "old world" (*dunia jah*) into the "modern world" (*dunia moden*), of which they are resolutely part. The former is strongly associated with the practice of *adat gawai*, rice farming, and longhouses, whereas the latter, which I explore in this chapter, is characterized by an inextricable combination of Malaysian nationhood, multiculturalism, ethnic and religious politics, and Malay hegemony. Recent decades have seen much scholarly interest in the relationship between these factors in national policy and discourse (e.g., Abdul Rahman Embong 2001; Hooker 2004; Kahn 1998; Loh and Kahn 1992; Mandal 2001; Shamsul 2001), and in how they have been manipulated by various politically active groups (e.g., Kessler 1992; Loh 1992; Shamsul 1997; Winzeler 1997). What remains understudied, however, is the place of ethnic minorities—particularly people such as Davina and her family, who are neither politically motivated cultural claimants nor completely oblivious to national discourses on culture and tradition—in this world. How do they construe and experience *dunia moden*?

Put differently, we might ask, following John Postill (2008), whether and how the Bidayuh have become Malaysian. In his recent book on the impact of mass media on Sarawak's largest ethnic group, the Iban, Postill argues that "state-led media efforts" at nation-building have been "amply rewarded" in rural communities by the fact that their inhabitants have "become thoroughly 'Malaysianised'" (2008: 3). "Thanks to decades of radio, television, school and face-to-face propaganda," he suggests, "Malaysia has become an unquestioned reality amongst the Iban" (ibid.: 192). Consequently, they view themselves and behave self-consciously as members of a larger nation, participating actively in its "mass public culture" (ibid.: 193) through rallies, concerts, football matches, television shows, and other outlets, aligning their communal and individual histories with those of Malaysia (ibid.). For them, the nation is "a lived-in world, a mediated community of practice," not simply an "imagined community" (ibid.: 194). Could the same be said of the Bidayuh?

This is the question with which the present chapter grapples. In the last few decades, Bidayuh communities have undergone a comparable process of "modernization" and incorporation into the nation-state. Like Postill's informants, they are highly aware of their status as Malaysians and genuinely want to be part of the *moden*, developed future toward which their leaders say the country is hurtling. Yet, aligning their lives with this trajectory is not a straightforward task. In becoming *moden*, Bidayuh villagers have had to engage in a whole series of negotiations with the state, the tourist industry, the media, and each other over what to do about the old ways—and indeed, what those old ways might consist of in the first place. Such negotiations are also tempered by a strong sense of marginalization and disgruntlement over national political realities, for Malaysian *moden*-ity, as I explain later, is not a level playing field but a highly uneven ethnic and religious terrain. Consequently, many Bidayuhs' experiences of Malaysian citizenship are marked by a complex blend of enthusiasm and resentment: of wanting to participate in statist arenas and policies while simultaneously buffering themselves from them. This ambivalence, as we shall see, pervades their thoughts, actions, and decisions, forming an important backdrop to their engagements with both Christianity and "culture." To understand how this situation came to be, however, we need to go back to the beginning and to work out how my acquaintances came to be "the Bidayuh" in the first place.

Troubled Taxonomies: The Making of Ethnicity in Sarawak and Malaysia

Let us begin with a moment of apparent clarity: a demographic portrait based on official statistics and categories in present-day Malaysia. The Bidayuh are one of Sarawak's indigenous groups. Numbering approximately 166,756, they make up just over eight percent of the state's population (2,071,506) and are its fourth largest ethnic community after the Iban, Chinese, and Malays.[1] Historically, they have lived in longhouse-based villages close to what is now the border with Indonesian Borneo and are related to certain Dayak groups in West Kalimantan, which many of them also acknowledge as their place of origin (Beccari 1986: 60; Brooke 1990: 47; Chang 2002: 20–22; Minos 2000: 8).

Already, the picture begins to be muddied. Members of these groups on both sides of the border consider themselves relatives (*bimadis*) who share common histories, languages, and ritual complexes; these links are cemented by cross-border visits that occasionally take place between kindred villages.[2] According to my Sarawakian informants, everybody in this relationship is "Dayak"—the endonym prevalent in Bidayuh villages and the official Indonesian designation for indigenous groups in Kalimantan. At the same time, those in Sarawak are acutely conscious of the national boundary that lies between them. Their Indonesian relatives may be Dayak, but they are not *quite* Bidayuh—and they are certainly not Malaysian. If the occasion arises (such as when the newspapers reported a surge in thefts in Kuching in 2005), my acquaintances have no qualms about differentiating themselves from those "Indons" who have come to live or work in Sarawak from Kalimantan.

This paradoxical sense of sameness and difference that characterizes such cross-border relations is not unique within Borneo. Nor is it confined to the areas around the national borders that, as a result of the island's colonial past, slice arbitrarily across large swathes of socially, culturally, and linguistically similar groupings (Bala 2002: 57–65). As anthropologists, historians, and government officials have discovered over the years, Borneo's populations have always seemed obdurately resistant to classification of any sort.[3] Jérôme Rousseau once described central Borneo as "a checkerboard pattern of ethnic units distributed randomly through the vagaries of migration" (1990: 1); this is a depiction that could aptly be extended to the rest of the island. Consequently, as Clare Boulanger suggests, terms such as "supraethnic," "ethnic," and "subethnic" can be used only in a "strictly... heuristic" sense in relation to the populations of Borneo (2009: 19), which, throughout its history, has had "people as well as 'cultural stuff' regularly oozing through whatever ethnic boundaries coalesced" (ibid.: 21).

"Bidayuh" literally means "people of" (*bi-*) "the land/hills" or "interior" (*dayuh*). Originally a Bukar-Sadong endonym (Geddes 1954: 6; Grijpstra 1976: 52), it was introduced in the run-up to Sarawak's independence from the British Crown in the 1950s as an ethnic label encompassing a large, motley collection of hill-dwelling communities in what was then the First Division. These groups had previously been bracketed together in the equally broad category, "Land Dayak," which James Brooke, founder of the dynasty of "White Rajahs" that ruled Sarawak from 1841 to 1946,[4] had more or less invented in the mid-nineteenth century (Keppel 1846, II: 174; Mundy 1848: 234; Roth 1980, I: 43). At the time of Brooke's ascension, most Bornean communities would have identified themselves through an overlapping combination of geographic features, lifestyles, leadership, and forms of political organization. Intermarriage was common, and frequent migration, skirmishes, and slave raids made the creation of new settlements and the absorption of individuals into different communities routine affairs.

The establishment of the Brooke Raj, however, heralded the start of a growing interest in establishing workable classifications that would facilitate the task of governance and control (Boulanger 2009: 35–36; Rooney 1981: 33). James's enduring contribution to these efforts was to divide the "Dayaks"—the common European name for non-Muslim natives of Borneo, which probably derived from the widespread indigenous term for "person" (Hose and McDougall 1993, I: 22; King 1993: 29–30; Roth 1980, I: 42)— into "Sea" and "Land" Dayaks in vague recognition of their habitation patterns (Keppel 1846, II: 174; Mundy 1848: 234; Roth 1980, I: 43). These became the cornerstones of an increasingly complex set of taxonomies, based variously on genealogy, "race," "tribal" identity, locality, and individual affiliation, which were built up as Sarawak's territories expanded. Their legitimacy was boosted by scholarly publications, which more often confused than clarified the situation as they made further refinements, additions, and omissions (e.g., Hose and McDougall 1993; Leach 1950; Roth 1980).

Such taxonomic maneuvers were riddled with caveats, betraying the authors' awareness of the inevitably conjectural nature of such classification exercises (e.g., Hose and McDougall 1993, I: 42; Roth 1980, I: 43). The schema they produced, however, acquired new political weight and a concomitant degree of fixed reality from the mid-twentieth century, as Sarawak was ceded to the British Crown (1946), then gained independence as part of Malaysia in 1963.[5] By the late-1950s, the combined efforts of administrators, scholars (including Edmund Leach, who was commissioned to produce a social scientific survey of Sarawak's inhabitants in the 1940s),[6] and others combined to produce a template of ethnic groupings that eventually gave rise to 30 official "native groups," as they became known in Article 161a of the new Malaysian Constitution (1963). In this milieu, "Dayak" in the European sense was adopted as the generic label for Sarawak's non-Muslim indigenes (Boulanger 2009: 42). The "Sea Dayaks" were renamed the "Iban," while various small communities in central Borneo were subsumed into larger groups, such as the pan-ethnic category "Orang Ulu" ("upriver people").[7] Meanwhile, the "Land Dayaks" formally changed their name to "Bidayuh," while incorporating new additions along the way—notably the Malayic-speaking Selako, who chose to "become Bidayuh" for fear of becoming "geographically isolated" in Sarawak's far southwestern corner (Winzeler 1997: 222).

The new name appears to have taken a while to gain currency. Some of my middle-aged acquaintances from Singai, for example, recalled how they initially shunned the idea of being called "Bidayuh," which they associated with the uncouth inhabitants of the Bukar-Sadong area. Many people in Benuk, on the other hand, accepted the validity of "Bidayuh" but did not know what it meant and carried on using "Dayak" as the closest thing to an ethnonym. Over time, however, the ethnic label has been accepted across the Bidayuh spectrum as a legitimate category of belonging intrinsic to their membership of Malaysia. As an elderly lady in Benuk put it, "We don't know which villages white people come from—London, America, Australia—so we call them all *branda*. The government doesn't know which villages we come from, so they call us all 'Bidayuh.'"

At the dawn of independence, then, what had mostly begun as local endonyms or taxonomically expedient innovations became the foundations for Sarawak's racial and ethnic order. The new ethnic groupings acquired added political mileage through the formation of bodies such as the Dayak Bidayuh National Association, the Iban-dominated Sarawak Dayak National Union (1956), and the Orang

Ulu National Association (1966). Such ethnically based forms of sociopolitical organization were relatively new to Sarawak (Leigh 1974: 7). However, their increasing salience from the 1950s paralleled a similarly pervasive preoccupation with race relations in next-door Malaya, to which it became wed in 1963 to form Malaysia.

Ketuanan Melayu: Malay Ascendancy and *Bumiputera* Politics in Malay(si)a

When Malaya gained independence from the British in 1957, it had long been depicted and governed as what the economist J. S. Furnivall famously termed a "plural" society (Hefner 2001: 16–17; Kessler 1992: 139; Shamsul 2001): a situation in which "two or more elements or social orders which live side by side, yet without mingling, in one political unit" (Furnivall 1944: 446). In the case of the British-ruled Malay states, such segregation took place along racial lines—a process set in train in the late-1870s, when the embryonic colonial government pursued an open-door policy of economic migration, encouraging large groups of Chinese and Indian laborers to work in tin mines, rubber plantations, and other industries.

This migratory influx had a lasting impact on the peninsula's demographic composition, creating a number of "enclave communities" that retained their own distinct languages, practices, and social norms (Hefner 2001: 19). The divisions were exacerbated by British economic policy, which attributed certain roles and occupations to specific groups: the Chinese, for example, to mining and commerce, and the Malays,[8] thought to suffer from a general "disinclination to work" (Swettenham 1948: 136), to peasant agriculture. This approach to governance formalized and probably generated further ethnic and racial divisions, notably through censuses, settlement plans, and other mechanisms (Hirschman 1987; Reid 2001: 307; Shamsul 2004: 145). By the mid-twentieth century, the idea that Malaya consisted primarily of three races (Malay, Chinese, and Indian) had become deeply ingrained in colonial epistemology and administration, as well as in the minds of many local elites.

Not all races, however, were equivalent in this framework. In the government's eyes, the Chinese and Indians would always be aliens in their adopted land, while the Malays, despite their apparent indolence and backwardness, deserved as indigenes to be buffered from the "rapaciousness of others" (Watson 1996: 10). During pre-independence negotiations in the 1950s, such paternalist sentiments evolved into explicit acknowledgment of Malay preeminence. Seen as occupying a disadvantaged niche within its own country, the Malay majority was deemed to require affirmative action in order to compete with other races, notably the rapidly growing Chinese (ibid.: 10). A report by the Reid Commission (1957), formed to offer recommendations for the new Malayan Constitution, advocated provisions for the "safeguarding of the special position of the Malays," which it suggested be reviewed or discontinued after 15 years (Parmer 1957: 149). This "special position" was duly enshrined in Article 153 of the Constitution, but the latter clause was rejected, thereby leading a contemporary commentator to predict that it held "little hope for the eventual attainment of equal rights for non-Malays" (ibid.: 150). The overall effect was that the Federation of Malaya and its successor, Malaysia, became a state "constructed around not simply a core culture, but a core ethnie"—the Malay race (Reid 2001: 309). This principle later gained candid expression in a slogan that has since endured both ideologically and in practice: *ketuanan Melayu* ("Malay dominance").[9]

Ketuanan Melayu is a claim to rightful (rectificatory) Malay ascendancy, based first on colonial policy and later on its postcolonial reincarnation as a "particular nationalist narrative of Malay indignity" (Kahn 2006: xv). In this regard, it coexists rather awkwardly alongside Malaysia's nominal ethos of racial and ethnic harmony, which has recently been reasserted through measures such as the National Integrity Plan (Hooker 2004: 161–164)[10] and National Service (Chapter 7). This combination, however, is not as contradictory as it sounds, for the very possibility of there being a dominant racial group rests on the existence of a racial and ethnic system for it to dominate. *Ketuanan Melayu* is in fact foundational to the Malaysian social, political, and economic structure, serving as the benchmark against which all other categories and privileges are defined (Shamsul 1998: 141–144). Put differently, the present Malaysian system is highly ethnicized precisely *because* it is "Malayized" (Shamsul 2001), with ethnic citizenship being an offshoot of the very conditions that make *ketuanan Melayu* possible.

This was the world that Sarawak and Sabah joined in 1963. During independence negotiations, it was agreed that their large and equally indigenous populations should be accorded the same "special position," protection, and privileges as the Malays on the Peninsula. Consequently, Article 153 of the Malaysian Constitution was expanded to include "Malays and natives of any of the states of Sabah and Sarawak." Collectively, these groups are known as *bumiputera* (literally, "sons of the soil")[11]: a title that indexes its claimants' indigeneity and their inalienable right to the land and its fruits. *Bumi*s, as they are popularly known, have access to substantial political and economic benefits, including entry quotas for the civil service and government-run higher education, entitlements to special bank accounts and loans, government housing and scholarships, as well as numerous incentives designed to increase their stake in the national economy. Although this system has since been sternly criticized by both *bumiputera* and non-*bumiputera*, it remains central to national development policies and has been repeatedly defended by the ruling United Malays National Organization (UMNO) as the only feasible means of righting historical injustices and persistent socioeconomic disparities in the country (e.g., Abdullah Ahmad Badawi 2006; Mahathir Mohamad 1991).

Malaysia's pro*bumiputera* policies, which were formally instituted in the New Economic Policy of 1970–1971, have amplified the importance of ethnic affiliation in Sarawak, for *bumi* benefits can be claimed only through a proven genealogical link with an eligible (i.e., indigenous) ethnie. In this way, ethnonyms devised in a late-colonial taxonomic fog, such as "Bidayuh" and "Orang Ulu," have acquired very real political and economic weight in contemporary Sarawak as determinants of access to *bumi* perks.[12] On a more quotidian level, such categories are also important organizing features of everyday Malaysian life. Like their fellow citizens, Sarawakians must state their ethnic affiliation when applying for jobs, enrolling their children in school, buying vehicles, or seeking medical attention. In this way, ethnicity and its assumed attributes, including "culture" and "religion," have become powerful idioms and modes of action in *moden* Malaysia. In this scheme, *moden*-ity, ethnicity, and indigeneity go hand in hand—a theme to which we shall later return.

Bidayuh *Moden*

In contemporary Malaysia, the *bumiputera* system overlaps considerably with another set of state policies, discourses, and practices: those revolving around the notion of *pembangunan*, or development. Their influence has been particularly pronounced in Sarawak, which, thanks to the Brooke Raj's deliberate insulation of native interests from commercial exploitation (Cramb and Reece 1988; Grijpstra 1976; Ooi 1997), entered the Federation as an economic backwater, with minimal infrastructure, impoverished rural populations, a rudimentary commercial sector, and untapped natural resources. Over the last few decades, *pembangunan* has become the "dominant paradigm underlying nearly every government action and expenditure in Sarawak" (Brosius 2003: 100)—the solution, it would seem, to "the pangs of rural poverty and backwardness" that keeps the state from taking its "rightful place in the 21st century," as the chief minister and firm advocate of development, Taib Mahmud, once put it (*The Sarawak Tribune,* September 9, 1995; cited in ibid.: 101).

In theory, *pembangunan* transcends racial and ethnic differences, uniting all Malaysian citizens in a march toward progress, modernity, and ultimately, First World Status—a notion reflected in numerous postindependence slogans and development programs. Of these, the most prominent in recent years has been *"Wawasan 2020"* ("Vision 2020"; Boulanger 2009: 60; Hefner 2001: 33; Hooker 2004: 150, 161; Postill 2008: 91–92; Rustam A. Sani 1994): a grandiose, if vague, agenda laid out by the then-Prime Minister Mahathir Mohamad in 1991.[13] Its "ultimate objective" is to turn Malaysia into a "fully developed country by the year 2020" (Mahathir Mohamad 1991); into

> a united nation, with a confident Malaysian society, infused by strong moral and ethical values, living in a society that is democratic, liberal and tolerant, caring, economically just and equitable, progressive and prosperous, and in full possession of an economy that is competitive, dynamic, robust and resilient. (ibid.)

In keeping with the general thrust of earlier New Economic Policies (and their successors, National Development Policies), Mahathir's agenda explicitly seeks to remove "the identification of race with major economic function," such that "economic backwardness" will no longer be identified with race (1991). This stated aspiration, however, glosses over the crucial fact that pro*bumiputera* policies—depicted by Mahathir as "affirmative action" to "build an equitable society" (1991)—continue to operate in this sphere, on the basis that old economic imbalances still need to be redressed. And it is here, ironically, that rosy ideals give way to harsh realities for many of my Bidayuh acquaintances.

While the *bumiputera* policy has bound Sarawakians ever more closely to a national ethnic template, it has simultaneously made them extremely conscious of the ethnic *in*equalities within it. Despite the notional parity of all *bumiputera* in Malaysia, there is a pervasive sense among Bidayuhs that they are only "second-class *bumiputera*" (Bruton 1993: 201) in comparison to their Muslim counterparts: to the Malays, who dominate government in Malaysia, and to the Melanau, the Muslim-majority group who dominates politics in

Sarawak. In my fieldsite, one of the most frequently cited examples of this gap between theory and reality was that of young, well-educated Bidayuhs who had applied for civil service jobs, deemed among the most prestigious in the nation. Recalling one of several stock cases from the village, people would point out that even though such Bidayuhs had "big schooling" (*sekolah-i baga*), they could not find work, because nine out of ten positions were reserved for Malays, even those less well-qualified (see also Boulanger 2009: 146).

For my acquaintances, then, Malaysian *moden*-ity has been a two-pronged affair. On the one hand, *pembangunan* promises a great deal: good jobs, a range of consumer and luxury items, sound infrastructure amenities such as electricity and piped water, and of course, the cash with which to afford all of this. To the extent that they seek to attain these perks by participating in development schemes and the national economy, they may be said to have become properly Malaysian. On the other hand, like most things Malaysian, this form of *moden*-ity comes with a string of ethnic, racial, and religious caveats. While all this has not diminished Bidayuhs' conviction that they are part of the wider Malaysian nation, it has certainly generated a widespread sense of alienation from its institutions and the powers-that-be.

This is not to suggest, however, that Bidayuhs have been roundly unsuccessful in *dunia moden*—a point that has been made repeatedly by a relatively small group of urbanized, self-professed "educated Bidayuh leaders" (Kiong 2003: 58). Many of them view themselves as having escaped from the "backward," myopic, "closed community" (ibid.) in which their rural counterparts live. In their speeches and writings, they often depict Bidayuh villages as bastions of conservatism and hindrances to progress; as Bidayuhs' "own small world, where there is a lot of petty and empty talks, of doing their things in the gardens and farms and, at times, talking negatively about what go [sic] on outside their villages or about other peoples or races or the government of the day" (Minos 2000: 59; see also Mamit, Sarok, and Amin 2003). In these discourses—which draw clear but, vitally, surmountable lines between progressive, urban elites and backward villages—rural Bidayuhs have only themselves and their "closed" traditional culture to blame for their lack of success in modern Malaysia. Tinged with genuine faith in the nation's developmentalist agendas, such discourses have filtered into rural villages through various channels and do exert an influence on some sections of the population—particularly the literate, relatively urbanized professionals who sit on village committees. However, even their perspectives tend to be marked by more complexity and ambivalence than those I have just described.

Although they are firmly committed to being part of *dunia moden* and making progress through education and links with the wider world, many rural Bidayuhs also see Malaysian "developmentalism" as inescapably ethnicized (Loh 2001). While thus ever hopeful that the politicians will "give" them development, my acquaintances also see them as complicit in a national politics of marginality—one governed, it is tacitly assumed, by profit and patronage rather than ethnicity—which hampers "ordinary" Bidayuhs from becoming fully *moden*. Such were the sentiments that surfaced during a chat I had with a man at a village barbeque on *Hari Merdeka* ("Independence/ Freedom Day")—Malaysia's national day, which commemorates Malaya's independence in 1957. Watching his children tear up and down the unpaved driveway of his house, waving little plastic flags, he reflected wryly, "*Merdeka?* There is no *merdeka* here. When we get proper roads and piped water [from the government and local Members of Parliament], then there will be *merdeka*." The implication of his statement, as live footage of the official celebrations in Kuala Lumpur blared on the television nearby, was clear. To be fully Malaysian—to have *merdeka*—is to have full access to the benefits of *dunia moden*. More pointedly, it is to have benefits to which *Malays* and other Muslims are deemed to have privileged access—a sentiment that is resurrected whenever another soap opera featuring rich Malays living in opulent air-conditioned houses and driving large cars airs on my informants' television screens (see also Postill 2008: 108–109). Such programs merge with a wider pool of evidence, including newspaper reports, politicians' broadcasts, and personal anecdotes, which are routinely used to argue that Malay-Muslim dominance of the country has hijacked *pembangunan* for everyone else.

In many lower-income village households, this sense of being trapped in a rut of imperfect *moden*-ity regularly manifests itself in the pressing problem of cash flow (or its lack thereof). For these families, *moden* amenities such as 24-hour electricity, mobile telephones, health care, vehicles, and education have proven mixed blessings. While now seen as necessities of life, these ultimately cost money to maintain: money that a large proportion of rural families, whose main wage earners bring home meager salaries from their work in factories or construction sites, can ill afford. The difficulties arising from these situations can swiftly turn to resentment when stories start creeping along the village grapevine about how some rural Malay communities are getting the *moden* infrastructure that has for so long eluded

Bidayuh areas (see also Harris 2001: 60), or that a spanking new community hall has just been built for a nearby village whose inhabitants converted en masse to Islam (Chapter 4).

Since independence, then, Bidayuhs have become Malaysian, ethnic, and *moden* all at once. These factors come as a single package and greatly heighten my acquaintances' consciousness of living in a world significantly different from before. It is a world that, in some ways, maps neatly onto what James Scott derisively calls "high modernism" (1998): a "muscle-bound" (ibid.: 4) ideology of human, scientific, and economic progress that disclaims the past and embraces the future (ibid.: 95; see also Baxstrom forthcoming). Malaysia, my acquaintances sense, is on a forward march to *moden*-ity, and they would very much like to be a part of it. Yet, there is also a pervasive anxiety that, through little fault of their own, they are somehow always out of step, or worse, lagging behind. *Moden*-ity has had its perks, but it has also left them constantly chasing after benefits that they as Malaysians and *bumiputeras* are entitled to but are persistently denied through Malay-Muslim dominance. In this respect, their transition to *moden*-ity has not been complete, leaving them lingering in an interstitial zone of hope, expectation, and, increasingly, resentment.

While my acquaintances' experiences of *moden*-ity have often left them feeling marginal and alienated, however, there is one arena in which they have been able to engage more positively with the wider Malaysian milieu. That arena, as I shall now explain, is multiculturalism—a peculiar genus of which has become a major political and economic force in Sarawak.

Living in a "Cultural Paradise": Multiculturalism and Modernity in Sarawak

> Head into Sarawak's interiors and your heartbeat will flutter at the fascinating and enchanting dances of the multi-ethnic tribes living harmoniously with each other... (http://www.sarawaktourism.com)

The Sarawak Tourism Board's official Web site alluringly depicts the state as a "cultural," "natural," and "convention" (i.e., meetings and conferences) paradise, where "nature meets modernity to get things done in a very different yet effective way." This combination of "nature," "culture," and "modernity" is less an alchemy than a juxtaposition of three elements that are seen as—and indeed must remain—incommensurable. Indeed, it is precisely their creative tension (Hold a meeting in a rainforest! Fly to a secluded upriver longhouse!) that lends Sarawak its appeal.

Such expectations, forged by official promotional material, foreign media, and travel guides, were rife among the visitors I met in Benuk, which has been a small-scale tourist attraction since the 1960s (Chua 2006a, 2009a). Intrigued by what they perceived as a mixture of the traditional and the new, they would often ask me, with the curiosity of the complicit, how the villagers had adapted to modern life. This was not lost on my informants, who, in turn, asked whether those tourists, like others of village lore, thought they were headhunters or monkeys who lived in trees. One woman recalled being incensed by a sightseer from Kuala Lumpur, who asked her daughter as she sat on the longhouse veranda whether she had ever visited Kuching. Her daughter, it emerged, worked in a bank in the city, and just happened to be home for the weekend. The mother herself had been an *amah* (nanny) for a Chinese family in Kuching, while her husband had worked as a cleaner in the Sarawak General Hospital; like many others, they had chosen to return to the village upon his retirement. "Who do these people think we are?!" she fumed in recollection, "Just because we live in longhouses doesn't mean that we are not *moden!*"

At the same time, this woman knew that what made Benuk interesting to tourists was its status as "a Bidayuh village," which distinguished it from an Iban or a Malay village. She knew that they were most interested in aspects of *dunia jah* that marked Benuk out as Bidayuh: the longhouse, the *pangah* (head-house), *adat gawai* paraphernalia, rattan baskets, and rice processing techniques, for example. She, like a number of other elderly women, had a regular stock of baskets that she would occasionally sell to interested visitors, and if they or their guide spoke Malay, she would often tell them to visit the *pangah* and the river where villagers bathed and washed their clothes. While thus not seeing *dunia jah* and *dunia moden* as incompatible, she was certainly aware of the multicultural ideal propagated by both governmental and touristic discourses in Sarawak: discourses that define ethnicity and culture within the *moden* world in resolutely *jah* terms.

More than emphasizing the pastness of these entities, however, official models push things a step further by depicting that past as continuing to shape and suffuse natives' lives in the present. In this respect, they are the diametric opposite of the "high modernist" developmentalist policies mentioned earlier, for rather than situating their subjects in a temporal progression, they obviate all traces of temporality and change. Such discourses draw on an international traffic of culture concepts, generating a model that "reifies culture and traces it to ethnicity, and...reifies ethnicity and postulates 'communities' of 'culture' based on purported ethnic categories" (Baumann 1996: 20). Here, both ethnicity and culture are made to look like "primordial attachments": "the 'givens'—or more precisely...the assumed 'givens'—of social existence" that arise from assumed "congruities of blood, speech, custom, and so on" (Geertz 1993d: 259). In Sarawak, "culture" is as natural an asset as the rainforests, caves, and rivers with which it coexists: a fundamentally time*less* phenomenon that has transcended the temporal shifts and ruptures of modernity.

The most prominent demonstration of Sarawakian multiculturalism takes place annually on June 1, during the state-sanctioned Gawai Dayak festival. Deriving from the Iban and Bidayuh term for "festival" or "ceremony" (*gawai*; see Chapter 2), this two-day public holiday has evolved into a statewide celebration of indigeneity—of "Dayak" in the encompassing sense. Originally devised in the 1950s and 1960s (Boulanger 2000: 50; Postill 2008: 170–171), Gawai Dayak draws inspiration from the pre-Christian postharvesting festivals celebrated by Iban and Bidayuh communities: massive, raucous villagewide affairs that marked the end of the old "rice year" and the start of the new. Although these rituals are now practiced in only a handful of villages, Gawai Dayak has persisted as a distinctively "cultural" affair—as the Dayak equivalent of Chinese New Year and the Muslim (= Malay) Hari Raya that marks the end of Ramadan. By occupying this "slot in the official calendar," Gawai Dayak enables indigenous Sarawakian groups to "symbolically claim a parity" with other races (Postill 2008: 178) and embed themselves in the wider, multiethnic state.

The annual Gawai Dayak celebrations in Kuching offer revealing insights into the way ethnic "culture" is defined in Sarawak. Every May, gaudy banners, often sponsored by state bodies or commercial firms (such as beer companies), appear at coffee shops, retail outlets, public areas, and government offices. These routinely contain images of young men and women decked in "traditional" Iban, Bidayuh, and Orang Ulu costumes, standing alongside each other in a picture of multiethnic harmony and "unity in diversity." Such visual displays are complemented by culturally themed street parades, restaurant buffets showcasing Dayak delicacies, and most extravagantly, an annual Kumang ("divine beauty"/"beauty queen") Gawai pageant, in which young representatives from each major ethnic category, dressed in a dazzling, jangling array of "traditional" costumes, parade to a soundtrack of "cultural" music before an appreciative audience in a large hotel ballroom. All these events draw upon and perpetuate a certain stock of artifacts and attire that have become metonyms for each major "culture" in the collective Sarawakian imagination. "The Bidayuh," for example, are almost always represented by young women dressed in what are essentially female *gawai* practitioners' clothes, including their distinctive red, black, and white hats and bead necklaces. In this field, ritual, ethnicity, and culture are thus folded almost seamlessly into each other: here, *adat gawai is* "the Bidayuh culture."

A similarly seductive kind of slippage occurs at another jewel in Sarawak's multiculturalist crown: the Sarawak Cultural Village (SCV). A colorful, 14-acre theme park located near Kuching, the SCV was set up in 1989 by the Sarawak Economic Development Corporation, with support from the Tourism Board and other governmental organizations (Latrell 2008: 44). Like many tourism initiatives, it is an explicitly commercial enterprise, tying "culture" to the state's economic development. As 1 of an estimated 15 such sites in Malaysia (Dellios 2002: 4), the SCV offers a whistle-stop tour of "culture" through architecture, "traditional handicrafts," food, and dance performances. In this spirit, it describes itself as a "living museum" where "it is possible to see Sarawak's ethnic diversity at a glance."[14] Each of the state's main official ethnic groups—Iban, Malay, Bidayuh, Chinese, Melanau, Penan, and Orang Ulu—is represented by a generic version of its "customary" dwelling, in which resident families live, dress in traditional garb, demonstrate traditional activities, and take care of bed and breakfast guests. SCV's spatial layout mirrors its multiethnic theme: Houses are clustered around a single lake in full view of each other, so that it is impossible to look out of the colossal "Orang Ulu longhouse" without catching sight of the "Chinese farm house" opposite.[15]

While multiculturalism is trumpeted as a feature of modern Malaysia, its substance in the SCV is uncompromisingly traditional. Before each model house stands a signboard introducing the ethnic group and listing its chief cultural characteristics, which are invariably rooted in a premodern past. These descriptions are written in the present tense, verbally instantiating the temporal compression intrinsic to the "living museum" concept. In the Bidayuh longhouse, for example, guides are dressed in adaptations of *gawai* ritual garb and periodically demonstrate the use of the wooden rice grinder and sugarcane press, both of which have long been replaced by machines in many villages. When I asked one of the ladies where the gongs and jars on display were from, she replied with practiced ease, "China," before launching into an explanation about barter trade and heirloom acquisition in past centuries. I was in fact trying to find out from where the SCV had obtained these items (the Sarawak Museum), but her instantaneous response reflected its ethos of privileging the distant past rather than the modern present. In the SCV, "culture" is the product of an unbroken ethnic and implicitly genealogical link with the past, and that which ethnic groups in the present can claim as inalienably theirs.

Here, the tension identified at the beginning of this section resurfaces. In Sarawak's multiculturalist discourses, "tradition" and "modernity" may coexist (just as ethnic groups coexist), but they do not meld. The SCV is an extreme but instructive expression of the notion that to be fully modern in multicultural Malaysia, an ethnic group must also have a fully traditional culture, which lends it national and international legitimacy. But how exactly are these traditions and cultures demarcated? As with other postcolonial states, Malaysia has long been concerned with the question of how to handle the relationship between modernization and local cultures, traditions and values, however these are defined.[16] Like modernization, economic growth, religious freedom (Chapter 4), and race relations, multiculturalism has had to be carefully managed in the decades since independence.

In Sarawak, this has been achieved through a series of five Cultural Heritage Symposia, held in 1988, 1993, 1998, 2003, and 2009. These events, which draw together representatives from each major ethnic group, have essentially served as means of delineating

> various aspects of indigenous culture that need to be preserved, modified and promoted,...focus[ing] on those positive aspects of indigenous cultural items that could be utilized and exploited for national needs and requirements,...[and] reviewing...cultural and ethnic identities, or images, for positive contribution to national aspirations. (Chin and Kedit 1989: vi)

These aims are rendered concrete through supplementary ethnicity-based workshops, in which community leaders, politicians, and researchers present papers and conduct discussions on what to preserve and to discard (Winzeler 1996: 20). In the first Bidayuh cultural workshop of 1988, for example, topics included overviews of "the Bidayuh culture," the impact of economic progress, ways of promoting Bidayuh heritage, and its contributions to Malaysian national culture.[17] But perhaps the most intriguing—and far-reaching—result of this event was the identification of an appropriate symbol that could feasibly stand for the entire Bidayuh community. This privilege was bestowed upon that elevated structure known variously as the *baruk*, the *pangah*, or the "head-house."

The *baruk* is an architectural feature unique to the Bidayuh (Leach 1950: 54) that has historically served as a meeting hall, men's ritual house, guest house, and, most sensationally, a store for the community's collection of skulls (Geddes 1954: 20–22; Winzeler 1997: 208)—most of them the heads of vanquished enemies who were then tasked with guarding the village.[18] By the time of the 1988 symposium, the ritual and political importance of *baruk*s had declined precipitously, leaving only a few such structures in certain villages, including Benuk, in which *gawai* rituals were still occurring. Participants at the workshop, however, thought that it would be a useful means of distinguishing the Bidayuh from other ethnic groups, and thus opted to revive—and certainly reinvent—its physical and aesthetic *form* as a key "Bidayuh tradition" to be maintained and endorsed (Winzeler 1996: 20). The hope was to turn it into a focal point of Bidayuh identity and loyalty, one that, as politician James Dawos Mamit put it, would bring

> pride into our hearts as Bidayuh. The *baruk* thus unite [sic] us as an ethnic group. It is recognized that the *baruk* is an integral element of the Bidayuh way of life; an institution where our rich culture is preserved and thus, more should be restored. (2003: 28)

In the last two decades, the *baruk* has been widely promoted by both Bidayuh leaders and non-Bidayuhs as a recognizably Bidayuh emblem, tourist attraction, and architectural prototype, resurfacing in the form of church halls, civic buildings (such as municipal halls and libraries), public pavilions, restaurants, printed icons, and even an online community.[19] One such edifice, filled with gongs, Chinese jars, baskets, drums, and other "traditional" objects, takes pride of place at the Bidayuh longhouse in the SCV, while another is used for community gatherings, discussions, and meals at the headquarters of the Dayak Bidayuh National Association in Kuching. It is in such explicitly multiethnic settings, where members of different groups regularly come into contact, that the *baruk* is most effectively transformed into a specifically Bidayuh cultural entity. In this way, it has become one of the many cultural emblems that jostle for attention on Sarawak's multiculturalist stage.

These efforts to prune and define an appropriately modern "Bidayuh culture" broach a number of questions that usually remain invisible in official multiculturalist models and discourses: Which elements of the past are commensurable with the present and future? Can these elements be modified or put to different use? And who or what determines their inclusion, exclusion, or appropriateness? As backstage negotiations to celebrations of "culture," such as the SCV and Gawai Dayak, they momentarily expose the "temporal sensibilit[ies]" (Guyer 2007: 409), as well as insecurities, of Malaysia's peculiar brand of "modernity." In this world, "culture," like "modernity," is not a given: it must constantly be defined, worked toward, and (re)aligned with other national priorities.

As Part II will reveal, such concerns are not the exclusive province of politicians and community leaders in Kuching. They are also shared by many Bidayuhs in rural villages—both in the context of Malaysian multiculturalism and in relation to their lives as Christians. The point to make here is that these village-based concerns have not arisen in isolation but are regularly being invoked, articulated, and (re)shaped by the wider currents of Malaysian *moden*-ity and multiculturalism. In the next section, we look at how some of these wider, state-level and even international "cultural" developments are being manifested in rural Bidayuh villages, while acquiring new dimensions in the process.

Culture in the Jungle

While Sarawakian multiculturalism is displayed most concertedly in Kuching, it is not confined to it. Like other aspects of Malaysian *moden*-ity, it generates a regular traffic of ideas, events, and artifacts between towns and villages—not least because many village residents move within the same urban circles as those who shape it. In recent years, the Sarawak government has put a great deal of work into bringing "development" and "modernity" to Bidayuh villages by building up their commercial viability as tourist attractions, often by channeling funds into what are deemed to be their "cultural" strengths. These efforts have usually been met with enthusiasm by village Bidayuhs, who generally participate wholeheartedly in rural "culture"-making exercises.

As with Postill's Iban informants (2008), their receptivity to such governmental schemes has been enhanced by the influence of mass media, particularly the satellite televisions that mushroomed across the villages when 24-hour electricity was introduced in the 1990s, and are now staples of social life. Television and radio programs often include documentaries about the heritage of various Malaysian states, live footage of multicultural parades in Kuala Lumpur and other cities, and catchy songs propounding racial harmony, to which children, who have already encountered these ideas at school, sing along. In recent years, moreover, Bidayuhs have been able to watch themselves, their villages, and their "traditions" on these very screens. Benuk's longhouse, for example, has been the setting for a number of national soap operas, documentaries about "the Bidayuh," as well as highly popular Iban and Bidayuh music videos, to which villagers warble along on karaoke sets at weekends. (Indeed, my adoptive aunt often suggested only half-jokingly that one day, she and her family would turn to the National Geographic Channel and find the photographs I had taken of them on screen.) In their own ways, these influences have generated a strong awareness of the cachet of "culture" (*budaya*), while also giving villagers a fairly consistent impression of what that "culture" ought to consist of—clothing, headgear, necklaces, dances, and baskets being routine examples.

Such media-based valorizations of "culture" have been supplemented in concrete ways by various governmental initiatives. While tourism itself is not new to Bidayuh areas, the 2000s saw an unprecedented surge in state-supported village "homestay" and jungle trekking programs, which allow tourists to spend a few days with a local family and experience "traditional" village life. This usually entails participating in a number of stock activities, such as "jungle trekking in [sic] tropical rainforest," "hunting with the blowpipe demonstration [sic]," rice harvesting, leaning to cook traditional foods, and watching "Bidayuh traditional cultural dance performance," as the Web site for the homestay program at Annah Rais near Benuk puts it.[20] Illustrated with photographs of white people doing precisely these things, it is filled with touristic catchphrases, revealing a familiarity with the perceived interests of an imagined visitor in search of both nature and culture.

Since the 1988 Cultural Symposium, the *baruk* has also grown increasingly prominent in rural "culture"-making exercises. In recent years, the few villages that still possess *baruks*—some of which are used for *gawai* rituals—have been given government funds to maintain and develop them as tourist attractions. Benuk's *pangah*, for example, underwent a major renovation with funds from the Ministry of Tourism from 2008 to 2009, reopening with a lavish ceremony presided over by the Minister for Urban Development and Tourism, Michael Manyin, who took the opportunity to spell out the government's plans to boost Sarawak's village homestay industry.[21] Meanwhile, several Bidayuh villages have built new *baruk*s as both community resources and tourist attractions, using them as chapels, gathering halls, and accommodation for visitors. One of the most prominent examples of this is the library of the Research and Development Movement of Singai Sarawak (REDEEMS) complex at Kampung Apar near Bau. REDEEMS was founded in 1997 as a community-based organization that, in its president's words, aims to "make the community to be actively involved in and contribute to their own development toward its vision for an orderly, disciplined and progressive society."[22] Since its establishment, it has been used regularly by the wider Singai community, and drawn Bidayuh villagers from throughout the Kuching Division to participate in its "cultural" activities, such as an annual pan-Bidayuh Gawai Festival, displays of traditional architecture and artifacts, and a Bidayuh Language Development Project (Rensch et al. 2006: 23–27).

All these developments have brought very tangible benefits to Bidayuh villages. Cash infusions are provided to village committees, for example, to beautify and upgrade their tourist attractions, such as bamboo bridges, *baruk*s, and riverside platforms. Homestay operators are also regularly given funds to improve their toilet and sleeping facilities such that they meet basic, government-defined standards of quality. Villages have further profited from various infrastructural developments, notably the extension of well-tarred roads through areas with tourist attractions and the gradual introduction of piped, treated water to rural areas. Moreover, as Chapter 7 reveals, being a well-equipped "cultural" attraction is a useful way of establishing relations with important political figures and local government officials, upon whose help the village might need to call in the future.

Casting a jaded scholarly eye over these developments, it is perhaps tempting to posit that, like so many postcolonial, non-Western people studied by anthropologists, the Bidayuh have either become canny operators manipulating the politics and economics of "culture" or are simply absorbing and reproducing the official models and frameworks propagated by the state. As contributions to the study of cultural consciousness (Introduction), these analyses have generally taken a cynical view of non-Western peoples' engagements with quintessentially Western essentialisms, often deconstructing them as political inventions or (more forgivingly) misapprehensions that create static, "stripped-down, simplified version[s] of...culture to stand in for the more complex and contradictory actuality" (Latrell 2008: 46). Such was the prevalence of this argument throughout the 1990s that

Marshall Sahlins, casting his own jaded meta-analytical eye over the field, declared that "pretty soon everyone will have a culture; only the anthropologists will doubt it" (1999: 402).

While not disputing the important contributions made by the literature on cultural consciousness, nor indeed the highly politicized nature of Sarawakian multiculturalism, I wish to make a rather different point in this book. My suggestion is that analyzing Bidayuh engagements with the "culture" phenomenon in predominantly political terms risks obviating the many complexities and ambiguities inherent in the situation—particularly those related to ritual and religious efficacy. Moreover, by assigning explanatory and analytical primacy to political processes, this approach risks treating Bidayuh exegeses on the situation as mere refractions of a more fundamental political reality that only the analyst can identify. The limitations of such a perspective will become obvious in the following example, which raises important questions that will remain salient throughout the book.

Beyond homestays and *baruk*s, the most conspicuous examples of "culture"-making in Bidayuh villages are the "cultural performances" held at various points throughout the year to mark official visits by politicians, government officials, large groups of tourists, and sometimes, film crews. These mostly involve young men and women clad in *gawai* attire performing carefully choreographed versions of *gawai* dances that would not look out of place in a Kuching hotel. However, in communities with practicing *gawai* populations—and even in those where *gawai*'s demise was relatively recent—it can be difficult to determine where ritual ends and "culture" begins, for the two often meld into each other. In Benuk, for example, "cultural performances" are carried out by two main parties: the regular youth dance troupe, and the elderly *gawai* practitioners themselves, who carry out scaled-down versions of normal rituals that nevertheless invoke real spirits and feature real ritual structures and offerings. On some occasions, their performances take place separately before coming together in a memorable dénouement, with both young performers and elderly practitioners circling the *sangar* (bamboo "altar") in an improvised rendition of the *gawai* "eagle dance."

Similar scenes often unfold during the village's yearly Gawai Dayak celebrations, which take place in accordance with the official government calendar. As I explain in the next chapter, *gawai* practitioners usually hold their own postharvesting rituals (*gawai sawa*) at the same time, so as to take advantage of the presence of younger, able-bodied Christians who have returned to the village for the holiday

Figure 1.1   Teenage girls performing a "Bidayuh cultural dance" for a documentary film crew from *Radio Televisyen Malaysia* (RTM), the national broadcasting corporation, Kampung Benuk, 2006.

and can thus help with the ritual preparations. During the height of the festivities, *adat gawai* rituals and "culture" frequently feed into each other: The elderly practitioners, for example, may dance to the tunes played by competitors in the village gong competition, in which teams vie to play the best renditions of ritual harmonies, while young girls may perform their "cultural" dances for the entertainment of the crowd during breaks in the ritual proceedings (figure 1.1). At these events, the term *budaya* acquires a certain elasticity, applying not only to the dance performances and gong competitions but also to the *gawai* rituals themselves.

For most of my informants, Christian and otherwise, there is little contradiction in saying that *adat gawai* in these situations is *both* an efficacious ritual practice and their "culture." However, this very ambiguity can also cause problems. On one of my visits to Kuching, I met up with a Bidayuh civil servant—a staunch Catholic from Singai who was heavily involved in state-level cultural management—who recounted his attendance at a recent Gawai Dayak celebration at REDEEMS. He told me that prior to its commencement, everybody in the audience stood up to recite a series of Christian prayers. These were important, he said, because the celebration was going to feature an actual *gawai* ritual performed by some elderly practitioners. Such affairs, he reflected, often made him and other Christians feel uncomfortable, because even though they were being performed as "culture," they would still attract spirits to the site. Moreover, he added, *gawai* rituals were hazardous affairs in which even one misstep, however unintentional, could bring misfortune to the whole community and its crops. The prayers, then, had two aims: to bless the whole ceremony, including the *gawai* ritual, which everybody hoped would go well, and to protect Christians from the potential spiritual dangers posed by its execution.

These sentiments—variations of which I have heard in both towns and villages—go some way to complicating the analytical frameworks and contentions of many other anthropologists of cultural consciousness. Such moments of ambivalence suggest that for many Bidayuhs, "culture" is not simply a political contrivance but can also have very real ritual ramifications. Understanding its significance in my acquaintances' lives thus requires more than an exploration of the politics of "culture" in Malaysia and Sarawak—it demands an appreciation of the ritual and religious factors at play in the same situation. "Culture" may be a vital means through which rural Bidayuhs can overcome (or at least challenge) the ethnic and religious politics of *moden* Malaysia, but it would be restrictive to presume that it can be fully analyzed through a political lens. In the next two chapters, then, we turn to the rest of the contextual jigsaw and examine *adat gawai* itself and the religion that has been at least as important as Malaysian multiculturalism in shaping Bidayuhs' conceptions of "culture"—Christianity.

Chapter 2

Following the Rice Year: *Adat Gawai*, Past and Present

As the last chapter revealed, multiculturalist discourses depict Sarawak's indigenous groups as existing in a timeless space of "tradition" not quite removed from, yet not quite commensurate with, modernity. What these portrayals often gloss over, however, is a topic of central importance to their very subjects: religion. While the omission of Christianity from official portraits of Bidayuh-ness is not surprising, it is striking that its predecessor, *adat gawai*, has not received much attention beyond its highly aestheticized "cultural" incarnations. This chapter attempts to fill in those blanks through an exploration of *adat gawai* as a ritual complex, both as it functioned in the pre-Christian past and as it has evolved in an increasingly urbanized, Christian present. As the next few chapters will reveal, it would be fallacious to describe *adat gawai*—and indeed *adat* in general—as an unchanging, bounded entity. This is particularly true in Bidayuh communities where Christians live side by side with the few remaining practitioners of the old ways. Although I devote separate chapters of this book to *adat gawai* and Christianity, then, it will become obvious that there is a constant, sometimes problematic, overlap between the two in reality; as contemporary phenomena, neither can be discussed without reference to the other. To begin, I recount one such scene of overlap—an entire saga, in fact—that unfolded over several months in 2005.

To *Bom* or Not to *Bom*: The White Crocodile under the Bakan Bridge

The main entrance to Kampung Benuk lies at the foot of the Bakan Range—a series of limestone hills flanking the Sarawak River as it meanders through Penrissen. The village is approached via a tarred road that hugs the curve of the mountain, its lush foliage overhanging and occasionally tumbling onto passersby. But falling vegetation is the least of people's worries: according to elderly inhabitants, the Bakan area has always been filled with spirits, whose presence, while diminished in this Christian day and age, remain very real and potentially harmful. Hints of these historical dangers can be found throughout the vicinity. Two small wooden statues (*tibudò kayuh*), each armed with miniature weapons, stand by the roadside; carved anew every year, they have guarded the area since it became the village's main entry point decades ago. Down the road was once a "ghost shop" (*kedai umot*) from which people could purchase charms, amulets, knowledge, and invulnerability before a skirmish. Closer to the mountain is a tall tree from which enemies heads were hung in the distant past (*jaman jah*), and on which the owl—a ghostly bird and the harbinger of death—perches in the dead of night.

For most of Benuk's residents, however, this is simply the road that links the core village site to its outlying neighborhoods, the Anglican and Sidang Injil Borneo churches, the clinic, farms, schools, and urban areas. People pass through it every day, heedless of spirits in the daytime and marginally more wary at night. Until mid-2005, its arterial importance was reflected by the state of Jambatan Bakan, the narrow bridge lying across the Bujang River at the village entrance. The width of a car and the length of two, it was a tired, overused structure guaranteeing a bone-jarring ride to the vehicles trundling across it. However, I thought nothing about this until it arose in a conversation with Nija, the then-Ketua Kaum (village head), about government-funded infrastructural projects. Jambatan Bakan was a nagging concern at the time: It was old and decrepit, he said, but most of his requests for it to be replaced or repaired had been turned down. This was not because the state was trying to withhold "development" from Benuk—an endemic suspicion in village circles—but because of an incident in the 1990s, when the village committee itself rebuffed governmental attempts to replace the bridge during a road-tarring project. To explain why the other villagers deemed the rejection valid, he told me about the crocodile under the Bakan bridge.

Like all the mountains surrounding Benuk, Bakan has a spirit associated with it. The reason that work on Jambatan Bakan had to be halted in the 1990s was that the government contractors working on this project wanted to blow (*bom*) it up and erect a new one in its stead. At this point, the village committee encountered protests from the *nyamba gawai* (*gawai* elders), who reminded them that the village's most important guardian spirit, a white crocodile, lived in the waters beneath the bridge. Some say that the crocodile was a pig that was about to be sacrificed for a *gawai* ritual in the old days. Miraculously, it escaped and ran into the river, where it transformed into a small white crocodile (*buai pedi*) with a lion's roar. Soon afterward, the spirit of the crocodile appeared in a dream to a ritual elder, telling him that from then on, it would surface whenever there was danger afoot. This would be a sign to those who saw or heard it to carry out a *gawai* ceremony to restore the peace and safety of the village. Now that most people were Christian, the crocodile emerged less often—and certainly not within living memory—but, the *nyamba gawai* pointed out, it was still there. Blowing up the bridge might kill the crocodile or chase it away, thereby depriving Benuk of its guardian spirit and unleashing untold dangers. Facing this situation, the village committee acceded to their request, and the old bridge was not demolished but patchily tarred over.

This, the Ketua Kaum lamented, put him in a difficult position. While he wanted to respect the *nyamba gawai*'s wishes, he was also responsible for village welfare and infrastructural improvements. Since taking up the job a few years earlier, he had submitted several applications to the Public Works Department requesting that it resume work on the bridge. Most were rejected—the authorities saw Benuk as having squandered its first "golden opportunity"—but when we spoke, he seemed confident about his latest application. He had told the government, he said morosely, that most of the opponents of the project had died and that the "new generation" wanted another bridge. It was not an easy decision to make, especially since the Tua Gawai (ritual chief) was his uncle, but he would just have to find a compromise.

Over the next few months, I mentioned the Jambatan Bakan crocodile to various people in the village, most of whom had at least heard of it. Some young adults were vaguely aware of the story, but reasoned that since they did not know what to do in the event of a sighting, the crocodile's fate was of little concern to them (Chua 2009b). Others pointed out that if there was once a crocodile, it was no longer there and they should not pay heed to "superstition." Still others figured that while it was not good to *bom* the crocodile's home, any unfortunate consequences could be dealt with by going to church—after all, the village was also protected by Christianity these days. Meanwhile, an Anglican woman suggested that the village could offer Christian and *gawai* prayers to let the crocodile know what was happening, and hopefully appease it. In sum, there was little consensus over what to do about the white crocodile under Jambatan Bakan—assuming it was even around anymore. Two consistent assumptions, however, underpinned these motley responses. First, there was no question over the veracity of the crocodile's existence: everybody acknowledged it existed or had existed in the past, even if its presence was hardly apprehended today. For most Christians, the key issue was whether it was of any consequence in a *moden*, Christianized village. Second, whatever people's opinions on the crocodile, they all agreed that they should consider the wishes of the *nyamba gawai* before taking action.

In July 2005, the Ketua Kaum's planning application received approval, and work on Jambatan Bakan commenced. A deal was reached: a new bridge would be erected on the same site, and the old one would not be blown up but dismantled and relocated to a nearby stream. One Saturday morning in late August, a *gawai* ritual was held by the river. Its aim was to bless the new bridge (the foundations of which had been established) and its temporary replacement nearby, and to keep malign influences away from the site. The story of the origin of the white crocodile was recounted by some Anglicans, who noted that we were standing on the very spot where the pig escaped. The ritual itself—performed by the Tua Gawai with the help of about ten (Christian) men—was not elaborate, although it was a typically merry, drunken affair, beginning with offerings to the spirits and ending in a huge communal meal of a sacrificial chicken and pig, cooked in metal vats over an open fire.

At noon, the Chinese boss of the bridge construction company, who had paid for[1] the sacrificial sow as a goodwill gesture, arrived and was dragged over to join the meal, where he was fêted with strong home-brewed *arak* (distilled rice wine). Passing vehicles—many carrying urbanites returning to the village for the weekend—were flagged down and stopped, and their passengers invited to eat something or donate money or food.[2] Most did both quite readily, for this was a normal, if infrequent, aspect of village life that they were happy to support. Not everyone knew why there was a *gawai* ritual being held at this spot, although it was not hard to guess that it was bridge related. (As we shall see, full knowledge on the part of nonspecialists is not expected or necessary for a ritual's success.) Nevertheless, not all villagers passed through in blithe ignorance.

Two days earlier, I spoke to a lady who had invited me to a party at a house on the outskirts of the village, just beyond Jambatan Bakan. She was afraid that the event, scheduled for Saturday night, might have to be cancelled if the bridge ritual was held that day. *Gawai* rituals often involve a "prohibition" (*păris/patang*) period that shuts off the ritual site (in this case, the bridge) to all traffic, making it impossible for people to pass. Disregarding such *patang*s constitutes an offence punishable by a cash fine and ritual compensation; it also exposes the culprit to spiritual punishment, such as illness, an accident, or even death. While an active member of the Catholic church, this lady was keen not to break the *patang:* it had to be respected; and besides, why take the risk? In the end, I made it to dinner as planned, as no such restriction was imposed by the Tua Gawai, who—possibly realizing the futility of stemming the flow of weekend traffic—simply went home afterward. Luckily, this calculated risk was justified in the following days by the absence of any untoward consequences or omens, and work on the bridge progressed.

This episode captures part of the experience of living in a world that my informants themselves depict as being in transition between *adat gawai* and Christianity. Because the old ways and their attendant regulations, artifacts, and spirits are still unavoidably part of village life, most Christians in Benuk have at least a passing familiarity with *adat gawai*; even those who know little about it have, at one point or another, had to navigate a potentially hazardous path between its many obligations and prohibitions (Chua 2009b). As I explain in Part II, their willingness to do so stems partly from their respect for their older relatives and neighbors, partly from a growing awareness that *adat gawai* is valued by the state, tourists, and other outsiders as "tradition" or "culture," and partly from a pragmatic desire to avert social discord or being fined as a result of flouting ritual regulations. Another important reason, however, is simply that these old ways constitute an *adat*, which by consensual definition is worth taking seriously. And it is to this concept that we must turn first in order to appreciate the role of *adat gawai*, and later Christianity, in Bidayuh life.

Ideals, Actions, and Effects: An Introduction to *Adat*

A concept of Arabic origin with cognates across the Malay world (Sather 2004: 123), *adat* is commonly translated as "customary law"—a reflection of its earliest manifestations during the fifteenth-century spread of Islam in Southeast Asia as a means of codifying indigenous beliefs and practices (Zainal Kling 1997: 45). This impulse was later extended by colonial scholars and administrators—particularly those in the Dutch East Indies (Schrauwers 1998: 208–211)—and inherited in various forms by their postcolonial successors. Today, *adat* is a multifaceted entity throughout the Malay world: brandished as a political weapon by indigenous rights movements in Indonesia[3] and "virtually exalted" (Boulanger 2009: 128) as a defining property of *bumiputera* groups in Malaysia, with far-reaching implications in inheritance and land tenure, as well as in "native" affairs falling beyond the remit of civil or Islamic courts (Boulanger 2008: 129–130; Hooker 1972; Langub 1994; Peletz 2002).

While distantly aware of its legal and political manifestations, most of my village acquaintances tend to see *adat* as simply a guide to life—a way of "being a person" (Koepping 2006: 60). Encompassing far more than "customary law," it is most commonly manifested in "rules and expectations" that govern "every aspect of existence" (Schiller 1997: 77), including politics, law, diet, religion, and economy. As Peter Metcalf, writing about Berawan *adèd* in central Borneo, puts it:

> The general category of things under which the usages of religion are subsumed is called *adèd*, but *adèd* involves much more than religion. Table manners, or the Borneo equivalent, are *adèd*; so are rules concerning who may fish where, and who may wear what kinds of beads, and how fruit trees are inherited, and a thousand other things besides. *Adèd* is everything from etiquette to law, everything, in short, that is governed by explicit rules or prescriptions, including ritual. (1991: 4)

This "wide but precise" definition of *adèd* as "simply 'the way of doing things'" (ibid.: 5) also sums up Bidayuh conceptualizations of *adat*. For most of my acquaintances, *adat* is less epistemological than experiential: it does not exist as a comprehensive body of abstract knowledge but emerges in shreds and patches, in and through specific things and practices. It is often said in Benuk, for example, that to "have *adat*" is to know which form of "you" to use when speaking to an older person, to eat or avoid certain foods on specific occasions, to wear appropriate clothing, and to use the correct implements for particular tasks. There are *adat*s for farming, village life, and city or urban life and those that were obeyed in the past (*jaman jah*). Spirits and certain animals too have their own *adat*, which humans may not fully comprehend but is "nevertheless presumed to exist" (Schiller 1997: 78).

The boundaries of these different sets of *adat* are porous and elastic, thereby allowing them to exist on multiple levels. At its most abstract and encompassing, *adat* is akin to an "immutable law of nature" (Zainal Kling 1997: 47) that dictates that heat burns and water wets (ibid.), that cocks crow and goats bleat (Hooker 1974: 75), and that the sun rises in the east and sets in the west (Sather 2004: 124). On an intermediate level, it may imply a long-standing norm, such as the Kayan adage that the *adat* of the Chinese—who have historically dominated commerce in Southeast Asia—is to be financially success-ful (Rousseau 1998: 6), or (as I often heard in Benuk) that it is *adat* for death to occur in old age. Finally, there is the more idiosyncratic level of *adat istiadat*—those diverse "procedural and ritualistic prin-ciples" (Zainal Kling 1997: 48) through which people engage with the human and nonhuman universe. At this prescriptive level, we find village *adat, adat gawai*, Christianity, and other similar sets of regu-lations. Although *adat* is most changeable and variable at this stage (ibid.), its performance has repercussions for the other levels of *adat*-reality; as such, it should still be followed diligently. In conversation, of course, the term *adat* may refer to one or all of these different levels, and it is only the analyst who attempts to delineate them, often without ready success. The vagueness of *adat* is thus its strength, making it a compelling mode of justification and injunction that can apply to potentially everything.

In Bidayuh societies, *adat* is broadly understood to maintain har-mony within the community and to preserve its general well-being (Adat Bidayuh 1994: i). In this prescriptive capacity, it is a tool for bringing about desirable outcomes—ultimately conceived as the establishment and maintenance of an ideal state of "coolness," or *madud* (see also Harris 2001: 62; Lindell 2000: 105–107), and the banishment of "heatiness" (*bŭngŭh* or *pǎras*), which is associated with conflict, imbalance, danger, and illness—the sorts of hazardous states that would have incited the white crocodile under the Bakan bridge to surface. In this respect, *adat* may be described as a science of ideals—even if, as my acquaintances acknowledge, reality does not always live up to theory. In reproducing their exegeses here, then, my aim is not to reproduce that fictitious "image of the harmonious *adat* community...entrenched in Indonesian [and other regional] stud-ies" (Tsing 1993: 152) but to highlight the way Bidayuhs often talk about and treat *adat* as a self-evidently valid and important feature of daily life. Like their legal, anthropological, and historical observers, however, they are fully aware of how unstable and open to interpreta-tion *adat* can actually be. As Chapter 7 explains, *adat* is often judged by its efficacy, such that verdicts on how well it has been done tend to be passed in retrospect (see also Rousseau 1998: 117; Wadley, Pashia, and Palmer 2006: 50). This gives its adherents considerable leeway in dealing with inconvenient situations or conflicts of interest, as hap-pened with the Jambatan Bakan ritual.

Adat: Indigenous Religion?

We shall return several more times in this book to the features of *adat* that I have just outlined. Before moving on, however, it is worth addressing an important analytical question: how does *adat* relate to "religion"? This is a critical consideration in the study of non-Muslim communities in the Malay Archipelago. Unlike their Muslim counterparts, many such communities have not historically distinguished *adat* from *ugama/agama* (Sather 2004: 124)—a Sanskritic term that in Malaysia and Indonesia has come to imply a broadly monotheistic, scriptural "world religion" (Atkinson 1983: 686–687; Kipp and Rodgers 1987). As Chapter 4 reveals, this notion of *agama* has grown increasingly important for Bidayuhs in recent years—but it has not completely filled the shoes of *adat*, which remains a key causal and conceptual framework in village life. This situation thus presents us with two analytical challenges. First, what is the difference between *adat* and *agama* if both can be (and have been) translated as "religion"? This will take a while to unravel and will be addressed more fully in chapters 4 and 5. The second challenge, with which I deal here, is whether there is a basis for asserting (as Borneanists often do; e.g., Metcalf 1991: 4; Rousseau 1998: 6; Schiller 1997: 77–79) that *adat* is the closest thing that many indigenous societies have to Euro-American concepts of religion.

The encompassing nature of *adat* is of pivotal importance here. Pragmatically, *adat* seems a suitable counterpart to religion simply because it deals with the things that we "first expect to constitute religious phenomena," such as "spirit beliefs, rituals, and cosmologies" (Kipp and Rodgers 1987: 28). It also fulfils many functions that anthropological convention has assigned to religions: "provid[ing] an impressive instrument for explanation, prediction, and control" (Horton 1971: 101), furnishing "models of" and "models for" reality (Geertz 1993b: 93; Turner 1967), perpetuating power imbalances (Bloch 1986) or certain social configurations, and enabling its adherents to construct social and spiritual realities (Schieffelin 1985). The fact that these functions and their attendant tutelary entities have repercussions in farming, politics, inheritance, and law may thus make it tempting to characterize *adat* as a primordial form of religion that has spilled over into everything else (Durkheim 2001).

While this overlap is a fitting reason to analogize the two concepts, however, it is also an impoverished one, for we could just as easily reason that *adat* is the closest indigenous equivalent to "law," "tradition," "custom," or "culture." The danger of this mode of definition-by-association is that it licenses scholars to use *adat* as a byword for a whole range of other concepts without having to address the question of what makes any of them tick. My interest, however, is in moving beyond this impasse by explaining just how *adat* is understood by its adherents to work and why certain types of *adat* may be discussed in religious terms. Drawing on an article by Alfred Gell, I suggest that my informants do distinguish certain forms of *adat*— which may be described as "religious practices"—from others. Yet, such *adat*s do not operate in a fundamentally different way from the rest, for they are essentially *homologies* of the basic *adat* model outlined earlier. While not losing sight of what makes them distinctive, we should also avoid assessing them in isolation, for their "religiosity" is merely one facet of their broader nature.

In his paper, "The Technology of Enchantment and the Enchantment of Technology," Gell makes a case for treating Trobriand magic as one of many "means of technical production" (1999: 181), such as gardening, marriage, and art, through which crops, persons, and social relations can be reproduced. These processes, he argues, are homologous modes of "the rational pursuit of technical objectives" (ibid.: 179) undertaken by any society. Yet, he also differentiates magic from the rest, because it is able to achieve those objectives without the same effort and drudgery entailed by "burdensome" activities such as gardening (ibid.: 180). Like art— which is able to "enchant" viewers through its "technical virtuosity" (ibid.: 173)—magic produces effects that most others are "at a loss to explain" (ibid.: 184) or replicate. In this way, Gell desacralizes both art and magic without homogenizing them. In treating them as homologous technical processes, he is able to examine how they might be understood to work; but in acknowledging their "enchanting" qualities, he also reminds us of why and how they might be distinctive to Trobrianders.

I wish to strike a similar balance in approaching *adat*'s multifarious incarnations. In Gell's terms, *adat* in its holistic form may be seen as a "technical base" or template through which Bidayuhs can produce effects. These may include anything from bountiful harvests to lucrative business ventures, good health to marriage. The precise means of attaining these goals, however, tend to vary along the lines of *adat istiadat*. When my acquaintances fall ill, for example, they usually turn first to vitamins, injections, and pharmaceutical drugs from the government clinic down the road, which they associate with a *moden*, biomedical modality intrinsic to Western *adat*. But if these fail, or if they want reassurance, they also have recourse to the healing rites of *adat gawai*, Christianity, or both. All these options are thus homologous technical processes stemming from a base model of *adat*, in the sense that they are geared toward the same *madud*-generating end. However, *adat gawai* and Christianity are distinguishable from Western biomedical *adat* by virtue of the added presence of spirits, God, and other nonhuman social others, with whom people can negotiate but not fully control.[4] In this, *adat gawai* and Christianity are akin to Gell's "magic" in enjoying the extra, often unfathomable, effort-relieving perks that only spirit entities can provide.

These are the kinds of *adat* that are described in this book as religious practices. In doing so, my aim is not to reify a conception of religion that is exclusively or primarily about "supernatural" entities but to acknowledge that *adat gawai* and Christianity are the only two *adat*s (for this is how Christianity is widely characterized) in Bidayuh communities that are specifically geared toward engaging with them. In the absence of a clear-cut definition of that notoriously slippery concept of religion, this characterization must thus serve to anchor the analysis that follows. This is a fine balance to maintain: while it is important to interrogate the very workings of *adat gawai* and Christianity rather than setting them aside as uniquely mystical phenomena, it is also vital not to lose sight of what makes them distinctive to their adherents. In sum, *adat* is not religion—not entirely, anyway. But in many rural Bidayuh communities, what analysts might recognize as religion is often *adat*-shaped.

Adat Gawai

The term "*gawai*" aptly condenses all the features of the events it describes: It is a feast, a ceremony, a celebration, and a religious (i.e., spirit-oriented) rite bundled into one (Nais 1988: 155). *Gawai*s are by definition *rami*—merry, raucous, and most important, crowded—affairs, which are essentially parties for humans and spirits alike (Geddes 1954: 23). As elsewhere in Borneo, "It would be impossible to have a serious [*gawai*] ritual without noise, confusion, and jocularity," for its "sociality . . . is an aspect of its sacredness, and not a byproduct or distraction" (Metcalf 1991: 9). Strictly speaking, then, *gawai* refers only to specific ritual occasions on which groups of people gather to eat, drink, and make merry.[5] In this narrow sense, *adat gawai* refers to the rules and regulations surrounding *gawai* performances, and the causative principles, paraphernalia, and spirit entities associated with them.

In day-to-day conversation, however, many Bidayuhs use the term *"adat gawai"* as a byword for *"adat jah"* (the old *adat*): a convenient term encompassing a range of procedures, understandings, and realities associated with the non-Christian past. Not all require the holding of a *gawai*, although many are performed by the same people and involve similar spirit entities, objects, and protocol.[6] Such overlaps make it difficult to distinguish between *gawai* and *non-gawai* rituals and observances, which often feed into each other practically and discursively—particularly in the last couple of decades, which have seen a rapid decline of the old ways. Such developments have cast a homogenizing pall over the practice of *adat jah*, drawing together its elderly practitioners as non-Christians by default, regardless of which "cult" (Geddes 1954: 31) they follow or their areas of expertise. This is not an impracticable solution, for at the end of the day these practices all share the same fundamental aim of making the village and its inhabitants *madud*, and banishing malicious influences that might generate a state of *păras*. In light of this, I shall take my cue from my informants, as well as from the anthropologist Fiona Harris (2001), and use *"adat gawai"* to encapsulate the full range of understandings, realities, and "rituals associated with the non-Christian life-world" (Harris 2001: 9).

As mentioned earlier, Kampung Benuk is one of an ever-shrinking number of Bidayuh communities to still have a practicing *gawai* population. When I arrived in 2004, there were 10 or 11 *nyamba gawai* in the village, only 9 of whom were fit enough to participate in rituals. Their population has since shrunk further, following a few deaths and one conversion to Christianity.[7] The elderly practitioners' situation was (and, at the time of writing, still is) tenuous. Their capacity to carry out rituals depended on the survival of their one male member—Bai Toyan, who had been Tua Gawai since the late-1970s—and Sumuk Nyangŭ, the only woman acquainted with the full set of female ritual chants (*băris*). Although elderly, both are fairly robust—Bai Toyan occasionally works as a security guard in Kuching, while Sumuk Nyangŭ tends a small vegetable farm—and have continued to lead *gawai* rituals up to the present. Should one of them die, however, the whole of *adat gawai* in Kampung Benuk will go with them, for every ritual requires a *tua gawai* and a senior *dayung băris* (literally, chanting lady) to direct proceedings. Eligibility to lead *gawai* is determined solely through ritual knowledge—even a Chinese person, I was often told, could become a *tua gawai* if he knew enough—but for these elderly practitioners, there is no one to whom they can transmit the knowledge they have accumulated orally and praxiologically over many decades.

Much of the following overview draws on fieldwork I have conducted with these *nyamba gawai*, during which I documented their ceremonies and practices and recorded their discourses and reflections on the ritual complex.[8] These people, however, were the first to point out that they were practicing a diminished form of *adat gawai*, steadily attenuated by the loss of personnel, knowledge, and memory over the years. Consequently, I shall supplement my description with information from other sources on *gawai*-related practices in Bidayuh villages, written at various points over the last century (e.g., Geddes 1954, 1961; Harris 2001; Lindell 2000; Nuek 2002; Roth 1980, I: 164–288; Sidaway 1969; St John 1974: Chapter IV). Although none are identical to those practiced in Kampung Benuk, they are underpinned by broadly similar principles, concerns, mechanisms, and causal sequences. Nevertheless, the following account makes no claim to comprehensiveness or coherence, for there are as many inconsistencies between Bidayuh regions and villages as there are similarities.

These expositions should thus be taken as ideal templates for what ought to be rather than as direct indices of reality. In keeping with the way many of my informants describe *adat gawai*, these will be articulated in distinctly material and performative terms, the significance of which will be dissected in Chapter 7. Because *adat gawai* is still practiced in Benuk in the form that I encountered it, I shall use the present tense in describing its basic features and principles. This should not, however, blind us to the fact that it is a dynamic, evolving phenomenon—a point to which we shall return later.

Gifts from the Skies

Like many other features of Bidayuh life, *adat gawai* originally came from elsewhere (e.g., Howes 1952: 74–76; Noeb and Noeb n.d.; St John 1974: 202–204). In one of several variations of its origin story, told to me by Sumuk Nyangŭ, it was brought to earth in the distant past by a woman who ascended to the skies. There, she encountered an elderly lady who taught her to chant (*băris*) and clothed her with a skirt (*jamuh*), hat (*sipiah*), and bead necklace (*sitagi*) that would enable her to *băris* in future (figure 2.1). One day, the woman looked down and spotted her husband, who was struggling to dibble and sow in their fields on his own.[9] Feeling great pity and longing for him, she asked the old lady whether she could return to earth to help. The old lady agreed and gave her a host of things to bring back. Upon reuniting with her husband, the woman revealed what she had brought as gifts from the skies, telling him that they must follow *gawai* from

Figure 2.1   Female practitioners (*dayung băris*) clad in ritual clothing chanting during *gawai sawa*, Kampung Benuk, 2005.

then on. These included chants, songs, clothing, yeast plants, young coconuts, fishing rods, sheets of split bamboo, and offering foods. She taught her husband to "do" (*nai*) *gawai* by showing him how to use these items, as well as the relevant actions to go with them. Since then, humans have followed (*tundak*) *gawai* correctly (*tŭnggun*; literally, straight), sacrificing chickens and pigs, dibbling, sowing, and chanting like old people in the past, because all this came from God (*Tăpa/Ieng*; see below).

Embedded in this story are several principles that, as we shall later see, have important implications for our understandings of ritual, religiosity, Christianity, and "culture." First, it is striking that what are effectively foreign practices, artifacts, and other entities are unproblematically accepted and incorporated into the lives of the man and woman. No explanation or recontextualization is needed beyond the fact that they are what God has given to humans. As later chapters will reveal, a similar willingness to take on novel or external phenomena as self-evidently valid can be found in many realms of Bidayuh life, ranging from intermarriage to the acceptance of new *adat*s. Once introduced, moreover, those things and practices can reshape people's lives. From here on, the man and woman realize, they have to follow *gawai* properly—to adopt new habits, relations, and an entire lifestyle. More than simply being incorporated into an existing context, then, the new additions are also actively changing it.

This change is facilitated by the fact that *adat gawai* is primarily a material and performative phenomenon, consisting equally of chants, clothing, plants, artifacts, knowledge, and actions. Its "straightness" thus lies not in the cultivation of an inner self or a deeper understanding of divinity but in "doing" and using things well in the here and now. If there is a religiosity to *adat gawai*, it seems to dwell less in the semantics of ritual recitations than in their pragmatics and performance, in tandem with actions and objects. As will become clear later, this does not imply a clear boundary between "meaning" and "materiality," but it does suggest that material forms and actions are often "crucial conditions of possibility" (Keane 1997: 13) for ritual efficacy. A final, related observation is that in this story, persons are not the only agents at work, for they are equally reliant on the agentive properties and capacities of objects in order to do *gawai* correctly. The woman can *băris* only when she is wearing the appropriate clothing, while the entire package of *gawai* knowledge, regulations, and paraphernalia is described as and indeed transmitted through an assemblage of gifts. As Chapter 7 explains further, what matters in this framework is thus a certain logic of combination and interaction between different entities, human and nonhuman, and the effects that these produce. But what exactly are those combinations meant to achieve? To answer this, we turn to the key concepts, principles, and players of *adat gawai*.

An Animistic Religion? On Souls, Life forces and Spirits

Over the last 150 years, scholars have sometimes described the Bidayuh as "animists" (e.g., Geddes 1961: xxv; Sidaway 1969: 141), largely in recognition of their tendency to attribute a spirit, soul, or life force—usually encapsulated by a single term, *simangi*—to material entities such as stones, trees, beads, jars, and humans. Like its Malay cognate, *semangat*,[10] *simangi* can refer simultaneously to several convergent phenomena. At its most basic, it is what Peter Pels calls "the spirit of matter" (1998): an undifferentiated "living principle" (St John 1974: 177) that "permeates the whole of the physical world" (Endicott 1970: 63), bringing persons and things into being (*jadi*) and sustaining them. In this capacity, *simangi* does not merely infuse materiality but is an active and intrinsic aspect of it.

At another level, however, *simangi* is the closest thing that Bidayuhs have to the concept of an individualized, discrete soul (cf. Endicott 1970: 37, 63): one that endows its bearers with a sensate awareness that enables them to be spoken to, cajoled, chided, and instructed. Unlike the generalized *simangi*-as-life force, soul-like *simangi* are detachable from their bodies, particularly when people dream (Lindell 2000: 102), get a sudden shock (Nuek 2002: 79–81), or fall seriously ill. Upon humans' deaths, *simangi*[11] persist as independent entities, often wandering the earth for a while before finding their way to an appropriate *rais* (village or community), of which there are several (e.g., Geddes 1954: 26; Lindell 2000: 123–124; Roth 1980, I: 218).

Finally, *simangi* is also the generic name for a range of spirits associated with the natural world, such as plants, waterways, and mountains. The most important of these is *simangi padi*—the soul or spirit of rice,[12] Bidayuhs' staple crop (Geddes 1954: 73). As we shall see later, many *gawai* rituals and observances are orientated toward the care of *simangi padi*, for it is an axiomatic understanding that rice enables humans to survive, "grow fat," and thrive. Consequently, most *gawai* rituals are designed to invoke, bless, and obtain the blessings of *simangi padi* (Harris 2001: 118; Nuek 2002: 141)—procedures that often involve the care and bathing of a number of rice stalks, which represent all the village's rice fields, such that the good done to a handful extends to all. Like a baby, however, *simangi padi* is easily frightened or shocked, which might cause it to weaken or flee the rice plant (Geddes 1954: 90–91; also see Endicott 1970: 23–24). This potentially calamitous outcome is averted through daily practice, farming techniques, and *gawai* rituals alike, which treat rice with gentleness and caution. In the not-so-distant past, for example, one had to immediately pick up spilled rice grains while uttering the term "*biya*" (to free from taboo or punishment) to sooth their *simangi*. This is the same thing that some adults mutter today when babies sneeze, as a habitual precautionary measure to prevent *simangi*-loss and illness.

Apart from *simangi,* there are numerous other characters in the *adat gawai* pantheon, which can only be described as vague and labile. Beings within it may morph from one form to another, and a single term may refer to various spirit types. We can safely begin, however, with a fairly universal entity: *Tăpa*, who is described by William Geddes (1954: 25) and others as a sort of "supreme being" and maker of the universe. His[13] name appears to derive from the verb *năpa*—to create or bring into being (Nais 1988: 298)—and he is the closest thing that exists to a monotheistic god. In this capacity, he is depicted as the same deity that is worshipped in Christianity, Islam, Buddhism, and other religious *adat*s, or "ways," as Babuk Ichau, headman of the Bukar-Sadong village of Mentu Tapuh, once explained to Geddes:

> "It is like this—" and then taking out his box of matches, he laid it down with four match-sticks pointing at it from different angles "—this first match here is the Christian way, this second one is the Malay way, this third one is the Chinese way, and this fourth one is our Dayak way. All ways lead to the True God, and it is well that all people should follow one way or the other." (Geddes 1954: 25)

As Chapter 3 explains, similar sentiments prevail in Kampung Benuk, with most Christians pointing out that they are still praying to *Tăpa*, albeit through a different *adat*. Aside from the ubiquity of his name, which is invoked in every *gawai* ritual, however, *Tăpa* seems fairly removed from the day-to-day affairs of men and spirits (Geddes 1954: 25; Sidaway 1969: 138; Roth 1980, I: 165). Consequently, while *Tăpa* is a useful mooring feature of *adat gawai*—and in recent years, of the process of conversion to Christianity—people are not unduly worried about his nature or role. It is to the other spirit entities that they direct most of their energies.

The term "spirit entities" glosses over a multifarious range of beings with whom humans may engage.[14] A small selection of these includes the ghosts of the deceased (*mindo*), named and unnamed ancestors, enemies from the distant past, spirits specific to particular localities (such as the white crocodile under the Bakan bridge), mischievous and potentially malevolent spirits (*gamut, umot*), omen birds,[15] and a range of other entities that dwell in the environs of the village that are not inherently prone to malice but can cause problems if offended or shocked. All these coexist in a nebulous pool in which new beings frequently appear and old ones vanish or acquire new guises. No moral hierarchy separates them, nor are certain groups considered more potent than others. Unlike *Tăpa*, who is by nature obscure and remote anyway, these beings are understood to be eminently manipulable by humans: They can be bribed, bargained with, indulged, and reprimanded through *gawai* rituals and observances. Ancestor spirits, for instance, are benevolently inclined toward their villages but must be invoked and entertained regularly in order to remain so. Conversely, *umot* are undesirable presences, but they can be fed, appeased, and told to depart, or simply fended off through ritual substances, structures, and incantations.

With these tutelary entities forming a populous backdrop to the practice of *adat gawai*, it is unsurprising that every ritual essentially involves managing relations with them. While their scopes and formats differ, they all follow the same basic template of invoking the help and blessings of *Tăpa* and all things benevolent, inviting spirits from the surroundings to partake of offerings of food, drink, tobacco, and other items, throwing a good party and providing entertainment at the ritual site, and then bidding them to do humans' bidding through an imaginative series of "pleas, commands and threats designed to persuade or coerce" (Endicott 1970: 131). In effect, every ritual comprises a series of transactions between humans and spirits, in which relations are established, obligations imposed, and expectations (hopefully) met.

Following the Rice Year

Given the direct relationship between the well-being of *simangi padi* and that of humans, it is hardly surprising that rice cultivation plays a major part in *adat gawai*. Many major rituals take place at different points in the agricultural calendar—a sequence sometimes described as "following the rice year." It is at these events that relations between humans and spirits are realized and reaffirmed in their fullest, liveliest manner; it is also here that the stakes are highest, for what hangs in the balance is the well-being of the *padi*, and by extension, the entire community. Up to the 1970s, when rice cultivation was the predominant activity in most Bidayuh villages, the agricultural cycle and the *gawai* calendar shaped each other. Their relationship was neatly summed up by Peter Howes, a fluent Biatah-speaker and later Archdeacon of Sarawak, who in 1960 wrote a thoughtful and sympathetic account of why many Land Dayaks were not Christian. In it, he recounted the words of a man who explained why he had "fought shy of accepting the Christian 'Law'":

> I have not become a Christian because I *can't*. You see for yourself that our *adat* is bound up with our work. Our worship goes with our work. We don't worship unless it has something to do with our work. We don't work unless it has something to do with our worship.... I need help on my farm, for planting, weeding, harvesting, and to get help I must give it in return. I can only get it and give it if I farm with others, and observe the same periods of work and rest as they do. It is not what I believe, but the way I have to live that keeps me from becoming Christian. (Howes 1960: 493)

Although this tight entanglement of "work" and "worship" later facilitated *adat gawai*'s decline (Chapter 3), it also served as a potent regulating force within Bidayuh communities. While rice cultivation was carried out by individual households, it also relied on large-scale "work exchange" arrangements (*pingiris;* see Nuek 2002: 19–28), whereby members of a collective would take turns working on each constituent farm, thus ensuring that major tasks such as *padi*-sowing could be accomplished quickly and effectively. In this way, entire communities were swept up in the same temporal structure over the course of planting. Following the start of the "rice year" around July—when the Pleiades, or star-sisters from which *adat gawai* is sometimes said to have originated (Lindell 2000: 98–99; Nuek 2002: 134), became visible above the horizon at daybreak (Howes 1952: 75–76; Lindell 2000: 99)—rituals would be held at every stage of cultivation to inform the spirits of the area about the proceedings, and to seek the blessings of *Tăpa* and other tutelary entities.

In the interstices of the work/worship calendar were various other ceremonies, notably healing rituals dedicated to retrieving or strengthening souls during severe illnesses (Geddes 1954: 25), initiation procedures for adolescent boys and girls ready to "enter *gawai*" (*mŭrŭt gawai*), and rites to mark major life stages, such as childbirth, marriage, and death. These usually took place within households (*rawang*), but, like the others already mentioned, shared the same basic concerns of engaging with spirits, strengthening their participants' *simangi*, establishing a state of *madud*, and banishing *păras*. Meanwhile, every village's *gawai* life would be punctuated by various improvised ceremonies devised for specific contingencies. In a river on Benuk's outskirts, for example, lies Batu Jung: a narrow, moss-covered rock that looks remarkably like a wooden boat. According to local stories, it was once a war-canoe bearing either Malay or Bisingai enemies coming to attack the village. Spotting the marauding party from a hill, the village elders immediately held a *gawai* to protect the community. This engendered a strong, chaos-inducing wind (*barui*) that swept over the vessel and turned it to stone. The occupants ran away—some say to safety, others, to the waiting blades of their intended victims. Occasionally, the story continues with Benuk's inhabitants taking the invaders' heads and installing them in the *pangah*.[16] This would have been cause for another major ceremony, *gawai mukah*, in which their spirits were bathed, fed, entertained, and persuaded to become village guardians (Noeb and Noeb n.d.). Up to about the 1990s, *gawai mukah* was repeated at regular intervals; while it is too large and complicated to perform today, the Tua Gawai still bathes, feeds, and blesses the skulls every year for the same purpose.

Finally, *gawai*s could be held to mark the visit of outside parties, such as a contingent from another village, a government representative (from the Brunei Sultanate to the current Malaysian state), or an important traveler. Apart from briefly livening things up, such episodes were vital ways of establishing relations between the village and the rest of the world. Indeed, in such situations, human visitors were effectively of a piece with spirits. As Geddes pointed out,

> In Dayak philosophy, the best way to win friends and influence people is to give them a party, be they Government officials or gods. If such august beings have any self-respect, this imposes an obligation on them to be helpful. Therefore the main festivals are parties put on for the ancestral spirits, for souls of various kinds, for demons prone to mischief and for distinguished visitors. (1954: 18)

Examples of Bidayuh engagement with these "august beings"—particularly European officials and other visitors—through rituals abound in the historical records (e.g., Nuek 2002: 103–104; Roth 1980, I: 242–244, 245–249, 250–251). Their regular occurrence suggests that ritual provided a means *through* which the villagers could engage with visitors, thereby extracting bargains, guarantees, and gifts from them, while also enlisting their participation in ritual sequences to bring about beneficial effects. In these instances, the religious, political, social, and economic dimensions of the visit were all collapsed into the *gawai*—a point to which we shall return in Chapter 7.

While fairly self-contained events, rituals usually entailed a host of attendant observations, proscriptions, and prescriptions that spilled into daily life. As mentioned earlier, almost every ceremony was followed by a *patang* ("prohibition") period, in which movement around the village was restricted, specific foods were banned, and certain activities, such as farming, collecting jungle ferns, or building structures, were momentarily halted. Such *patang*s were considered necessary to purge the village, household, or individual of all *păras* influences and could last from one to eight nights. Breaking them could, in theory, cause a serious imbalance in relations between humans and sprits (Adat Bidayuh 1994: i), engendering illness, petrifaction, and numerous supernatural punishments.

Apart from incurring hefty fines for such transgressions, however, offenders also risked falling out of step with the rest of the community. Indeed, this was the key problem posed by the few Bidayuhs to convert to Christianity from the late-nineteenth and early twentieth centuries. As Howes' interlocutor explained, their "worshipping" in a different manner effectively forced them to follow a different order of "work," sociality, and even residence to their *gawai*-following peers (Lindell 2000: 228; Winzeler 1996: 15), because they would inevitably break the latter's communal *patang*s and live and farm by an alternative schedule (Howes 1960: 493–494). Like Geddes (1954: 24), I found that people were marginally more willing to take their chances with spirits than with their social peers (Chua 2009b). While disregarding or strategically reinterpreting a *patang* could sometimes be retrospectively vindicated (as happened with Jambatan Bakan), the benefits of doing so had to be weighed up against the risk of social censure (see also Wadley, Pashia, and Palmer 2006: 50).

This sense of needing to balance collective obligations is part of a broader, and still salient, moral framework, examined in Chapter 6, in which a notional collective is both the object and the gauge of proper (*patut*) behavior. To be a "good" follower of *adat* is, first and foremost, to be a good social being—whether in terms of relations with spirits or with fellow villagers. Conversely, failure to "do" *adat* properly (such as by breaking a *patang*) does not only bring about supernatural sanction but also the community's disapproval; no sympathy is accorded to those who reap what they have sown (see also Harris 2001: 108). Put differently, while *adat gawai* possesses recognizably "religious" attributes, it is also inextricably embedded in wider social networks, practices, and ideals. For my acquaintances, *adat* always implies a larger collective and networks of sociality: an idea that, as Chapter 6 reveals, works well in theory but can prove problematic in practice.

Adat Gawai in Kampung Benuk

In the last few decades, it has become increasingly difficult for *nyamba gawai* to follow their *adat* in any comprehensive or regular sense. In Benuk, only a few rice-related *gawai*s are now conducted annually: *gawai nyipa'an* (usually abbreviated to *pa'an*), held to bless the rice plants prior to harvesting; *gawai sawa*, which marks the end of the harvest and the consumption of the new rice; and *gawai bayan*, held a few days or weeks after that to formally "close" (*nutŭp*) the old rice year. While the last is held in individual practitioners' households, the first two are observed at the longhouse as large-scale communal events, the blessings and benefits of which extend to the entire village, its crops, and its inhabitants.

The most important of these is *gawai sawa*, the Bidayuh version of the postharvesting rituals on which the official Gawai Dayak festival (Chapter 1) is based (figures 2.2 and 2.3). Up to relatively recently, each village would hold its own *gawai sawa* shortly after the end of the rice harvest in April. (In Benuk during the 1970s, this date was fixed annually as May 5 by the then-Tua Gawai, Otor anak Sunjam.) More recently, however, the increasingly frail *nyamba gawai* have found it expedient to align their rituals with the official Gawai Dayak holiday on June 1 to take advantage of the availability of large numbers of able-bodied villagers who can lend their help and support to the proceedings. Indeed, it is no exaggeration to say that the continued practice of *adat gawai* in Benuk is almost entirely dependent on these Christians, who gather ritual materials such as bamboo from the jungle, handle and cook the sacrificial animals (chickens and sometimes pigs), and play drums and gongs for the practitioners' offertory processions and dances (*birăjang*). It is for the same reason that *gawai* rituals that fall outside the Gawai Dayak holiday are usually held at weekends rather than during the working week;

Figure 2.2 Calling the rice spirit from the river and jungle during *gawai sawa*, Kampung Benuk, 2005.

Figure 2.3 *Gawai sawa* ritual at the longhouse, Kampung Benuk, 2005.

this was further circumscribed during my fieldwork by Bai Toyan's working schedule, which sometimes required him to be in Kuching on Saturday nights.

Although *adat gawai* continues to revolve around rice, then, its very survival has depended on its keeping pace with distinctly *moden* schedules. This is sometimes complicated by village church calendars, which themselves hold special prayer services at important stages of the rice cycle (Chapter 3). February and March 2005, for example, saw a string of *gawai pa'an* observances in Benuk: first by the Catholics, then the *nyamba gawai*, followed by the Anglicans. The reason the Catholics marked *gawai pa'an* early—well before the rice had ripened—was that Lent was about to begin. Lent is commonly understood as constituting a lengthy *patang* on being *rami* (i.e., having fun and socializing): when no birthday parties or discos should be held, for example. Because *gawai pa'an* was considered a *rami* affair, church leaders decided that they could not celebrate it closer to the actual time (which would fall during Lent), choosing instead to observe it the weekend before Lent. A few weeks later, when the rice was ripening, it was the *nyamba gawai*s' turn: two nights of alcohol and gong-fuelled rituals on a weekend when Bai Toyan was not working. I was told that there were more Anglicans in attendance than

Catholics because the latter were trying to observe the Lenten *patang* on being *rami*. Finally, the Anglican church, seemingly unconcerned by this *patang*, held its *gawai pa'an* service that same Sunday, to which several of us who had been at the previous night's ritual turned up, looking and feeling more than a little ragged.

In a curious twist, then, the developments of the last few decades have turned *adat gawai* into a quintessentially *moden* entity, whose survival is greatly dependent on continued Christian support. Up to about the mid-1990s, the eventual conversion of all *nyamba gawai* to Christianity seemed a foregone conclusion; as the next chapter explains, it was just too difficult for them to carry on otherwise. Since then, however, this process has juddered to a halt. The few *gawai* practitioners that were left by the time I started fieldwork were not would-be converts; most of them would carry on practicing it until they died, or until it became impossible to continue—such as if the Tua Gawai or senior *dayung băris* died, or they had to move away from the village. The upshot of this momentary halt in conversion is what a close village friend described as a "not yet pure Christian" village: one in which the old ways, already on the verge of disappearance in the collective imagination, continue to exist alongside the new, with no definite end in sight.

Why did things turn out the way they have? What made Christians lend their full moral and material support to the increasingly attenuated practice of *adat gawai* at such a crucial moment, thus halting what might otherwise have been its natural demise? In Part II, I shall suggest that this situation has come about as the result of several interwoven factors, including the pressures of ethnic and religious politics, the influence of multiculturalism, and indeed the policies and content of Christianity. Before that, however, let us look at the other *adat* that has played such a significant part in Bidayuh life: Christianity.

Chapter 3

The Making of a "Not Yet Pure Christian" Village

In 1969, David Sidaway, a missionary at the Benuk Anglican Dispensary, lamented that

> Christianity has made comparatively little impact on the Biatah-speaking Land Dayak, and, as one might expect, when they do become Christian their interpretation of the faith is coloured by their former traditional beliefs since they come from a pagan world in which magic and superstition are everything. (1969: 139)

Sidaway's pessimism was not unwarranted. Although Christianity had by then been in Sarawak for over a century, large-scale success in conversion had eluded its representatives. Yet, whether or not he realized it, he was writing on the cusp of significant change. A scant 20 years after Sidaway's ruminations were published, the vast majority of Bidayuhs had become Christians of various denominations. Today, Christianity is deeply ingrained in village sociality, and closely, though not inextricably, associated with being Bidayuh.

What brought about this turn of events? How did Christianity grow from being a distinctly marginal religion followed by small pockets of Bidayuhs to a key *adat* governing communal life? Unlike some of their Sarawakian neighbors, such as the Kelabit (Amster 1998: 282–314), Bidayuhs experienced neither a collective epiphany nor a sudden, ruptive change when they became Christian. Instead, conversion began as a tentative, often drawn-out, process, which only later acquired a momentum of its own. Its erratic historical trajectory meant that Christianity was not adopted comprehensively as "a new culture whole" (Robbins 2004: 3) but was engaged from the start in a complex dialogue with *adat gawai*, village sociality, and later, a host of postindependence, *moden* developments. To understand the shapes it takes in Bidayuh villages today, then, we need to examine the peculiar circumstances in which conversion occurred.

Early Forays

While never subject to direct oppression or excessive political control, Christian institutions and personnel in Sarawak have not been completely free agents either. Since the mid-nineteenth century, Christianity has been linked in one way or another to the state— particularly the Brooke Raj (1841–1946) and later the Malaysian government (1963–present).[1] As such, its development should be viewed as part of a broader process of negotiation, collaboration, and occasionally, conflict with political authorities, whose policies have directly and indirectly shaped its nature and presence.

Christianity first entered Sarawak under the auspices of Rajah James Brooke, who began soliciting funds for the establishment of an Anglican mission in his new kingdom while visiting England in 1847. The foundation of the Borneo Church Mission Institute (BCMI) soon followed, as did the first missionaries, Reverends Francis McDougall and William Wright, who arrived in Kuching with their families in June 1848. From the outset, their efforts centered on the moral and material uplift of Dayak communities, whom Brooke depicted as living in a "condition of unparalleled wretchedness" (*The Colonial Church Chronicle* 1847: 28); Muslim communities remained strictly off-limits in accordance with his earlier guarantee not to intervene in the "laws and customs of the Malays of Sarawak" (Payne 2004: 56; Saunders 1992: 19).

Brooke clearly envisioned the Church in Sarawak as both a "civilizing" and a "converting" force (Saunders 1992: 6): here was no place, he felt, for "zealots, intolerants and enthusiasts ... who preach on tubs and begin the task of tuition by a torrent of abuse at what their pupils hold sacred" (cited in Ooi 1991: 284). Under the watchful eye of the government, missionaries' energies were thus channeled into health care, education, and general native welfare (Ooi 1991: 283). As other denominational representatives began entering Sarawak, the Raj effectively carved up the country between them. While the Society for the Propagation of the Gospel (SPG, into which the BCMI was absorbed in 1852) established its foothold in the First and Second Divisions, the Catholic Mill Hill (London) priests, who arrived in 1881, moved into Bau in the First Division

(Lindell 2000: 226–227; Westerwoudt 2002), as well as the Rejang and the Baram in the Third and Fourth Divisions. There, they were followed by the American Methodists, who ministered to Sibu's immigrant Chinese population from the early twentieth century (Ooi 1991: 286). Over the next several decades, these three pioneering churches would be joined by several more strains of Christianity, including Baptists, Seventh-Day Adventists, and the indigenous Sidang Injil Borneo (SIB; Borneo Evangelical Church), more of which we shall see later.

James's early preference for missionaries who would "live quietly, practise medicine, relieve the distressed…and aim to educate the children" (Ooi 1991: 284) set the tone for its manifestations in Sarawak over the next century. Throughout Brooke rule, the work of the Christian missions was most clearly embodied in schools and medical facilities in both urban and rural areas. These were open to all comers, Christian and non-Christian, and received land, funding, and political backing from the Raj. Such establishments, moreover, were deemed by government officials to be useful instruments of sociopolitical control. While concerned about the emasculating impact of Western-style education on the Dayak character (Ooi 1991: 287; Saunders 1992: 191), for example, the second Rajah, Charles Brooke, hoped that the mission presence would calm local skirmishes, undermine slavery (Ooi 1991: 285–289), and encourage shifting communities to settle, thereby facilitating "the population stability" that he and others saw as "a necessary pre-condition to any lasting development in Sarawak" (Rooney 1981: 33). Up to the mid-twentieth century, then, church and state could, in spite of divergent motivations, opinions, and efforts within, be broadly described as "partners in a common enterprise" (Saunders 1992: vx).

While the missions consolidated their position in Kuching, however, they struggled in rural areas. Early European missionaries worked as individuals or small groups in remote, arduous conditions, often facing hostile or indifferent populations (Ooi 1991: 289; Rooney 1981: 39–40; Westerwoudt 2002) and hindered by poor funding and institutional support (Saunders 1992: 196–197). Nevertheless, there were some notable successes among the Land Dayaks. Following a difficult start, the Mill Hill Fathers managed to retain a small but dogged presence in Singai near Bau, with Father Albert Reijffert leading a group of converts to establish their own village, Sagah, in 1905 (Chang 2002: 47; Lindell 2000: 227–228). Meanwhile, the Biatah-speaking village of Kuap (Quop), which provided the language for a new vernacularized liturgy, became a pioneering center for Anglican education and proselytization (Kedit et al. 1998: 51–52), particularly under the leadership of the Reverend William Chalmers (1858–1861) and the redoubtable Peter Howes (1939–early 1950s), keen student of Biatah and later Archdeacon of Sarawak and Brunei. While not winning many other converts, Kuap nevertheless enabled the SPG to maintain a small presence in the area (Kedit et al. 1998: 108; Ooi 1991: 312).

Similar instances of small-scale but relatively isolated conversions dot the history of Christianity in Bidayuh areas. These, coupled with the existence of mission-run schools and clinics, ensured that Christianity remained, at the very least, a known entity among local populations. This pattern is clearly illustrated by the slow, piecemeal spread of Christianity in Kampung Benuk. Anglican influences had been in the village since at least 1926, when a student from the Kuap school opened a class there (Kedit et al. 1998: 61). As elsewhere in the First Division, this early attempt at mission education enjoyed limited success (ibid.: 96); indeed, Howes remarked in the 1930s that the schools in the area were "practically dead" (Ooi 1991: 312–313). Such efforts, however, persisted; and in 1953, Benuk's rudimentary school was reestablished under the control of the Church as St Paul's Anglican Primary School. Its first teacher was Nisserd Robert, a Bidayuh from Kuap. This institution provided an important educational foundation for many children in Benuk and the surrounding areas, who would later spearhead large-scale conversion to Christianity.

From 1956, the SPG's efforts in the area received a significant boost from the Padawan Community Development Scheme (PCDS), which was set up by the British government in collaboration with the Anglican Church to improve health and educational provisions for local communities (Howes 1956; see also Kedit et al. 1998: 109). Run by Howes, the scheme enabled Dayak and European teachers, agriculturalists, nurses, and other trained workers—most of whom spoke Malay or Biatah—to minister to Land Dayak villages in the region. While much of their work took place on an itinerant basis, they also set up a number of permanent facilities. One of them was a clinic in Benuk, established in 1958 by Miss Simit, an Anglican health visitor (Chang 2002: 63; Kedit et al. 1998: 61). It would later be run by a succession of nurses-cum-missionaries (Kempton 2008), including Gwynedd Nicholl, of whom elderly Benuk residents still speak with fondness as "Muk Dawan" ("Grandmother Padawan") (Kedit et al. 1998: 109; Kempton 2008). The clinic, like the PCDS, has since been taken over by the government, but its continued presence near the church and school serves as a physical reminder of their joint origin.

Despite their early failure to establish a large Christian flock, then, missionary efforts to improve material conditions in rural areas appear to have created "a favourable climate for conversion" (Horton 1971: 86) without directly instigating it. Instead, large-scale conversion did not begin to occur until about the early 1970s, when Christianity finally began to replace *gawai* as the majority *adat* in Bidayuh communities. The existence of Anglican-run schools, clinics, and other schemes had been a useful precondition for this phenomenon, but they were evidently not sufficient propagators of change. As Geddes found in Mentu Tapuh in the 1940s (Chapter 2), Christianity seems to have been accepted as part of the *adat* landscape, alongside Islam and Buddhism, as one more inherently valid "way" of engaging with *Tăpa* and other spirit entities. At this time, however, its large-scale expansion was a distinct possibility but not a foregone conclusion. What, then, tipped the balance in Christianity's favor?

Christianization: The First Waves

By way of illumination, let us look at some of the first conversions to take place in Kampung Benuk. The earliest documented case I have come across was that of 14-year-old Denis Miset Sembus, who was baptized in St Thomas' Cathedral in Kuching on July 3, 1955. Denis's father had been village head in the 1950s, and had become friends with Peter Howes, who often stayed with him when traveling to and from St Peter's Church in Pangkalan Empat, Padawan. Denis recounted how, on one such visit, Howes asked him whether he would like to go to school in Kuching, eventually convincing him that he should get a proper education. Through Howes's intercession, Denis became a pupil of Batu Lintang School,[2] boarding there during the week and returning to the village at weekends.

It was in this setting that Denis became exposed to Anglicanism and decided to become Christian. From then on, he would tell his peers about the new religion whenever he went back to the village, eventually drawing several of them into the fold.[3] Soon, this nascent group of Anglicans began holding prayer gatherings at the home of Mr. Nisserd, the teacher at St Paul's. For several years, Anglicanism continued to spread, in Denis's words, "from friend to friend." The group soon outgrew the schoolteacher's house and began meeting in a small bamboo building. In 1963, St Paul's Church was consecrated on a piece of land near the school that had been donated by one of the converts, Goper. It was administered from Kuap until 1971, when it became a parish church with its own permanent priest, Father

Christopher Lewis; today, it has 15 village chapels under its remit (Kedit et al. 1998: 129).

A different but analogous process of conversion to Catholicism took place slightly later. Concerted missionary efforts in the Penrissen region began comparatively late, when the Mill Hill priests established St Ann's mission at Tenth Mile bazaar (now Kota Padawan) in 1963. This was later taken over by the Franciscan Friars, who now run it as the regional parish church. Even before the 1960s, however, Catholic influences had been creeping into local Bidayuh communities. Some of them took root in 1952 in Kampung Simpok (Chang 2002: 135), a village in Padawan with close links to Benuk. It was from here that Catholicism arrived in Benuk in the early 1960s, via John Lambo, who had married a Benuk woman. Together with another Catholic, Matthew Pueh, he was responsible for garnering the first "RC" population in the village.

These early converts were not, like Denis and his friends, young, educated villagers, but often rice farmers who seized on Catholicism as an easier alternative to *adat gawai*. Their numbers, however, remained small—no more than a handful of households—until a cohort of younger adults and teenagers, many of whom had received an education and were now wage earners, began to actively spread Catholicism. Key among them was James Sakas, a dynamic young man who converted in 1975 after the birth of his third child. The fact that he had a basic education was, he told me, important, as this enabled him to go on a course for prayer leaders run by St Ann's. Unlike older, illiterate Catholic converts, who could only repeat stories they had heard and preach what they already knew, he and his peers could read around and draw on wider church resources in order to spread the word. Leading a similarly youthful group of villagers, many of whom had converted while studying or working, he went from house to house talking to relatives and friends about Christianity, reading aloud Bible stories (through which, James said, you could hear the voice of Jesus), and organizing carol services. This time, more villagers began converting, often in familial or neighborly clusters, and St Matthew's Chapel was built on a piece of farmland on a small mound donated by Bai Jewi. Today, its congregation consists of just over a hundred households.

Through these cases, it is possible to discern the multiple, overlapping reasons that enabled conversion to take off in the 1960s and 1970s. First, there were certain "push" factors that convinced some people, such as the earliest Catholic converts in Benuk, that life would be better under Christianity than it was under *adat gawai*. The three that I most commonly recorded were that *adat gawai* entailed too many awkward ritual, omen, and *patang*-related commitments and restrictions, many of which could scupper carefully laid work plans and whole days of planting (Chua 2009b); that *gawai* rituals themselves were tedious, time-consuming, and hard to follow; and that the old death *adat* was expensive and burdensome, obliging the bereaved to carry out costly postmortem rituals, to bury valuables with the deceased, and often pay designated undertakers—of whom there were few—large sums of cash, heirlooms, or parcels of land (Sidaway 1969: 144). For certain subsistence farmers—the people most heavily affected by these regulations—Christianity offered freedom from such onerous responsibilities. My elderly acquaintances often told me that they found it much "easier" to follow, particularly since it mainly involved "sit[ting] down" in church once a week (see also Grijpstra 1976: 75; Harris 2001: 158–159) rather than spending hours gathering and preparing ritual paraphernalia[4] and observing difficult *patang*s.[5] Moreover, Christianity had the added value of protecting converts from the wrath of spirits that might take offense at their rejection of the old rites (but cf. Chua 2009b).

A second important factor was that by the mid-twentieth century, many rural Bidayuhs had developed a genuine respect and affection for the schoolteachers, health visitors, and other mission representatives with whom they had been interacting for many years. While some, such as Denis's father and Benuk's then-Tua Gawai, Otor anak Sunjam, maintained friendly relations with them without converting, others were sufficiently impressed to contemplate adopting their *adat*. This appears to have been the case for Denis, who said that he and his friends had been taken with how kind and generous the missionaries were, and figured that living a Christian life would be the best way to progress in the world. Similarly, some elderly Christians in the nearby Bengoh area told me that they were won over by the fact that the church actually gave moral, logistical, and sometimes financial support to bereaved families, encouraging the whole community to pitch in to help with arrangements rather than forcing them to spend money on rituals, as happened in the past.[6] This perception of Christianity as a caring religion was undoubtedly further given shape and advanced by its stories and songs that missionaries, and later indigenous advocates such as James Sakas, used to spread its message in lieu of outright proselytization. In this respect, the content of Christianity and its real-life manifestations acted as mutually reinforcing draws to potential converts—a point to which we shall return in Chapter 6.

While these two reasons influenced many Bidayuhs' decisions to become Christian, they alone do not explain why conversion gained such momentum from the late-1960s and 1970s. Here, we need to look at a third factor: the shifting social, economic, and political developments in rural communities following independence, for it was in this milieu that the young villagers who became Christianity's most successful proponents shone. These converts were from the first generation to really reap the benefits of mission-run healthcare and basic education, which set them on different trajectories to those of their rice-farming parents. Abetted by the postindependence developments described in Chapter 1, they began moving to towns and bazaars, thus generating a slow population trickle from the villages that drained the agricultural workforce. Many of them were only partial or temporary émigrés, often making regular visits home, or returning after several years' employment. Encouraged by governmental schemes, moreover, growing numbers of villagers—including urban returnees—turned to cultivating cash crops such as rubber, pepper, and cocoa (Grijpstra 1976: Chapter 11), thereby becoming further entangled in the *moden* economy.

Every subsequent generation from the 1960s thus produced fewer swidden farmers. Cumulatively, these developments precipitated a decline in the villages' relative self-sufficiency, and a mounting reliance on cash as the primary medium through which clothes, medicine, tools, and later, *moden* accoutrements such as vehicles, radios, television sets, chairs, and display cabinets could be acquired (see also Grijpstra 1976: 104). Within a couple of decades, the economic and social landscape of the village thus underwent a significant transformation, marked most clearly by the shrinkage of rice cultivation. According to my acquaintances who were young adults during this time, Christianity was better suited than *adat gawai* to this self-consciously *moden*-izing world for several reasons. For a start, its rhythms and temporal regulations were more routine and less haphazard than those of the old ways, which, as Chapter 2 revealed, involved constant *patang*s and omen-based interruptions. Indeed, as Fiona Harris points out, the very idea that such old practices were "time-wasting" was probably forged by the mission schools, which inculcated in their pupils specific ideas about time management and work ethics (2001: 98; see also Comaroff and Comaroff 1991). These understandings would have been accentuated by the growing prominence of what Postill calls the clock-and-calendar time (2008: Chapters 8 and 9) of postcolonial Malaysian public life.

Faced with the demands of regular occupational and educational schedules, young Bidayuhs became less able and prepared to observe communal *gawai* restrictions on movement and work. Christianity's appeal as an alternative *adat* was further enhanced by the fact that apart from Sunday services, its adherents were generally able to pray wherever they were, whenever they wanted, and in any social configuration. In contrast to the collective, highly localized, and predominantly agricultural rituals of *adat gawai*, Christianity was thus better suited to the "macrocosm" (Horton 1971) in which these young adults were now moving.[7] Intrinsic to this *moden* world, moreover, was a deepening association between Islam and political hegemony (Ackerman and Lee 1988)—one that rapidly turned religious affiliation into a highly politicized affair throughout Malaysia. Against this backdrop, as the next chapter reveals, Christianity also came to serve a new, critical purpose for many young Bidayuh villagers: acting as a buffer against Malay-Muslim domination, while still enabling them to tap the benefits of *moden* life.

The Second Wave: 1980s to the Present

When the first Anglican conversions occurred in the 1950s, Denis Sembus recalled, the relationship between *gawai* people and Christians in Benuk was "not too hot, not too cold": Most of the former did not take up the new *adat*, but they seldom objected to their children joining it.[8] Because *gawai* was still practiced by the majority, the new converts continued to abide by its *patang*s and other communal regulations; if a *patang* fell on a Sunday, for example, they would simply skip their prayer session. Such decisions were often pragmatic: At the time, most village leaders were *gawai* followers who could level severe fines on those who breached community-wide taboos. In this climate, Christians in Benuk thus took the path of least resistance in the interest of keeping the peace.

During the 1970s, however, the situation gradually reversed. As the last chapter revealed, *adat gawai* and rice cultivation were historically inextricable, with each sanctioning and supporting the other. This enmeshment of "work" and "worship" made it exceedingly difficult for Christianity to dislodge *adat gawai* in predominantly rice-planting communities, for the latter was not simply "the old religion" but an encompassing way of life. Yet, it was precisely this bond that later triggered the decline of *adat gawai* in most Bidayuh villages, and the concomitant rise of Christianity in its stead. Without its agricultural base and a sufficiently large and able-bodied population to carry out its labor-intensive rituals, *adat gawai* became progressively more difficult to follow, especially for its older adherents. At the same time, the unwillingness of young, *moden* residents to observe *patang*s on movement and participate in night-long rituals—particularly in longhouse-based communities such as Benuk—meant that *gawai* practitioners had to become increasingly flexible in accommodating the Christian majority's movements and habits.

It would be wrong to assume, however, that Christianization during these years was a straightforward process. Indeed, not all converts remained converts: reversions to *adat gawai*, though uncommon, did happen, while many Christians continued availing themselves of *gawai*-based rituals, objects, and substances (Sidaway 1969: 148–151). As I later explain, the fact that Christianity was recognized as an *adat* more suited to the *moden* world did not render *adat gawai* false or less (potentially) efficacious, and in the 1970s it remained a viable option for many people. Father James Meehan, a Catholic priest who ministered to rural Bidayuh congregations during this period, recalled, for example, that there were couples who would "hedge their bets," with one following *gawai* and the other Christianity, in order to take advantage of whichever worked better. A similar logic underlay the occasional conversion *between* different Christian denominations. During this time, there appears to have been little perceived difference between Anglicanism and Catholicism—something that, in many ways, has persisted up to the present. Both were described as "*adat Kristen*," and the choice of which denomination to adopt was often made on the basis of kinship ties, friendships, or other group affiliations. Consequently, it was not uncommon for an entire row of houses to "follow" (*tundak*) one denomination, or for rival factions within a community to go their separate ways (Grijpstra 1976: 74; Harris 2001: 169).

In sum, conversion to Christianity in the 1960s and 1970s was not a one-way sequence but an erratic process shaped by local politics and "religious skepticism and selectivity" (Kirsch 2004: 702; Wadley, Pashia, and Palmer 2006), as villagers figured out, often through trial, gossip, and error, which *adat* to follow. It is instructive, then, that similarly pragmatic impulses underlay the next major wave of Bidayuh conversion from about the 1980s. This largely took place among older, rice-planting villagers who "followed" their children into their respective denominations. At this point, Christianization became more or less inexorable, causing *adat gawai* to diminish at an accelerated pace. A number of key factors contributed to this shift. By the 1980s, villagers had had over a decade in which to compare the relative merits of *adat gawai* and *adat Kristen* in addressing basic concerns such as health, material success, and crop growth. During this time, the two were essentially placed in direct competition as effect-producing *adat*s, with their most potent demonstrations often taking place in the arena of healing. Indeed, it was not uncommon for villagers to deploy both "pagan" amulets and ceremonies and Western medicine prescribed by the Anglican dispensary (Sidaway 1969: 148–151)—the latter being shored up by Christian prayers, rosaries, crosses, holy water, and medallions (some of which, Father Meehan recalled, also circulated among *dayung bǎris* as sartorial accessories). A significant number of Christians were born from these episodes, with the converts choosing the *adat* that had proven most efficacious in curing their ailment, reviving their rice fields, or bringing about some other positive outcome.

The trajectories of many young converts also helped to convince others of the viability of Christianity. Such people tended to do well in *moden* terms, with their educational qualifications enabling them to attain relatively well-paying jobs in urban areas. Their wealth was manifested quite tangibly in the large, detached cement houses that they erected in the village, motor vehicles, radios, display cabinets, and other such trappings: items that, Harris (2001: 100) suggests, took the place of gongs and cannons as barometers of wealth and influence (*rajar*). In effect, these people were beginning to occupy the niche of affluent leadership once filled by successful rice farmers (Chua 2009a: 35; Geddes 1954: 90–92; Harris 2001: 85). In the hierarchy of *moden* governance, moreover, their educational qualifications enabled them to ascend to new, state-sanctioned positions of authority that older, illiterate leaders were ineligible to fill (Grijpstra 1976: 75–76). While these developments did generate tensions within villages, they also served as compelling evidence of Christianity's usefulness in the *moden* world; whether or not it was directly responsible for their success, it had certainly proven to be commensurate with it.

Finally, the fate of *adat gawai*—or more pertinently, concerns about its efficacy—also influenced elderly people's decisions to become Christian (also see Harris 2001: 169). As chapters 2 and 7 explain, *adat* of any sort is said to work best when it is being "done" (*nai*) correctly, as part of a collective effort. By the 1980s, however, *gawai* practitioners in Benuk faced the dual problem of declining manpower and ritual knowledge. The second was a function of the first: as elderly *gawai* people died, they took with them advanced ritual expertise that they had not yet taught others. Over time, certain ceremonies thus had to be simplified or discarded. This, in turn, generated the sense that *adat gawai* was no longer being done well, which, in turn, detracted from its actual (though not potential) efficaciousness. Conversely, as Christianity flourished, it became seen as an *adat* whose efficacy was augmented by the collective efforts of large numbers of practitioners. The clearest illustration of this understanding lay in the gradual consensus among *nyamba gawai* in the 1980s and 1990s that converting to Christianity would safeguard the fate of their souls (*simangi*). By this stage, most of their children had become Christian, and they feared that when they died, their bereaved relatives would not know the appropriate *gawai* rites with which to send their souls to the correct village (*rais*)—or worse, that those rites would be improperly performed. Rather than risking this outcome and becoming lost souls, many of them opted to "enter" (*mŭrŭt*) Christianity, secure in the knowledge that the collective efforts of those they left behind would get them to Heaven (cf. Connolly 2009: 499; Lindell 2000: 232–233; Schiller 1997: 144).

By the late-1990s, then, the vast bulk of Bidayuhs in rural areas had become Christian. While the majority were Anglican or Catholic, several other denominations had also entered the picture, including Methodists, Seventh-Day Adventists, and the Borneo Evangelical Church, or the SIB. The last—the successor to the multidenominational Borneo Evangelical Mission established in 1928[9]—was introduced to Benuk in the early 1990s. Its congregation consists mainly of former Anglicans, who depict "becoming SIB" as a process of spiritual renewal, true repentance, and hence rupture from the past. In this respect, their conversion narratives conform to a recognizable charismatic template that situates Christians within a "sloping temporal order in which people are forever pitched forward" (Robbins 2004: 164) in anticipation of the Second Coming. We shall examine these narratives—and SIB religiosity at large—more closely in Chapter 5. For now, it will suffice to point out that since the SIB's establishment in Benuk, its numbers have grown slowly but not significantly. The majority of Anglicans and Catholics, moreover, view its services and practices with a modicum of suspicion, for reasons that will be discussed later and in Part II. However, none of this detracts from the fact that the SIB is now integral to the community's Christian landscape, and very much included in the common refrain that "*kieh sopŭrŭg Kristen*" ("we are all Christian").

Before moving on, it is worth pausing to consider the handful of elderly practitioners who have defied convention and continued to observe a much-attenuated version of *adat gawai*. As Chapter 2 explained, their capacity to do so is tenuous, for once Bai Toyan and

Sumuk Nyangŭ pass on, the remainder will probably have to become Christian too. But why, we might ask, did they not convert with everyone else? This is admittedly an awkward question, and my queries were mostly met with noncommittal grunts or silence. Like many Christians, *gawai* people view all *adat* as being inherently valid; their objection is not with Christianity per se. What they express reservations about, however, is having to learn a whole new *adat* from scratch, particularly since *gawai* has worked for them for so long. Bai Toyan also mused, quite without prompting one day, that he did not subscribe to the widespread opinion that *adat gawai* was difficult and Christianity "easy." "Christians have to go and pray every Sunday," he pointed out, "But if you follow *gawai* you only have do rituals a few times a year."

These responses arguably stand as skewed reflections of the efficacy-related considerations that convinced others to convert from the 1970s. However, they also reflect the current state of the relationship between *gawai* and Christianity. By the 1990s, *adat gawai* had clearly become a minority practice that everyone acknowledged would soon be "lost" (*mǎnyap*). Yet, by this time, *adat gawai* had also been rehabilitated, so to speak, and redefined through a combination of official multiculturalist discourses (Chapter 1), Christian "inculturation" policies (Chapter 5), and certain aspects of Christian theology and practice (Chapter 6) as a fundamentally worthwhile aspect of Bidayuh life. As Part II will suggest, these developments appear to have spurred many village Christians, ensconced as they now were in the majority, into lending their wholehearted support to the dwindling practice of *gawai*. In a curious paradox, then, the very people who once left *gawai* because they found it difficult have now made it an easier *adat* for its remaining practitioners to follow.

Christianity in Kampung Benuk Today

As we have just seen, Christianity is treated very much as an *adat* in Bidayuh communities. While clearly possessing what I described in the last chapter as a "religious" dimension, it is also "suffusive" (Schiller 1997: 78) of sociality, temporality, morality, and many other features of village life. This section examines certain aspects of contemporary Christianity in Kampung Benuk, as a way of introducing the thematic explorations of Part II. Accordingly, it focuses mainly on the role and place of the three churches in village life, while touching only briefly on their ethnotheological content and practices, which will be explored more fully in the next few chapters.

"We are All Christian"? A Tale of Three Churches

Although villagers constantly reiterate their unity as Christians, there are noticeable distinctions between Benuk's three churches. St Paul's Anglican Church (figure 3.1) is by far the largest, ministering to the majority of Christians in the village and those in the surrounding area (Kedit et al. 1998: 129). As the regional parish church, it has two resident priests, four subdeacons, a large roster of village prayer leaders, lectors, altar boys, a choir, and various interest groups, such as the Women's and Youth Fellowships. Housed in an imposing concrete building on a hill by the main road, its services routinely feature vernacularized versions of old English hymns, the heavy smell of incense, thick white cassocks, Communion at the altar, and rigid physical protocol—all constituting an impressive display of High Anglicanism in the middle of Borneo.

St Matthew's Catholic Chapel is an altogether more modest establishment. A simpler concrete building located in the main village site, it serves a congregation of just over a hundred households. As a satellite of St Ann's Catholic Church in Kota Padawan, it is visited several times a year by the Friars, who celebrate full masses and sometimes hear confessions. Like other Catholic chapels, it relies the rest of the time on a corps of village prayer leaders who run regular Sunday services and preside over wakes, rosary sessions, and other events.

Figure 3.1   St. Paul's Anglican Church, Kampung Benuk, 2009.

Catholic services are also filled with physical and spoken protocol but are markedly less formal than those of their Anglican counterparts, using a vernacular liturgy and contemporary hymns sung in Biatah, Malay, and English. Finally, standing in stark contrast to its older counterparts is the SIB, which, like its brethren elsewhere (e.g., Amster 1998; Lees 1979), runs more open-ended charismatic (and sometimes Pentecostalist) services. These events are far less mediated by the paraphernalia and prescribed action that characterize Anglican and Catholic services, consisting instead of Bible readings, lengthy sermons, "praise and worship," and spontaneous eruptions of individual prayers, testimonials, and even glossolalia.

Since the 1960s, weekly services have been the chief focal point of village Christianity. Every Sunday morning is *simayang* (prayer) time in the village, when Christians of all ages, dressed in their good clothes, gravitate toward the three churches clutching hymnals and prayer books. They are often joined by their city-based relatives and friends who have returned to their village houses for the weekend. In this way, Sunday church attendance has become the only consistent point of contact for Benuk's full-time residents and its urban diaspora. The temporal regularity imposed upon the community by these services, moreover, has turned each church into a node of *moden* governance, through which the village committee (JKKK) propagates announcements and organizes collective activities. Several times a year, for example, Benuk holds a *gotong-royong*[10] Sunday: a day of villagewide "maintenance" dedicated to sprucing up communal areas, roads, and riverbanks. The dates of such activities are circulated through announcements at Sunday services, with each congregation taking charge of specific areas. Similarly, information about village celebrations, such as the annual *Pra Gawai*—a government-sanctioned, community-oriented day of food, games, and "cultural" performances held before Gawai Dayak—is propagated via church channels; lucky draw tickets for such events are also sold after services. Village Christmas carols, meanwhile, are also organized along denominational lines, with each church's choir calling on households from its own congregation throughout Advent.[11]

The status of churches as nodes of village organization exemplifies the complex nature of Christian unity in a community with three coexisting denominational strains. While these divisions largely remain irrelevant in daily life, there are occasions throughout the year when they become palpable. Apart from the *adat gawai* question, which we shall examine in chapters 5 and 6, an especially sensitive topic on this front is interdenominational marriage. In Benuk, as elsewhere, there is a pervasive understanding that according to *adat Kristen*, spouses must attend the same church. Consequently, couples-to-be from different congregations are asked to state at their engagement who will "follow" whom. There are no hard and fast rules governing such internal conversions, with decisions being made according to individual circumstances. When they do occur, however, they occasionally engender a denominational territorialism bordering on belligerence. SIBs, for example, occupy an uncomfortable niche in this pattern of internal conversion: While Anglicans and Catholics are usually willing to "enter" each other's churches, they are often less keen on switching to SIB, and vice versa. However, I sometimes also heard middle-aged Catholics asserting that "RC" was the *asar* (original) church and the Anglicans and other denominations its "children" (*anak*), so it was only right that non-Catholics "return" to it if the opportunity arose through marriage.

This was the firm opinion of one of my close female friends, whose daughter's marriage plans caused some consternation shortly after I left the field in 2005. Several years earlier, when the girl started going out with a boy from a different Bidayuh village, her mother told his SIB parents that she would allow the relationship to continue only if he agreed to convert to Catholicism upon marriage. At the time, the parents agreed. Around 2006, however, they and the groom-in-waiting began vacillating about the prospect of an "RC" wedding and suggested a civil ceremony as a compromise. Neither the young lady nor her parents were willing to entertain this, and the relationship duly ended. A few months later, she got engaged to an Anglican from the village who agreed to "follow" her into the Catholic Church. Friends and neighbors mused that this was an appropriate decision, because the groom's father was a Catholic who had "entered" Anglicanism through marriage; now it was only right that his son should go the other way and balance things out.

This episode reveals the tensions, considerations, and negotiations that can arise in such multidenominational settings. At the same time, however, the divisions between the three churches should not be overstated. As mentioned earlier, "we are all Christian" is a common and heartfelt adage among villagers, who tend to identify themselves first as Christian, and only secondarily as "Anglican," "RC," or "SIB." Moreover, it is rare to find families, households, or neighborhoods that subscribe uniformly to one denomination, as individual variations within them are fairly common. In theory, then, all of Benuk's Christian residents are "the same": a notion reiterated whenever a community-based event is held.

One such affair, a villagewide prayer procession held in October 2004, illustrates both the workings and difficulties involved in maintaining a unified Christian front. The event was held in the midst of an unusual spate of deaths that was widely attributed to an overly "heaty" (*păras*) atmosphere in the village, possibly caused by malignant spirit presences. Consequently, the village committee decided that the entire place needed a proper blessing to restore its "coolness" (*madud*) and to keep evil spirits and Satan at bay. Held on a Sunday morning, the event began outside the community hall, where leaders from the three denominations took turns reciting prayers and sprinkling holy water over a large crowd of villagers. After singing a few songs, everyone dispersed into separate denominational trains, each led by prayer leaders, choirs, and (in the Anglican and Catholic cases) volunteers carrying crosses, candles, incense, and holy pictures. Each group covered specific sections of the village: the Anglicans the longhouse and center, the Catholics its hilly peripheries, and the SIBs, in their minivan, the outskirts of the main site.

Over the next two hours, the groups moved along their routes, stopping at points to recite prayers, sing songs, and sprinkle holy water on the surroundings. With the circuits complete, they reassembled at the opening spot. A pig had been slaughtered, and everyone partook of a large meal—a staple at Christian events—after each choir had sung more songs. Part of the reason the joint prayer session, touted strongly as a village-unifying affair, worked so well was that each group used its own hymns, paraphernalia, protocol, and wordings— even the Lord's Prayer is recited differently in each church—as mixed groups would have made coordinated participation difficult. Yet, it was vitally important that everyone started and ended in unison, for, as with *adat gawai*, the ultimate beneficiary of their efforts was not individual churches but the community at large.

Beyond Church Walls

Churches are, however, only one feature of the village's Christian landscape. On a day-to-day basis, all villagers regularly encounter denominations other than their own through various prayer gatherings in private settings such as homes, farms, schools, and shops. These are held on a range of occasions, such as when there is an anniversary to be marked, an achievement to be celebrated, or a problem to be solved. Each gathering is conducted by a church leader (or priest, if he is available), and usually involves Bible readings, collective recitations of prayers (or the rosary for Catholics), the sprinkling of

Figure 3.2 A Catholic household altar, Kampung Benuk, 2008.

holy water, and the consumption of a large meal prepared by the host (Harris 2001: 150) (figure 3.2).

While church services have introduced a distinctly Christian mode of temporality and praxis to the village, their privately held counterparts constitute mixtures of indigenous modes of sociality and Christian "fellowship" gatherings, both of which emphasize communion and commonality. Such events are more fluid and less hierarchical than Sunday services, for what matters here are collective presence, *rami*-ness, and commensality. Birthdays and engagements are observed in this manner throughout the year, as are prayers for sick or pregnant people, which, while not (always) viewed as curative devices, are seen to strengthen their *simangi* and protect them from Satan, diseases, and "heatiness." These gatherings are also integral to the lengthy succession of postmortem rites and obligations that people have come to associate with *adat Kristen*.[12] The death of a Christian villager inevitably initiates a sequence of prayer gatherings, beginning with several consecutive nights of prayers (the body is usually buried on the third or fourth day), followed by similar gatherings a month, 40 days,[13] a hundred days, and a year afterward. Meanwhile, one-off prayer gatherings may also be organized for specific "technical" objectives (Chapter 2). A glance through my field-notes indicates that within the space of a few weeks in 2004, for example, I went to several birthday parties and wakes, prayer sessions at a rice farm, the blessing of a recently deceased man's farm hut that his children were taking over, a going-away party for a boy about to begin National Service (*Khidmat Negara*), and prayers in a nearby village for a car that had just been repaired following an accident.

These and similar occasions are attended not only by members of the host's own church but also by relatives, neighbors, and friends, regardless of their affiliation. In this way, villagers acquire a certain familiarity with the texts, objects, procedures, and modes of prayer associated with other churches in the village. The extent to which they participate in such affairs varies: many Anglicans and Catholics try to keep up with each others' formulaic recitations and actions[14] but often find the personal, spontaneous orations of SIB prayer gatherings difficult, whereas most SIBs eschew the ritualized actions and recitations of Anglican and Catholic sessions. However, amid these divergent attitudes, there exists a broad tolerance and awareness of the many forms that *adat Kristen* can take. In this way, the notion that "we are all Christian" acquires an added resonance, a sense of commonality that, in daily life at least, supersedes the differences between the three denominations.

This conviction is enhanced by the sense that as an *adat*, Christianity is not confined to specific ritual events but must serve as a guide to daily life and sociality (Chapter 6). The upshot of this is that church leaders have acquired an informal and widely accepted moral authority within the community. Even though they cannot levy fines or liaise with the government as the village head can, they do take responsibility for monitoring and regulating people's behavior. I became strongly aware of this when, late one weeknight, a habitual drunkard tried forcing his way into my house, where I was working alone. Thankfully he was too inebriated to get very far and was eventually hustled away by another man—but not before he had attracted the attention of my neighbors. Over the next few days, word of the incident spread rapidly, and when I arrived at St Matthew's for a service shortly afterwards, I was met by a cluster of prayer leaders who apologized profusely for the man's actions. They would take him to task, they said sternly, although I should also report him to the village head if he harassed me again. And besides, they added, "We wouldn't want you to go away and tell others that this village is full of bad people." As Christian (not simply Catholic) leaders, these men were acting as unofficial social arbiters and representatives of the village itself. Their actions reflected the widespread understanding, elaborated in Chapter 6, that Christianity cannot be disassociated from day-to-day sociality: Like *adat gawai* before it, it is an encompassing guide to and regulator of village life.

The Look (and Feel) of Religiosity

While prayer leaders possess a certain gravitas in communal affairs, their authority is, unsurprisingly, strongest within their own congregations. During fieldwork, I was frequently told by villagers to "ask the prayer leaders" whenever I had any Christianity-related queries, in the same way that they referred me to Bai Toyan and Sumuk Nyangǔ whenever I asked about *adat gawai*. Like senior *gawai* practitioners, I suggest, Christian leaders are invested with a potency that derives not from some innate power but from how much they know and how well they perform their religious duties (cf. Harris 2001: 176). Most of them are working or retired men in their thirties to sixties[15]— ordinary (but, crucially, literate) village residents who have undergone basic theological and pastoral training courses run by regional parish churches. From this position of ritual responsibility and power, they lead Sunday prayer services, deliver sermons, choose the readings and hymns for prayer gatherings, and handle a range of problems and requests within the village.

Over the years, this structural configuration—shaped by the exigencies of conversion—appears to have combined with the *gawai* ritual dynamics described in the last chapter to create a specific mode of religiosity that still characterizes Anglicanism and Catholicism today. This may have been foreshadowed in the 1960s and 1970s, when missionaries such as Sidaway (1969: 151) and Father Meehan noted that their congregations generally remained silent or distracted while priests led prayers at the altar. They attributed this tendency to the persistence of *gawai*-based notions of ritual efficacy, in which physical presence rather than full participation and knowledge on the part of nonspecialists mattered most. In the intervening decades, villagers have become more vocal and participatory, with Anglican and Catholic services now resounding with the dutiful recitations of the congregation. Yet, in many ways, the early emphasis on ritual practice and presence—itself encouraged by the missionaries (Chapter 5)—rather than knowledge of doctrinal intricacy remains a defining characteristic of much Bidayuh Christianity.

During services, the most commonly used prayers and hymns are recited from memory, and great attention is paid to physical protocol such as genuflecting, making the sign of the cross, and bowing. In my experience, concertedly saying and doing the right thing at the right time is at least as crucial as taking in the words of the readings or the sermon; indeed, attendees often become restless and unfocused during those lengthy interludes that involve no physical or verbal input on their part. In this way, most Bidayuhs appear to experience Christian services in what Leo Howe, writing about pre-Reformation Christianity, describes as a "ritually doctrinal" mode:

> By this I mean that the...liturgy and associated doctrines were converted into performative ritual, the doctrine being embedded in the ceremonies....The laity may be uninformed about the niceties of theology, but they knew how to do the rituals, or at least how to behave when they were being performed by the priest. (2004: 137)

As chapters 5 and 6 will reveal, this tendency on the part of many "ordinary" Bidayuhs toward "orthopraxy" (Harris 2001: 162–163, after Geertz 1993c: 177) does not suggest that Christianity is devoid of content for them. It does, however, bear out the important point, recently made by several anthropologists (e.g., Hirschkind 2001; Keane 2008; Luhrmann 2004; Mahmood 2001; Mitchell and Mitchell 2008; Morgan 2010a), that religiosity can often be intrinsically, irreducibly material, rather than primarily an inner state "defined by a cognitively drawn notion of 'belief'" (Howell 2007: 373) or extensive doctrinal knowledge. During fieldwork, I was struck by how, for my Anglican and Catholic acquaintances, praying "properly" (and teaching ethnographers to pray properly) largely entailed recourse to a large corpus of material entities both at home and in church. Cars almost always had small crosses, rosaries, or medallions dangling from their rearview mirrors, while nearly every household owned a small altar, consisting of a cross, candles, pictures of Jesus, Mary, or saints, small plastic bottles of holy water, palm ribs from that year's Palm Sunday services, medallions, rosaries, and perhaps a Bible and liturgical calendar. These altars formed the focal point of house-based prayer sessions while also providing useful daily resources: it was not uncommon, for instance, to see people daubing holy water on injuries, or keeping rosaries around their necks or fingers when feeling ill.

To an extent, the centrality of material things and actions to Anglicans' and Catholics' experiences of Christianity may be said to reflect the tendency, examined in chapters 2 and 7, to think of *adat* in highly substantive and praxiological terms. However, we should not lose sight of the part that Christianity and conversion themselves have played in cultivating this interest (Chua n.d.). Despite some reservations about the hazards of "pagan" artifacts in Bidayuhs' lives (Sidaway 1969), the Anglican and Catholic missionaries appear not to have undertaken the same concerted projects of "purification" (Keane 2007, after Latour 1993) as those carried out by the Dutch Calvinists in Sumba, for example. Instead, they—and later the local catechists—selectively deployed both Bidayuh and Christian artifacts and ritual performances as a means of spreading and consolidating Christianity. Early Christians, for example, were occasionally given holy water, crosses, and medallions as protection from harassment by the old spirits when they converted (Chapter 5). Such entities have since become important focal points for Christian prayer, without which Anglicans and Catholics often say they feel bereft or "empty." Added to these were prescribed actions and tasks, such as saying the rosary and reciting prayers before meals and sleep, both of which James Sakas used to prepare villagers for baptism. Meanwhile, major occasions are often prescribed by the institutional churches in highly tangible terms: All Souls' Day, for example, is known widely as "*simayang kubur*" (grave prayers) in recognition of the custom of cleaning and lighting graves in the churchyard, while Holy Saturday is described as "*simayang di-an*" (literally, prayers with candles) in reference to the rite, followed by churches worldwide, of lighting the Pascal candle and spreading its flame among the congregation.

In short, rather than being distinct from inner or individual religiosity, the performative and material features of Christianity are arguably constitutive of it—a notion that, as chapters 2 and 7 argue, appears to characterize Bidayuh conceptions of *adat* in general. This point is widely recognized by Anglicans and Catholics, who sometimes describe these artifacts and practices as ways of helping them pray to and think about God, whose greatness and power lie beyond the realm of true human comprehension. On this point, however, their opinions diverge sharply with the SIB minority. As I explain in Chapter 5, SIB Christianity is shaped by strong charismatic and Pentecostalist influences, which emphasize "live and direct" (Engelke 2007) communion with God and the Holy Spirit. An SIB elder told me that pictures, candles, and incense were unnecessary distractions from one's relationship with God; since they were not in the Bible, why use them? Even the cross, he added, was not needed at SIB services: "You yourself are the cross," and it was what was "inside" the person that mattered.

Such self-conscious asceticism and stress on the "inner life," however, confounds many of my Anglican and Catholic acquaintances, who confess that they cannot understand how SIBs can pray properly without material accoutrements and physical protocol. What kind of Christianity was this, asked a friend who once rented a house in Kuala Lumpur with some SIB students, when it consisted only of "*minyu, minyu, minyu, nga* 'sharing'" ("talking, talking, talking, and sharing")? Such austerity is, moreover, deemed to spill into their homes, which an Anglican elder described as very "clean" (English)—that is, devoid of altars, candles, pictures, and other accoutrements. SIBs are also known throughout the village for their relative abstinence and self-discipline—a tendency that is usually attributed to their peculiar Christian *adat*. Indeed, another Anglican parishioner pointed out that the SIBs were no different from *gawai* practitioners, because they too did not know how to use Christian paraphernalia!

It is worth pointing out, of course, that from an analytical perspective, the SIBs' typically charismatic mode of religiosity could not be characterized as purely immaterial. For a start, despite their professed disinterest in material accoutrements, there are specific artifacts—notably the dog-eared, bookmarked, and thumb-worn personal bibles carried by nearly all SIBs—which are invested with heightened significance in services and daily life. The "marked sensational dimension[s]" (Meyer 2010: 744) of SIB prayer sessions, moreover, are manifest in actions such as the laying of hands on those in need of healing, praying with one's eyes tightly closed and hands outstretched, or swaying and clapping as one is moved by the Holy Spirit—all of which are inseparable from the words that overtly characterize them (Coleman 2007). While moved by very different understandings of Christian practice, then, SIBs arguably share their Anglican and Catholic neighbors' commitment to getting things right, as well as their concerns about the potential agency and hazards of material things—including those of *adat gawai*, as we shall see in Chapter 5.

The point to take away here, however, is that in introducing an overtly different model of ritual practice to village life, the SIB has engendered a degree of reflexivity among many Anglicans and Catholics about what Christianity means and entails—and, as chapters 5 and 6 will reveal, about how the *gawai* question and the relationship of the past to the present should be handled. (Indeed, many of my own insights came about during fieldwork conversations about what made the SIB mode of prayer so discomfiting for others.) In this respect, such divergences provide fertile ground for both analysts and Bidayuhs to contemplate the nature and extent of conversion, transformation, sociality, and religiosity—all themes to which we shall return in Part II.

Christianity and (Dis)continuity?

Before moving on to Part II, it is worth pausing to address a question that has lurked in the background of this chapter: To what extent has conversion to Christianity entailed "real" change in Bidayuh society? The subtext of this question is, of course, what Robbins identified in his article on "continuity thinking" (2007): How well have anthropologists coped with the models, processes, and discourses of change often precipitated by conversion to Christianity? From one angle, this chapter's "thick" historical and ethnographic narrative may appear to perpetuate the very continuity-seeking tendency that Robbins criticizes as being endemic to anthropology (2007: 6). As we have seen, Christianity came to Bidayuh communities not as a bolt from the blue, but in a gradual, contingent succession of events, many of which were inextricable from the wider Malaysian milieu that was simultaneously reshaping Bidayuhs' lives. The fact that these developments gave rise to a series of "long conversations," in which Bidayuhs and missionaries struggled over the "terms" and "media" of Christianity (Comaroff and Comaroff 1991: 224) well before its "substantive message" (ibid.: 199) was taken on board, cannot be ignored or dismissed as insignificant.

However, acknowledging that such "conversations" took place does not mean that anthropologists should discount the fact that conversion did enact fundamental social, cultural, and other changes in their adherents' lives. What is intriguing about the Bidayuh case, I suggest, is that such changes did not only generate discourses of change and difference but also gave rise to a strong, and in many ways, more pervasive, sense of connection with the past: of continuity and contiguity between *adat gawai* and Christianity, and between *nyamba gawai* and Christians (chapters 5 and 6). Like rupture and discontinuity, such discourses need interrogation and explanation—and it is to this task that the second part of the book turns. Its central problematic is how and why those notions of continuity and contiguity that characterize the majority of my acquaintances' engagements with *adat gawai* (and thus "culture") have emerged the way they did—and why, conversely, the SIBs' insistence on breaking with the old ways has not garnered more support. In the following chapters, I shall focus on how Christianity played a vital social, moral, theological, and political role in these developments, shaping Bidayuhs' attitudes toward *adat gawai*, "culture," and indeed the world at large.

What this book does *not* seek to do, then, is assess Bidayuh Christianity in purely *analytical* terms as evidence of either structural and cultural continuity or complete rupture. As we shall see in Part II, what the analyst would identify as continuity and discontinuity have both featured strongly in the Christianization processes of recent decades; and to try to identify one or the other as dominant would be to descend into an endless, and rather pointless, intellectual spiral. More importantly, it would tell us very little about how Bidayuhs themselves discuss, articulate, and debate their experiences of conversion, Christianity, and the question of "culture." My priority here, then, is to explore their own projects of continuity and discontinuity (Robbins 2007: 31): projects that, as we shall see, are styled by a combination of Malaysian politics, institutional church arrangements, and the doctrinal and moral frameworks of Christianity itself. Each chapter in the rest of this book thus opens with a specific project—or, more often, a specific problem—that preoccupies my acquaintances, and from which my analysis proceeds. And it is by thinking through these issues *with* Bidayuhs, I suggest, that anthropologists can gain a fuller understanding of what really matters for them in this complex, not yet pure Christian world.

Part II

Chapter 4

Why Bidayuhs Don't Want to Become Muslim: Ethnicity, Christianity, and the Politics of Religion

Shortly after starting fieldwork, I got into a convivial conversation with Paka and his wife, Sumuk Meroi, about marriage *adat* before the coming of Christianity. Over sweet coffee and biscuits, the couple coyly recalled their brief teenage courtship and subsequent wedding: a boisterous, full-blown, villagewide celebration that lasted all night. But weddings today, they mused, were different: People got married in church in an altogether less *rami* (merry, raucous, crowded) fashion. Moreover, going to church was only one of many possible marriage options in the *moden* world, because Bidayuhs were now marrying more people from other *bangsa* (ethnic groups or races)[1] who might do things differently. Drawing with a modicum of pride on personal memory, they reeled off a list of people whom Bidayuhs could wed: Iban, Orang Ulu, Chinese, Indians, and Europeans. Impressed, I remarked that it sounded like Bidayuhs could marry anyone in the world. At this, Paka's face grew dark. "But there is one *bangsa* that Bidayuhs cannot marry," he said quietly, "Bidayuhs cannot marry Malays—Islamic people." Not entirely surprised by this observation, having heard anti-Malay rumblings elsewhere in the village, I pressed him on why this was so. "Because," he replied immediately, "they do not eat pork."

It is with this seemingly trivial remark, variants of which I would hear many more times, that I begin my exploration of the ethnic and religious politics that infuse my acquaintances' lives. More than reflecting local dietary preferences, Paka's comment illuminated a certain model of ethnicity, transformation, and agency that, I shall

argue, shapes rural Bidayuhs' perceptions of—and anxieties about—
their status as Malaysian citizens. The present chapter reveals how, in
this highly politicized sphere where ethnicity and religious affiliation
are thoroughly intertwined, my acquaintances have used Christianity
as a vital buffer against Malay-Muslim political hegemony, and thus
as a means of preserving a freedom of movement that they associate
with being Bidayuh. Yet, more than acting as a bulwark, Christianity
has also given them an officially sanctioned means through which to
participate more fully in the political and economic system of *moden*
Malaysia—particularly, as the next two chapters suggest, by fostering
and legitimating a concept of *adat gawai* as "culture." To understand how and why this has happened, then, let us return to the
more immediate gastronomic concern of pork consumption—or its
lack thereof.

Why Bidayuhs Do Not Want to Become Muslim

As a regular dietary feature and component of major *adat gawai*
(and now Christian) ceremonies, pork has historically been the
most important meat for Bidayuhs. The inability to consume it is
always the first reason cited by villagers when explaining why they
would not become Muslim,[2] and flagged as the main problem that
Malays encounter or cause when visiting Bidayuh communities (see
also Connolly 2009: 499). Such aloofness, my interlocutors concur,
makes it impossible for Malays to live in Bidayuh villages, for if, as a
young teacher put it, they do not eat the same food and sit apart from
everyone else, how would they learn the language and the lifestyle?

To an extent, then, Paka's comment highlighted the importance
of commensality as a basis of belonging and sociality in Bidayuh
communities (Chua 2010). However, it also threw into problematic
relief a set of much broader concerns about ethnicity, *adat*, religious
affiliation, and sociality. He and his wife explained that the pork
proscription was simply the most prominent of a gamut of Islamic
rules and restrictions—including praying five times a day, avoiding
alcohol, and dressing in specific ways—which Bidayuhs associate
with being Malay. Such rules, they say, have to be obeyed by Malays
at all times, no matter where they go and what they do. By religious diktat, Malays can thus only ever be Malays, retaining their
speech, dress, habitus, and diet for the rest of their lives. While
this does not generally perturb Bidayuhs—Malays, after all, must
abide by their own *adat*—it can generate tensions when intermarriage occurs, because the Bidayuh spouse will (by convention, and

now, state law in Malaysia) have to convert to Islam. In the process, my informants roundly agree, he or she will "become Malay" (*jadi Kirieng*): an inevitable outcome across Southeast Asia, where Islam and Malay-ness have historically been mutually generative and coterminous (Benjamin 2003: 31, 50; Connolly 2009: 497; Harrisson 1970: 27; King 1993: 36; Kipp 1993: 5; Milner 1986; Reid 2001: 309–310; Shamsul 2004: 143). And this, they also agree, is not a good outcome.

In their aversion to marrying Malays or becoming Muslim, my informants are not alone; similar recalcitrance has been documented among indigenous minorities across maritime Southeast Asia (e.g., Aragon 1996; Benjamin 2003; Chou 1997; Kipp 1993; Lenhart 2003). But why, given the high incidence and generally unproblematic acceptance of marriage to other *bangsa*, does Malay-ness seem to provoke such obdurate antagonism? Anthropological studies of these groups tend to attribute their responses to the fear of assimilation and a concomitant loss of ethnic identity—the implication being that, like other communities studied by social scientists, such people need to define and maintain a sense of their corporate distinctiveness. In this chapter, however, I wish to approach the issue from a different, less constructionist, angle. Drawing on my acquaintances' exegesis, I shall suggest that for Bidayuhs, the situation is less about creating an identity than it is about preserving a certain freedom of movement and the capacity to become and un-become different things—a notion on which I shall now elaborate.

The Flux of "Becoming"

Like other Bornean communities, Benuk has its fair share of spouses from outside the village; in 2005, these included Bidayuhs from other regions, Ibans, Chinese, a Melanau, and a Kenyah. Most of them, however, are not easily pinpointed, because they speak the same dialect, eat the same food, weave the same sorts of baskets, grow crops in the same farms, and pray at the same churches as everyone else. While their origins are never forgotten, villagers often say with undisguised approval that he or she "has now become Dayak." These spouses' eligibility to be incorporated into village life is thus unquestioned: What is important is not who they are or where they came from, but whether they do (*nai*) Dayak things. Conversely, the handful of spouses who do not learn the language or attempt to integrate into the community are viewed with suspicion and disdain, and frequently referred to by their ethnic origin.

Perhaps the most decisive gesture of incorporation for intermarried spouses is their acquisition of a teknonym upon bearing children. An intrinsically relational designation, the teknonym identifies its bearers through their offspring, firmly situating them in social networks exclusive to the village. Most adults in Bidayuh villages are known by these monikers rather than their personal names, and even those who are childless but of a suitable age are assigned one by their friends and relatives.[3] The widespread use of teknonyms is seen as a means of showing respect to their bearers (Geddes 1961: 35), and of affirming, and thus reproducing, social relations; as a lady with whom I planted rice put it, they show that the villagers who use them are all related (*bimadis*), both biologically and socially. Their pervasive importance both reflects and consolidates Bidayuh communities' general lack of interest in descent as a criterion for belonging (Geddes 1954: 26), as Chapter 7 explains further. Orientated toward present and future generations, teknonyms help to cultivate a certain "genealogical amnesia" within their corporate groups, thereby adding an "elasticity" and "adaptability" to their memberships (Geertz and Geertz 1964: 94).

It is worth noting, however, that the amnesia engendered by teknonymy and intermarriage is not absolute. As my informants' reflections on intermarriage reveal, "becoming Dayak" (*jadi Dayak*) is both an expected and idealized facet of living in a Bidayuh village. But what happens when those incomers go back to their place of origin? Such return movement is not uncommon: Occasionally, marital splits cause one partner to leave the village, a woman may move back to her parents' house during and just after pregnancy, and most commonly, a spouse may leave briefly to attend a wedding, funeral, or some other occasion. When this happens, the returnees are expected to also reacquire the language, habitus, and other features associated with their original *adat:* in short, to "un-become" Bidayuh and "re-become" Iban, Chinese, Melanau, and so on. The same applies to their children, regardless of where they have been brought up. A boy of Bidayuh-Iban parentage who lived in Benuk, for example, told me that whenever he went to his mother's Iban village, he would speak Iban, eat their food, and generally follow other aspects of their *adat*—in effect, become Iban. In displaying such flexibility, he was not unique. Just as my acquaintances expect incomers to become Dayak, they too are prepared to adapt to other *adat*s and un-become Dayak when the occasion demands.

The freedom and capacity for maneuver implied by the trope of "becoming" (*jadi*) was brought home to me toward the end of my fieldwork, when some of my informants began talking about me in the way that they discussed intermarried spouses: Because I spoke Dayak, ate Dayak, planted rice, visited the houses of deceased villagers, and socialized with everyone in the village, they said, I too had become Dayak. This was usually accompanied by some jocularity, because I had not been there much more than a year, and despite hopes that I would marry a Benuk man, I was clearly going to leave. However, had I settled down and had children—the "logical conclusion of the process of assimilation which had been set in train when I began fieldwork" (Carsten 1997: 279)—I too could have laid serious claim to Dayak-ness, even though everybody continued referring to me as that "Chinese girl from Singapore." While my origin was thus never occluded, it was never incommensurate either with the dizzying succession of ethnies that, some women at the longhouse once declared, I regularly underwent. When I was in Benuk, they said, I was Dayak; when I was at school in England, I would *jadi branda* (become a white person); when I returned to my mother in Singapore, I could *jadi Cina* (become Chinese); and the next time we met in Benuk, I could *jadi* Dayak again.

Like *adat*-crossing objects and spirits, then, Bidayuhs depict themselves—and, ideally, others—as "translatable figures" (Siegel 1986: 297) able to traverse ethnic and other boundaries, and to "comprehend [and perform] within others' codes" (ibid.) when required. This happens on various scales and can be applied to anything from international travel to intervillage relations. In Benuk, for example, I was frequently told of a young man who had gone to study in Korea, learned the language, and now worked there, as well as of a few women who had married *branda* (white people) and gone to live in their countries. At the other end of the spectrum, I once spent an evening at a wedding with a group of young women from different villages in Penrissen, all colleagues at a small company near Kota Padawan. Although all communities in the region officially speak Biatah, the primary unit of linguistic sameness is the village, such that everybody else, whether five minutes down the road or in Germany, is said to have a different *tong* (way of speaking). At this wedding, I was treated to a remarkable display of intervillage mimicry by my companions, who explained that they could tell which village a person was from simply the way he or she spoke. Their awareness of these differences, however, did not engender chauvinism or insularism. Instead, the women explained that whenever they visited another village or encountered its inhabitants, they would try to use the other *tong* and speak like them.[4]

This impulse toward "translatability" has important implications for our understanding of Bidayuh conceptions of ethnicity, identity, and, as we shall later see, conversion and Christianity. Undergirding it is a tendency to obviate, but not obliterate, genealogy or the past: that amnesia identified by Geertz and Geertz is never complete. Unburdened by their origin, persons are able and indeed expected to move between different *adat*s when necessary. In this sense, their identity at each stage is not a given but elicited through the combination of words, actions, material objects, spirits, and other entities associated with that *adat*. Put differently, the closest thing that my Bidayuh acquaintances have to a definition of ethnicity is one that pivots on performance—human action in its most holistic, tangible sense—rather than on genealogy or provenance. In this respect, an ethnie, like other corporate groups, is not seen as a primordial essence acquired through birth, but a collection of shared, *adat*-based attributes, artifacts, and other features that humans must constantly bring into being.

The *analytical* description of ethnicity as a performative phenomenon is not of course new to anthropology, which has long adopted an antiprimordialist stance on the topic (e.g., Banks 1996; Barth 1969; Cohen 1978; Jenkins 1997). What I am presenting here, however, is a form of native exegesis: a model of transformation, sociality, and responsibility, which is both well articulated and embraced by my informants. And it is this model—this ideal of "becoming"— that sheds light on the problem that opened this chapter. For many Bidayuhs, the notion of becoming something else through marriage or migration is not in itself problematic; indeed such transformation is positively encouraged and expected. However, what my acquaintances find so vexatious about becoming Malay is not the fact that converts acquire a different *bangsa* but the fact that having become it, they can no longer *un*-become it. Once a person "enters Islam" (*mŭrŭt Islam*), it is said, he or she will find it very difficult to leave. Lingering on the topic of pork, Paka and his wife explained to me that whereas Chinese, Indians, and white people also had different *adat*, they could still eat the same food as Bidayuhs. And even if a Bidayuh married a non-meat-eating Buddhist or Hindu—the existence of whom I pointed out—it would not matter, because the Bidayuh spouse would still be allowed to eat Bidayuh food and do Bidayuh things upon returning to his or her village. By contrast, Bidayuhs who married Malays had no choice but to follow *adat Islam*; they would not only have to give up pork but also dress, speak, and pray like Malays.

This was especially galling whenever converts from the village who had moved elsewhere came back to visit their relatives. It was then, while watching the returnee emerge from a car clad in Malay garb, often with Malay children in tow, that the grumbles became most vehement; that sullen mutterings of "s/he has forgotten how to become Dayak" were heard. Donning sartorial markers such as the *tudung* (headscarf), declining pork and alcohol, and sometimes even eating from separate receptacles, they remained steadfastly Malay in a situation where they were *expected* to re-become Bidayuh. Such people thus reinforced the pervasive impression that becoming Malay was not a reversible process. As Sumuk Meroi put it, unlike Christianity, Islam did not allow Bidayuhs to "return to their own *adat*" (*pari adat adŭp*)—a point on which we shall later touch. This did not, however, engender a great deal of sympathy among my informants. The converts, they said, had made their choice and now had only themselves to blame for landing in such a predicament—and worse, for adding to the strength and numbers of Malay-Muslims in the world.

For my Bidayuh acquaintances, then, the problem with marrying a Malay and becoming Muslim is one of permanent entrapment within a fixed performative regime or *adat*. This change, moreover, must be "constantly *cultivated*, as a means of supplanting whatever went before," which means "regularly glancing back at [but not joining] what one has left behind" (Benjamin 2003: 20; italics in original). Unlike other ethnies or corporate identities that momentarily still the flux of transformation in which Bidayuhs expect to participate, Malay-Muslimness thus *halts* it, making it impossible for its adherents to be and do anything else.[5] In the process, it causes a rupture not only from one's friends and family (Connolly 2009: 499) but also from both the past and the potential future, bringing to an end any further possibility of "becoming." What my acquaintances most fear losing, I thus argue, is less a distinctive ethnic identity than a freedom of movement that they associate with being Bidayuh—but that does not have to culminate in a fixed Bidayuh identity.

Up to independence, these sorts of quandaries would mostly have played out within and between small-scale communities. In the last few decades, however, they have grown increasingly entangled with the religious and ethnic politics of the postcolonial Malaysian state, which, as Chapter 1 revealed, is organized around a specific framework of Malay ascendancy. In this framework, the customary connection between Malay-ness and Islam has been rendered constitutionally inalienable, such that becoming Malay or Muslim is now no longer a purely social affair but has unavoidable political and legal ramifications. In the next section, then, I shall examine how rural Bidayuhs have mapped their concerns about fixity and flux onto the contemporary Malaysian system: a world to which they are strongly committed, but of which they are also suspicious and resentful.

Fixity and Flux in the Malay(sian) Ethnic System

As Chapter 1 explained, a key aspect of Malaysian citizenship is membership of a recognized racial or ethnic category, or *bangsa*. These categories, however, are not neutral, and while my acquaintances recognize the validity of the ethnic label "Bidayuh," they nonetheless have little love for the system in which it is entrenched. For many of them, it is this very system—and the genealogical notion of ethnicity on which it is built—that has fixed them in a national pecking order shaped explicitly and implicitly by Malays, who are deemed to enjoy political and economic advantages over everyone else.

My informants' disgruntlement with the Malaysian ethnic system, however, is fanned by another allied factor—a modicum of fluidity that, I would argue, disturbs them more than its overt fixity. This is the fact that a non-Malay can become Malay, and thus access certain privileges allocated officially or otherwise to that particular ethnic group (Muhammad 1992: 263–264; Nagata 1974: 337; Siddique and Suryadinata 1981: 666, 671). This prospect is legally facilitated by Article 160 of the Constitution, which defines a Malay as "a person who professes the religion of Islam, habitually speaks the Malay language, [and] conforms to Malay custom."[6] In other words, "Malays cannot be but Muslims in Malaysia" (Shamsul 1997: 209). While "set firm in constitutional terms" (King and Wilder 2003: 205), this definition thus allows for a certain amount of flux in the form of movement *into* but not *out of* that particular group.

The few exceptions to this rule illustrate the sheer difficulty of challenging it. 2006 saw a brief flurry of reports about the Seremban Syariah Court's decision to posthumously recognize the non-Muslim status of an 88-year-old Malay woman, Nyonya Tahir, who had been raised a Buddhist through adoption, and married a Chinese man in 1936. Her long-drawn efforts to gain official acknowledgment of this fact, which would allow her to be interred next to her late husband, culminated shortly after her death. Facing the prospect of having her buried as a Muslim by dint of her recorded ethnicity, her family testified that she had lived and died a Buddhist and should therefore be buried according to Buddhist rites—a plea to which the court eventually acceded. Two years later, Penang's Syariah High Court allowed a Chinese woman, Tan Ean Huang, to rescind the Muslim identity she had adopted upon marrying an Iranian man (who subsequently left her), and return to practicing Buddhism. The decision to permit a living Muslim to renounce Islam—wrangled from the courts after two arduous years—was the first of its kind nationwide.[7] These cases, however, are anomalies that do little to alleviate the pervasive understanding in both national and village circles that officially unbecoming Muslim is well-nigh impossible.

This was reaffirmed in a lengthy and intensely public legal battle undertaken between 1999 and 2007 by Lina Joy, a Malay woman originally named Azlina binti Jailani, who converted to Christianity of her own volition and was baptized in 1998. In 1999, she succeeded in changing the name on her national identity card,[8] but failed on several subsequent occasions to get the word "Islam" removed from it. According to the National Registration Department, it was not within its remit to allow the renunciation of the religion, which such a move would entail.[9] Although Article 11(1) of the Malaysian Constitution states that "[e]very person has the right to profess and practice his religion," the National Registration Department argued that Joy could not deconvert from Islam through personal fiat but would have to produce a certificate or some other form of permission from an Islamic authority—one essentially condemning Joy as an apostate—which would enable it to remove "Islam" from her card. Put differently, the only means by which she could un-become Muslim was with the unwilling—and still unforthcoming—acquiescence of a Syariah court.

Joy attempted to circumvent the religious authorities by taking her case—based principally on Article 11(1)—to the High Court in 1999, the Court of Appeal (2005), and finally the Federal Court (2006), where it was ultimately rejected by a 2-1 majority.[10] Apart from the constitutional difficulty posed by the fact that she, as an ethnic Malay, couldn't not be Muslim,[11] the consistent dismissal of her case rested on the assertion that Muslims remained under the religious jurisdiction of the Syariah courts, and could not therefore renounce Islam of their own accord. For my informants, many of whom heard about the Lina Joy case and other similar occurrences, the judgment simply cemented in legal and constitutional terms what they already knew through experience: that becoming Malay rules out the possibility of un-becoming it again.

What complicates matters in the *moden* Malaysian context, however, is that such one-way conversion is not an entirely unpalatable prospect, for it is often perceived as the only official mechanism of flux available to Bidayuhs who wish to "rise" (*maad*) from their disadvantageous position in the ethnic hierarchy (Chapter 1). And become Malay some Bidayuhs do. The village gossip network was rife with stories, apocryphal or otherwise, of ambitious Bidayuhs converting to Islam to obtain job promotions or other benefits. There were also tales of certain Bidayuh villages converting en masse in response to governmental promises to improve the local infrastructure. One nearby settlement—its mosque prominently situated by the roadside—was often pointed to as an example of this phenomenon. "They have become Malay; they don't want to become Dayak," it was commonly said.

As with intermarriage, then, the official process of converting to Islam and becoming Malay is a deadening one, a one-way flux that ends in stoppage and definitive rupture from the past and the relations associated with it. As such, many Bidayuhs look disdainfully upon it as a high price to pay for improved *moden* amenities, better salaries, or more prestigious jobs. This dangerous, yet tempting, flux is not only articulated through the trope of "becoming" (*jadi*) but also in very physical terms, many of which center on that crucial communal unit, the village. The longhouse in Benuk—which, up to the 1970s, was effectively the village itself—has been enshrined in collective memory as a potent embodiment of the pre-*moden* (i.e., pre-Malaysian) past. In those days, people recall, the longhouse was huge; one could walk around the village without ever having to step on the earth (*mijog tanah*). It was, as they often say in English, "steady": a term that implies literal sturdiness as well as stability, success, and well-being.[12] There was nothing to fear when visiting at night, there were no "gates" in front of individual apartments, people were seldom ill, and the entire place was simply more *rami* than it is today.

The longhouse appears to have served as a physical and conceptual anchor to village life in this golden age of the past, as well as to the flux of persons, spirits, and things passing into, around, and through it. Its gradual disintegration and replacement by standalone concrete houses in the 1980s, however, is also associated with Benuk's real entrance into *moden* Malaysia: a world marked by Christianity, Malay dominance, and economic and political marginality. As one elderly lady, having reminisced at length about the old structure, put it:

> Now everything is *hancur* (destroyed, fragmented, falling apart), and everyone wants separate modern houses made of cement. And all our money is flying away, like leaves in the wind.

In their own poetic way, these remarks capture the almost visceral sense shared by many of my informants that they are in constant danger of being "pulled" (*tarik*) toward the center of Malay power, Kuala Lumpur (usually abbreviated to "K.L."), and to a lesser degree, Kuching. "K.L." is commonly used as a byword for both "Malaysia" and its Malay-dominated government: It is the center that defines the *moden* ethnic hierarchy and its unequal distribution of resources. As the geopolitical hub of Malay(sian)-ness, K.L. thus enacts the same sort of imbalanced flux that my village acquaintances associate with becoming and staying Malay.

This is especially concerning whenever young adults from the village move to K.L. or elsewhere in West Malaysia—as they commonly do—for further education or employment. I was told by a number of students, for example, of how they were constantly pressured by their Muslim peers at university to convert—a "pull" they resisted by going to church and socializing primarily with Christians. Meanwhile, their parents have their own anxieties and disappointments to cope with. A woman who lived down the road from us complained that her son had "gone to K.L. and become Malay" by marrying a Malay woman, and now would or could no longer buy a ticket home—not even, she said ruefully, on the budget airline, AirAsia. For Bidayuh villagers, then, the increased opportunities for long-distance travel offered by the *moden* world have also exacerbated the historical danger posed by Malay-ness, by widening the range of things into which Bidayuhs can be "pulled." Worse, persons are not the only things being drawn inexorably toward K.L.; following them too are precious resources, such as wages, which would not have broken off from the "steady" longhouse-village of the past. Money may fly away like leaves in the wind, yet it is not randomly swirling over the heads of villagers, but moving toward the Malay(sian) center of power, K.L.

In this center lies a dangerous, tightly entwined Malay-Muslim bundle of ethnicity, religion, and politics, from which the difficulties and disadvantages faced by my informants in the *moden* world are seen to originate. At the end of the day, however, there is no escaping the fact that Bidayuhs are Malaysian citizens, and therefore part of this world. How, then, have they dealt with this situation? To a degree, the irksome anti-Malay mutterings that can often be heard in Bidayuh villages and the widespread stigmatization of conversion to Islam may be seen as forms of low-level resistance—what James Scott calls "small arms fire" (1985)—to Malay hegemony in *moden* Malaysia. However, it would be injudicious to overstate their reactive character. As we have seen, people in Benuk are very consciously part of the *moden* world; it is not contradictory, for example, for the most vociferous critics of K.L.'s "pull" to send their children to college there to improve their job prospects, or to aspire toward the affluent standard of living shown on Malay soap operas. If Bidayuhs are resisting the political and religious dangers posed by Malay-Muslimness, they are not doing so by sole recourse to means "indigenous to the village sphere" (Scott 1985: 273) but also through active engagement with some very *moden*, quintessentially Malaysian, channels. The rest of this chapter looks at two such modes of engagement that, in very different ways, have enabled Bidayuhs to counteract the deadening pull of Malay-Muslimness by maintaining, rather than halting, the flux that they so value.

Making Disassociations

As tangible means of making "individual citizens officially legible" (Scott 1998: 71) to the state, entities such as the national identity card, regular censuses, and virtually every form of official documentation have also had the effect of impressing upon Bidayuhs the concreteness and relevance of official *bangsa* categories. At first glance, the genealogical model of "being" that underpins such categories seems incommensurate with the performative model of "translatability" that remains so salient in their lives. In the following pages, however, I shall suggest that, in a curious twist, the official *bangsa* model has also given Bidayuhs the conceptual tools with which to circumvent the problems posed by Malay-Muslim-ness.[13]

At this stage, it is important to point out that the terms "Bidayuh" and "Dayak" are not identical, although, like my acquaintances, I have been treating them as equally real and interchangeable. As Chapter 1 explains, people of all ages tend to use "Dayak" as their endonym within the village, particularly with reference to speech, dietary habits, ways of farming and weaving, and all the other performative attributes mentioned earlier. Conversely, while accepted as legitimate and self-evidently valid, "Bidayuh" is acknowledged to be a fixed *Malaysian* category: as something that distinguishes them from their equally "Dayak" relatives across the Indonesian border, for example. As my informants' most salient mode of identification in *moden* Malaysia, it is also constitutive of their relationship with the state, giving them access not only to health care, education, and other state services but also to benefits reserved solely for *bumiputera*, such as government scholarships, special bank accounts, and certain kinds of jobs. Most importantly, I suggest, "Bidayuh" is also coming to be understood as an innate, genealogical trait—something that one is born with and retains throughout one's life—which thus lends it a fixity and permanence lacking in the more performative concept of "Dayak." While this distinction does not usually preoccupy my acquaintances, there are certain contexts in which it is becoming increasingly important—as I discovered during a lengthy conversation with two young women.

Cathy and Gian had dropped by one Friday evening, having just returned from a staff outing with their colleagues in the company where they worked. As we sipped our soft drinks and languidly discussed our weekend plans, Cathy (who lived in nearby Kampung Sikog) casually mentioned that she was going to attend her uncle's[14] wedding in the village the next day, adding as an afterthought that he was *Kirieng*—Malay. Intrigued and not a little surprised by the thought of a Malay wedding in a Bidayuh village, I immediately began pressing her on who this uncle was. Well, he was Bidayuh, she said—but of course he would be because he lived in a Bidayuh village. With further interrogation, it emerged that Cathy's uncle was of mixed parentage—his father was Malay and his mother Bidayuh, and he was brought up as a Muslim. The lady he was going to marry was also Bidayuh, but she had already converted to Islam for the wedding. And were they going to live in the village after they married? I persisted. Yes, said Cathy; in fact, there were already a few (Bidayuh) Muslim households in Sikog. Like the handful of Chinese, Indians, Seventh Day Adventists, and Baha'i followers who also lived there, everybody was Dayak; they were all *sambut* (accepted, welcomed). With everyone else's stern pronouncements about how Muslims and Bidayuhs could not coexist in the same community whirring through my head, I began mumbling feebly about how difficult it must be for people like her uncle to live there. Following a momentary pause, Cathy and Gian explained to me that "*madin mŭh sănang*"—it was now easy for them to do so. These families, they said, stayed in their own houses, where they prayed, were *Kirieng*, and practiced Islam. The rest of the time, however, they simply lived as part of the village.

What should we make of this conversation, and the bewildering array of terms with which Cathy described her uncle—Malay, Bidayuh, Muslim, Dayak? Following a great deal more probing and discussion, the three of us managed to work out what all these labels implied. First, Cathy's description of her uncle as *Kirieng* was neither a denial of his Bidayuh-ness nor an insistence on the primacy of his paternal descent. She and Gian explained that *Kirieng* was more like a "lifestyle" (English) than a *bangsa:* One is *Kirieng because* one wears a headscarf, doesn't eat pork, follows Islam, and so on. In this sense, *Kirieng* is analogous to "Dayak" in being a primarily performative category. This was counterbalanced, however, by a second point: The fact that, for Cathy and Gian, Bidayuh-ness was a constant. The former's uncle was, of course, Bidayuh (in this case used interchangeably with "Dayak") because he lived in a Bidayuh (= Dayak) village, but what mattered more was that he and the other converts were Bidayuh in *bangsa*—it was fixed on their identity cards. Even when converts changed their names to Muslim ones, my interlocutors added, they would always keep their Bidayuh names as aliases on those very cards.[15] In this way, they depicted Bidayuh-ness as permanent and inalienable: a product of genealogy rather than of anything anyone did. The upshot of all this was that it was perfectly feasible for Bidayuhs who became Muslims to live as *Kirieng* in their homes while being Dayak like everyone else in the village (apart, they said with regret, from eating pork), *and* still remaining Bidayuh in *bangsa*.

By working through these different conceptual terms with me, Cathy and Gian helped to elucidate what I suspect is a growing understanding, particularly among younger Bidayuhs: the fact that what was customarily conflated under the encompassing rubric of *adat*, namely, ethnicity, "lifestyle," and religion, can in fact be disassociated (Kipp 1993). Consequently, although *normative* assertions that Bidayuhs cannot marry Malays and that Muslims cannot live in Bidayuh villages continue to be upheld and propagated by people of all ages, there exists in reality a much wider and more complex range of opinions on the matter. This is particularly important in places such as Sikog—and I have come across several more villages like it— and even in Benuk where, although there is no permanent Muslim presence, growing numbers of people have kin or other acquaintances who have married Malays, or converted to Islam for one reason or another. Some of these instances have been swept under the proverbial rattan mat, while others have been criticized in an unusually forthright, even venomous, manner. In between these two extremes, however, appears to be one further, relatively new response. In recent years, I suggest, Bidayuhs have found within the Malaysian state various discursive and conceptual means of dealing with the situation— chief among them, as Cathy and Gian's constant references to the identity card suggest, the explicitly genealogical notion of *bangsa* found in national politics, official policy, and public discourse.

With *bangsa* being increasingly understood as an innate, unchanging attribute, Bidayuhs Muslims are now able to avoid what was once (and in many ways, remains) a highly unpopular inevitability: complete and irreversible transformation into a Malay. Paradoxically, then, the recognition of their inalienable Bidayuh-ness by no less than the state has restored some freedom of movement to these people, allowing them to shuttle legitimately between genealogical Bidayuh-ness, performative Malay-ness, Islam, and sometimes even performative Dayak-ness, as the situation demands. This was certainly the rationale behind the admittedly controversial actions of an elderly man in the Singai region—a former Tua Gawai who had converted to Islam[16]— who told me that it was acceptable to still help out at *gawai* ceremonies, some of which involved pig sacrifice, since he was still Bidayuh and not fully *Kirieng*. It may also have underlain the behavior of a girl of Malay-Bidayuh parentage, who would simply *be* Bidayuh when she visited her mother's village, taking off her *tudung* (headscarf) when she returned for festivals and other occasions, and redonning it when she left. Although such instances were, in my experience, relatively uncommon, it is possible that the *bangsa*-based logic underpinning them will become increasingly widespread in the coming years.

While this is unlikely to result in a surge of Bidayuh conversions to Islam, it does give both Bidayuh Muslims and the non-Muslim majority a useful means of challenging, or at least alleviating, some of the problems associated with Malay-Muslim hegemony. By conceptually and praxiologically disassociating *bangsa*, "lifestyle," and religion, these people are able to maintain not a distinctive identity but some of that translatability that they value so highly. While Malaysian citizenship has thus not afforded my acquaintances the same freedom of "becoming" as "Dayak"-based village membership, it has nevertheless given them certain indirect routes through which to avoid getting completely trapped within a dangerously politicized ethnic and religious system. Such disassociation, however, is not the only means by which they have sought to achieve this end. In the next section, we turn to quite a different strategy through which the majority have dealt with the situation: the conflation of Christianity and Bidayuh-ness.

Making Associations: Christianity and the Politics of *Agama*

Although Christianity is routinely apprehended in Bidayuh villages as an *adat*, its adherents are also conscious of its status as an *agama*— an officially recognized world religion distinguishable from *bangsa*, *budaya* (culture), and other facets of life. In Malaysia, the standard benchmark of *agama* is the state religion, Islam, adherence or nonadherence to which can have considerable social, political, and economic

implications (Chapter 1). The other official *agama* categories recognized by the state include Christianity, Hinduism, Buddhism
and "traditional Chinese religions" (including Confucianism and
Taoism), as well as the euphemistically titled "tribal/folk religions"
(*agama suku kaum/folk*), under which *adat gawai* is listed. This last
category, however, is an *agama* only in a tenuous sense, encompassing an unspecified jumble of practices and ritual complexes that bear
none of the institutional, codified features conventionally implied by
the term. In that respect, it is, if anything, a second-tier *agama*, closer
to what is described in Indonesia as "*kepercayaan*" (beliefs), "*tradisi*"
(tradition), or simply "*adat*" (way of life; see Kipp 1993: 118; Kipp
and Rodgers 1987: 23; Rössler 1997: 280–283; Schiller 1997: 114;
Tsing 1993: 273).

Here, the parallels with the situation in Indonesia are illuminating.
The first tenet of the *Pancasila*, or Five Principles, on which contemporary Indonesian nationhood is based, is belief in a single supreme
God (*Ketuhanan Yang Maha Esa*; Kipp and Rodgers 1987: 17; Schiller
1997: 116). This, along with the existence of a prophet and scripture
(or at least written traditions), forms the foundation of an officially
recognized concept of *agama*. While this model applies unproblematically to Islam and Christianity, "it is an open secret" that Hinduism
and Buddhism, and more recently, Confucianism,[17] have had to conform "in public dialogue to a Middle Eastern monotheism" (Atkinson
1983: 688). Excluded from this definition of *agama*, however, are a
great many "tribal" or "ethnic" religions, the practitioners of which
are, tellingly, labeled "*orang yang belum beragama*"—people who
have not *yet* got religion (ibid.: 688; Kipp and Rodgers 1987: 23). In
this unabashedly evolutionist equation, "[a]n *agama* identity marks
one as a modern Indonesian citizen" (Kipp 1993: 91); those lacking
it, by contrast, "appear disloyal national citizens, uncommitted to the
values of Pancasila, not to mention intellectually and morally backward" (Kipp and Rodgers 1987: 21–23).

Although the distinction between *agama* and everything else is
less pronounced in Malaysia than it is in Indonesia, there is a comparable hierarchical imbalance between them. This is a point of which
my informants are aware, and although they sometimes describe *adat
gawai* as their *agama lama* (Malay for "old religion") in conversation with outsiders, they also know that Islam and Christianity are
entirely different kettles of fish. Such *agama*s are seen as enjoying a
certain status and influence in the *moden* world that *adat gawai* does
not (see also Rousseau 1998: 7–8). Indeed, it is common to hear my
informants using pejorative English words such as "superstitions" and

"paganism"—picked up from certain churches, television programs, and urban settings—to describe *adat gawai*. Similarly, a 15-year-old girl I knew came home from school one afternoon saying that her teacher had told her that *gawai* was not a proper *agama*, but "animism" (English), which she worked out was somehow inferior to, say, Christianity or Islam (see also Lindell 2000: 233). While such terms are not always used in a hostile or dismissive manner, they do reflect the unequal status of world religions and their "folk" counterparts in Malaysia. In this regard, as Asad has noted of the very concept of "religion," *agama* is not simply an "abstract and universalized" category, but very much "attached to specific processes of power and knowledge" (1993: 42) in the *moden* world.

If their forebears did not have *agama*, however, contemporary Bidayuhs can now lay claim to one. More than converting to Christianity, my acquaintances have in fact converted to a *religion* (Broz 2009) in the official Malaysian sense. In this capacity, they use it as both an assertion of their status as *moden* citizens and a buffer against the dangers of living in a Malay-Muslim dominated world. Its efficacy rests on its legibility (Scott 1998) within this milieu as a *moden agama* that, officially at least, is on a par with the state religion. While *gawai* practitioners are fair game for a "conversion to modernity" (van der Veer 1996) through conversion to Islam, Bidayuh Christians have thus already got there. Like the mountain minorities in Burma and Thailand about whom Cornelia Kammerer writes (1990: 285), my acquaintances see "conversion to Christianity...[as] simultaneously a claim to difference from and a claim to equality with" the Malay majority (see also Aragon 1996: 360). In possessing an *agama*, they too are *moden*—but they are not, crucially, Muslim.

Yet, even though Christianity is not ethnie-specific in the way that Islam conventionally is, it is increasingly held up by Bidayuhs as their de facto religion. "Bidayuhs," I constantly heard during my fieldwork, "are *memang* (naturally, of course) Christian." Conceiving of the relationship between Christianity and Bidayuh-ness in this manner has enabled my acquaintances to frame and channel their discontentment with the state in ways that are quintessentially Malaysian. There were rumblings of disapproval, for example, when all non-Muslim civil servants in Sarawak had to attend a compulsory educational convention on Islam on Holy Saturday in 2005, sandwiched as it was between the public holidays of Good Friday and Easter Sunday. The complaints grew louder the next day, when the village was plunged into a blackout lasting well into the next morning—an uncommonly long spate for a fairly common occurrence. A running joke at some of the Easter celebrations I attended was that, like the civil service convention, this was a deliberate slight against *Christians* by the *Malays* who ran the state electricity company.[18] In this way, the relationship between my acquaintances and the government was enunciated in terms of *agama* and *bangsa*—even if it involved, as it often did, an admission of the former's disadvantageous position.

Unlike official *bangsa* categories, Christianity is rooted and legitimated in a world that transcends Malaysian boundaries. Indeed, it is strongly valued by many Bidayuhs for the fact that it ties them to a larger worldwide community of fellow adherents (see also Harris 2001: 62)—something that *adat gawai* could never do. This sort of connectedness is concretely manifested in the periodic visits to the village of church groups from outside Sarawak (such as Singapore), which sometimes result in generous cash donations to local chapels. It is also reinforced during village church services, which often feature announcements and prayers relating to world affairs: for the soul of the late Pope John Paul II and the successful pontificate of Benedict XVI (2005), for the new U.S. president (in 2004 and 2008), and all too frequently, for peace in the Middle East. Indeed, my acquaintances' sense of involvement in a global Christian community was regularly manifested in their commentaries on contemporary issues, such as the ongoing Israel-Palestine conflict and Islamic terrorism in Southeast Asia. When these topics flickered across village television screens, they would often provoke a storm of remarks that framed specific events in terms of a worldwide conflict between Christianity and Islam—one in which my interlocutors saw themselves as somehow enrolled, if only very remotely.

Meanwhile, when Bidayuhs move into urban centers across Malaysia and neighboring countries, they find in Christianity a consistent anchor and form of protection. I knew several young adults, for example, who had spent years studying or working in West Malaysia. During this time, many of them recalled feeling "targeted" by the Muslim majority around them. One man who went to university in Kuala Lumpur recalled how, facing constant harassment by his Malay peers to convert, he found solace and solidarity with a group of other Sarawakians with whom he regularly attended church. In his narratives, he, like my Holy Saturday companions, identified himself as a Christian facing an onslaught of Malay proselytization. Indeed, he virtually conflated Christianity with his *bangsa*, thus assigning Bidayuh-Christianness an equivalent counterposition to Malay-Muslimness. This was not unusual, for I often heard similar sentiments among other Bidayuhs. One afternoon in Kuching, for example, I struck up an idle conversation with a middle-aged lady—whom I later discovered was a Bidayuh from Bau—and asked if she was Malay. "No," she replied immediately, "I am Christian."

These examples reveal an interesting countertrend to the recent tendency toward disassociation identified earlier. While dealing with the problem of Malay-Muslimness by disentangling *bangsa*, "life-style," and religion, Bidayuhs have concomitantly begun to entangle Christianity and Bidayuh-ness, often treating them in practice as indivisible and interchangeable. Yet, what remains crucial is the knowledge of their separability in theory: a notion that is periodically reiterated in day-to-day conversation and during church services. This happened, for example, when I brought my British husband and in-laws to the Catholic Holy Saturday service in Benuk in 2010. During a characteristically eloquent sermon, the presiding prayer leader used their presence to underscore the inclusivity of Christianity. It was not just Europeans, he said, who could be Christian, because Christianity was for all *bangsa*—even, he added, to a few wry smirks from the congregation, Malays.

Allied to this awareness of Christianity's relative openness is the conviction that, as Sumuk Meroi put it, it also allows Bidayuhs to "return to their own *adat*." As we shall see in the next two chapters, this does not necessarily mean returning to *adat gawai* or resurrecting every aspect of the past. Nor, indeed, does it mean that everybody agrees on what the "return" or the "*adat*" in that comment might entail. The key point is that Christianity is largely viewed as a religion that, unlike Islam, does not demand rupture from existing relations and practices, and does not permanently entrap people in an ethnoreligious package from which there is no escape. In short, it is a religion whose adherents always possess the *potential* for further movement and translation: a freedom that is most palpably manifested in the continued ability of Christian Bidayuhs to eat pork, drink alcohol, and do things that seem commensurate with being Dayak. And it is this characteristic, I would argue, that makes Christianity such a crucial interface between rural Bidayuh communities and the *moden* Malaysian state. As is the case in numerous other settings worldwide, "the ethnicization of religion" in Malaysia means that "conversion acts ha[ve] social consequences that reach...far beyond specifically theological concerns" (Pelkmans 2009: 6). Here, Christianity is political precisely because it encompasses so much more than just politics, narrowly defined.

This, however, is not the only reason that Christianity is so important to contemporary Bidayuh communities, and it would be inadequate to characterize it as merely a means of resisting Malay-Muslim political hegemony. As the next two chapters will reveal, its institutional, ethnotheological, and moral features have also played vital roles in encouraging Bidayuhs to engage far more positively with the contemporary Malaysian state—particularly through participation in the multiculturalist arenas described earlier. In the following pages, we shall take a closer look at how Christianity has contributed to the conceptualization and valorization of *adat gawai* as "Bidayuh culture," by shaping both its adherents' understandings of conversion and the past (Chapter 5) and their sense of obligation and responsibility toward their *gawai*-practicing kin and neighbors (Chapter 6). These reveal how contemporary Bidayuh attitudes toward the *adat gawai* question have been influenced not only by Malaysian multiculturalist politics but also by Christian tenets, models, and institutional policies. The task to which this book now turns, then, is an examination of the very Christianity of "culture."

Chapter 5

Speaking of (Dis)Continuity: Cultures of Christianity and the Christianization of "Culture"

Saturday, June 4, 2005, was a busy day in Kampung Benuk's *adat gawai* calendar. Having spent the previous 72 hours conducting post-harvesting rituals around the longhouse (*gawai sawa*; see Chapter 2), the *nyamba gawai* now turned their attention to the health, safety, and well-being of the village community at large. In the morning, the male ritual chief, Bai Toyan, held the annual *gawai* for the two pairs of wooden guardian spirits (*tibudò kayuh*) that had protected the village's old river entrance for as long as anybody could remember. With the aid of some Christians, he built a *sangar* (bamboo altar) with offerings for the spirits, and carved them entirely new bodies, replete with miniature weapons, to ensure that they would continue watching over the place. As dusk fell, he, a small group of female practitioners, and some family members then gathered in the *pangah* to bathe, feed, and bless the ten skulls hanging from its rafters—to persuade them, as their forebears had done, to keep defending the village from enemies, illnesses, and other dangers. Balancing precariously on a wooden sawhorse, Bai Toyan carefully wet the skulls using a bundle of leaves and smeared them with ritual substances, including turmeric, oil, and chicken blood, before also daubing everyone else present.

When the ritual ended, three of the *gawai* women set off on a walk around the neighborhood carrying the same substances, which they would offer to all the households along their route. Called *nawar*—literally, to relieve pain and sickness (Nais 1988: 301)—this traveling rite would extend the blessings and protection accrued during the day's rituals to the entire community.[1] The departure of this small, wizened party from the *pangah*, however, was barely noticed by the people thronging the center of the village. As it was the first Saturday after the statewide Gawai Dayak celebrations, Benuk was still heaving with revelers, many of whom had taken a whole week's leave for the occasion. The atmosphere that evening was decidedly carnivalesque, and if people were not out gambling at the longhouse[2] or attending the disco at the village hall (featuring a popular Bidayuh boy band), they were at home eating and drinking, entertaining guests, watching television, or perhaps belting out the latest karaoke hits. Weaving their way through the crowds, past the flashing lights and cacophonies, the elderly *gawai* women looked diminished and incongruous—as if they were about to be swallowed up by the entire ebullient scene. Yet, as they moved from one household to another, an intriguing pattern began to unfold.

Whenever they approached a house, the women would rap on the door or sometimes walk straight in, and announce that they were there for the *nawar*. At this point, almost all the people inside recognized what was happening, and immediately ushered the visitors into the living room. Without prompting, they would present themselves and their children to the *nyamba gawai*, sitting, squatting, or bowing their heads as they, like the skulls, were "bathed" with the leaf bundle and anointed with various ritual substances. Most recipients gave the old ladies cash, beer, food, and other tokens, although some also asked to be "treated" for specific ailments: A bedridden stroke patient, for example, had turmeric and other health-restoring substances massaged into her, while another woman was "beaten" with the leaf bundle, amid much laughter, to chase out her illness.

While these people were all Christian, it was manifestly clear that they were used to this sort of visit, and treated it as part and parcel of life in the village. Some older residents told me that they had known this ritual since their youth and just did what they must, while others pointed out that the *nawar* was acceptable because it was basically "good"—simply the "old" or *asar* (original) way of blessing and protecting them. And so this pattern of reception persisted—until the *nyamba gawai* arrived at one house and had the door slammed in their faces. Having got distracted along the way, I caught up with the group and asked what had happened. Their answer was accompanied by a shrug of resignation but not surprise: The people in the house were "SIB"s.

As this episode reveals, life in a community with a persistent *adat gawai* presence is not always straightforward or unproblematic. While the Anglican and Catholic majority are mostly amenable toward its continued practice (even when it enters their homes), SIB adherents generally take a sterner stance, seeking instead to distance themselves from the old ways. In the face of such contrasting views, it may be tempting to draw a clear dichotomy between continuity-seeking Anglicans and Catholics on the one hand and rupture-mad SIBs on the other. To do so, however, would mean oversimplifying what is in reality a far more complicated and ambiguous situation, in which all Bidayuhs—Anglican, Catholic, SIB, and *gawai* alike—are struggling with the same thorny questions about conversion, Christianization, continuity, and discontinuity.

This chapter seeks to elucidate some of those questions, paying particular attention to how, over the last few decades, the different churches and their representatives have shaped villagers' thoughts, discourses, and actions vis-à-vis the old ways and the Christian present. Rather than trying to reach a clear *analytical* conclusion about the continuity or discontinuity of Christian conversion, I shall examine how Bidayuhs' discourses and lived experiences of (dis)continuity are constantly feeding into or contradicting each other. As we shall see, their constant interplay makes it difficult to either achieve complete rupture or to maintain complete continuity with the past. Before moving into such messy territory, however, let us begin with a conviction broadly shared by all my informants: the idea that Christianity has "freed" Bidayuhs from the dangers and difficulties of the old days.

On Being "Freed" by Christianity

Although Anglicans, Catholics, and SIBs have their own opinions on the relationship of the past to the present, there is one proposition on which they almost all concur: the idea that life really has changed as a result of Christianization. The assertion that "this village is now Christian" ("*rais ati madin mŭh Kristen*") was something that I heard regularly throughout fieldwork, as was the consensus that things were very different compared with when everybody followed *adat gawai*. To an extent, such remarks conflate the growth of Christianity with the rapid and very tangible postindependence changes that turned Benuk and other Bidayuh villages into self-consciously *moden* communities (Chapter 1). However, they also reflect the fact that the Christianity itself has spurred them into crafting their own models and discourses of temporality, change, and transformation.

This is perhaps best encapsulated by my elderly informants' occasional use of the term *biya* to describe their entry into Christianity. In *adat gawai*, *biya* refers to the lifting of those *patang*—prohibitions or "taboos" on movement, behavior, work, and food consumption—that usually accompany rituals. As Chapter 3 explained, such tedious and costly prescriptions were among the "push" factors that spurred some of the first converts into leaving *adat gawai* and adopting *adat Kristen*. For these people, Christianity must have been akin to one large, encompassing *biya*, which enabled them to abandon those onerous obligations and responsibilities while still protecting them from the vengeance of the old spirits. As elderly converts would tell me, following *gawai* could be very difficult, but with Christianity, everybody was now "free" (*bebas*).

If Christianity freed people from the dictates of *adat gawai*, it is also said to have freed them from fear (*tăru*)—the state in which people in the past are often depicted as living (see also Postill 2008: 116–117). In this old (*jah*) world, ghosts, spirits, and other unseen entities appear to have been particularly plentiful and capricious. Several of my acquaintances, for example, recalled with genuine shudders how they, as children, were locked inside their houses immediately after a death in the village and only allowed to peek out through cracks in the door, because the deceased's spirit was roaming about, causing fright-illnesses to those it encountered (Lindell 2000: 125; Nuek 2002: 81). Prior to Christianization, moreover, few people were willing to handle or come into close proximity with corpses (Sidaway 1969: 144); accordingly, death rituals were often abrupt affairs, with the body being wrapped in a mat and thrown into the jungle after a day or two.[3] Set against this past, Christianity is portrayed by many Bidayuhs as having stopped them from feeling afraid. Indeed, freeing the bereaved from fear and sadness is an explicit theme in Christian postmortem prayer sessions, which focus on commending the deceased to the mercy of God and marking the end of his or her suffering on earth (see Chapter 6). In this way, Christian protocol has transformed death into a rather more edifying and significantly less disconcerting matter than it used to be.

Finally, it is also commonly said that Christianity liberated Bidayuhs from a past filled with incessant warfare and headhunting. Although the Land Dayaks were stereotyped by nineteenth-century European writers as timid, peaceable natives who made "ideal victims" for Iban headhunters (Runciman 1960: 57), they were certainly not averse to skirmishes, raids, and head-taking,[4] tales of which pepper my acquaintances' depictions of the past. While this fractious history does not feature strongly in their day-to-day thoughts and conversations, it sometimes acquires a retrospective significance in the context of conversion. While chatting with friends in the Padawan village of Rejoi, for instance, I was told that "Rajah Brooke" brought peace (*damai*) to Sarawak by ending all the fighting that had gone on prior to his arrival. Without any allusion to the Raj's many punitive measures to this end, my interlocutor attributed this to the fact that the Rajah had brought in Christians to teach Dayaks to live well—which, in turn, made them stop fighting and taking heads. In this narrative, variants of which I have heard elsewhere, Christianity was thus credited with teaching Bidayuhs about right and wrong (see Chapter 6), and giving them the freedom to move about without fear or harassment.

This example highlights a crucial point that has remained implicit throughout this section: the fact that my acquaintances' discourses of freedom from the past are themselves shaped by the present, and more specifically, by priorities and concepts relevant to their lives as Christians. Indeed, it is instructive that *biya* is not the only notion of "freedom" invoked by my acquaintances. As we shall later see, it has also been cemented and elaborated by a particular missionary discourse of emancipation and deliverance from fear and "bad" aspects of the old days. In this respect, it is not always easy to tell where the images, idioms, and principles of Christianity start and end in my acquaintances' reflections. Does the conviction that Christianity has freed people from fear, for example, derive from missionary exhortations, or from genuine relief at not having to worry about random encounters with jungle spirits? To what extent has the Christian trope of "peace" colored people's views of the "bad" old headhunting days? While such questions are analytically intriguing, the point I wish to make is that in many ways—and certainly for my informants—those distinctions are of no consequence. What matters, rather, is the effect that they have on my acquaintances' lives, social relations, and conceptual understandings.

This brings me to a related point: the fact that "our attention to language has to be complemented by an attention to lived experiences" (Engelke 2010: 196). Taken at face value, the *discourses* of freedom that I have just described may seem consonant with Robbins's argument that by "keeping the discontinuity that marked its birth at the forefront of its followers' minds," Christianity induces its converts to "represent the process of becoming Christian as one of radical change . . . [as] a rupture in the time line of a person's life that cleaves it into a before and after" (2007: 11). However, a closer look at the situation in my fieldsite suggests that far greater complexity exists; that talk of freedom does not always equate to actual rupture, or indeed to a thoroughly millenarian stance that leaves people "wait[ing] in a constant state of expectation" for the Second Coming (ibid.: 12).

For a start, it is important to note that despite their sense of being released from the past, my acquaintances do not portray the old days as entirely bad. In fact, the very people who complain about the difficulty of following *gawai* are often also the first to reminisce about how much more *rami* (boisterous, fun-filled) and enjoyable its rituals were in comparison to Christian prayer services. Similarly, they see no contradiction in asserting one minute that the old *gawai* days were filled with fear and pointing out the next that the longhouse-village was a much friendlier and more sociable place back then (Chapter 4), when people could wander all over without worrying about getting lost, robbed, or hurt. While these reflections cannot be disassociated from the shifting political circumstances around them, they do offer a cautionary reminder against mapping discourse too readily onto reality.

This admonition is especially pertinent when we consider the *patang*s and omens from which Christians proclaim they have been freed. As I explain elsewhere (Chua 2009b), their numbers and significance may have decreased in recent decades, but they have not been entirely excised from village life. Indeed, during fieldwork I became well acquainted with several common *patang*s, which, while not as severe or extensive as in the past, were nonetheless accepted as part of communal life. Every death in the village, for example, mandated a light *patang*, which by vague consensus usually translated into a one-day suspension of manual work within the village and the prohibition of movement around certain areas.[5] Trying to abide by them could involve a healthy degree of interpretation and negotiation on the part of Christians. In July 2010, for example, my adoptive mother, Ndŭ Pin, got home after a long day of clearing a newly bought piece of land on which she intended to plant rice, to hear the disheartening news that a neighbor had just died. Drawing on past practice, her mother (one of the village's earliest Catholics) reminded her that a death on the first day of work was a bad omen that mandated a yearlong *patang* on the planned activity—in this case, rice cultivation. Frustrated but resigned, Ndŭ Pin pointed out that there wasn't much she could do: Had she not been told about the *patang* she might have gone ahead, but now that her mother had asserted that it ought to exist (Chua 2009b), she would probably grow corn or vegetables instead that year.

In sum, while Christianity has brought about real change in Bidayuh societies—more of which we shall see in the next chapter—their discourses of freedom must still be situated in relation to their lived experiences, as well as to other discourses and models in their lives. To suggest, as have Matthew Engelke (2004, 2010), Olivia Harris (2006), and Birgit Meyer (1998, 1999), among others, that assertions of rupture are not as watertight as they seem is thus not to downplay my acquaintances' experiences of change but to highlight the very real complexity and ambivalence that often surrounds them in practice. The next chapter will have more to say about the lived realities and moral dilemmas precipitated by Christianization. In the following section, however, I would like to turn to some other discourses and ideas about the past, *adat gawai*, and the present, which are equally relevant to Bidayuh Christianity today. While not incommensurate with the proposition that Christianity has "freed" Bidayuhs, these have had the cumulative effect of mitigating this perception of rupture, tending instead to foster a sense of continuity and contiguity between the old ways and the Christian present. To understand how this situation came about, we need to examine the traffic of ideas, arguments, and actions that took place during the height of conversion, from the 1960s to the 1980s.

On Good Fields and Bad Fields: Ruptures and Realignments with the Past

Although the first mission presences in rural Bidayuh areas tended to creep rather than crash their way into people's lives through health care and education, they nevertheless placed severe demands on those who did convert. Many early twentieth-century missionaries were disparaging of *adat gawai* and other aspects of the old ways, which they sometimes denounced as "bad" or "*kaper*" (from the Arabic *kafir*, i.e., infidels or unbelievers).[6] Several of my elderly informants recalled that they would confiscate or destroy converts' *gawai* paraphernalia, encourage them to break communal *patang*s, and generally teach them to "throw away" (*tăran*) earlier practices and artifacts (see also Nuek 2002: 108). Their intention, in short, appears to have been to obliterate all links with a "pagan world in which magic and superstition [were] everything" (Sidaway 1969: 139).

While moderately successful in the short run, such tactics may, however, have backfired, as was suggested in a conversation that I had with Sumuk Jewi, one of Benuk's first Catholics. Recounting the "RC"'s' struggle to expand their nascent congregation in the

1950s, she remarked that the other villagers were then "stupid," because they thought that becoming Christian would mean permanently becoming *branda* (white people) and abandoning their own *adat*. Yet, looked at from a different angle, such "stupidity" may have been a reasonable response to the very tangible enactments of rupture entailed by conversion. In essence, I suggest, the missionaries were demanding the same sort of one-way movement associated with conversion to Islam (Chapter 4): a complete social and temporal break with the past, which would not allow converts to "return to their own *adat*." To become Christian would thus mean shunning not only the old rituals but also all the attributes of being "Dayak" and the social relations implicit in them (see also Chapter 6; Connolly 2009).

As the 1960s wore on, however, missionary tactics evolved from complete disassociation to strategic rapprochement, with many Anglican and Catholic missionaries adopting more measured approaches to conversion and religious guidance. This shift was arguably precipitated by several convergent factors, including growing missionary familiarity with "pagans" and their practices (e.g., Aichner 1955; Howes 1960; Sidaway 1969), the increased presence and influence of native catechists in rural missions, and, as we shall see, a mounting tendency on the part of international church establishments to vernacularize Christianity. The result was a reorientation of missionary priorities throughout Sarawak (e.g., Postill 2008: 133, n.1; Varney 1968) toward compromise and coexistence between Christianity and the old ways. Their relationship, however, was never one of full equivalence, because not all aspects of the past were deemed compatible with the Christian present, as this story, recounted by Father Meehan, reveals:

An Iban man had a dream in which he met a Dutch priest. "Where are you going?" he asked the priest, to which the latter responded, "Heaven." "I want to come with you," said the Iban man. But the priest replied, "You cannot come with me, because you are pagan." And then the priest showed the Iban man two fields, and told him that in order to get to Heaven, he would have to abandon one field and cultivate the other. When the Iban man awoke, he went to see a Bidayuh Catholic schoolteacher, wanting to know what the dream was about.[7] The latter interpreted it thus: "You have to become Catholic," he said, "but not Dutch Catholic. You have to be Iban Catholic. The bad field is full of *patang*s and other bad aspects of your old religion. The good field is full of good Iban customs which you must keep when you become Christian."

Rather than insisting on a complete desertion of Iban *adat*, as would have happened previously, the schoolteacher's interpretation bifurcated it into good and bad "fields." It thus made the crucial point that becoming Christian did not necessarily mean un-becoming Iban; it simply meant weeding out those elements of the old *adat* that were not commensurate with Christian living. But what exactly was "good" and what was "bad"? Answers to this question did not come easily, and for some years, missionaries, catechists, and local converts seem to have found it easier to identify the latter than the former. Headhunting, for one, was a popular candidate for renunciation. Having effectively been eradicated by the Brooke Raj by the start of the twentieth century (Haddon 1901: 395–397; Hose 1994), it was sufficiently proximate in collective memory to have some resonance, but sufficiently remote in collective experience for its disavowal not to matter. Associated with this was what came to be portrayed by the church and later, Christian Bidayuhs, as a state of constant strife and warfare. Whether this was a natural offshoot of the "pagan" hothead-edness that came from not knowing God (as the missionaries put it), or a threat to "cool," harmonious sociality (as many Bidayuhs would have seen it), discord within and between communities was incontrovertibly undesirable—and thus something that all parties could agree should be abolished. A third example was, of course, the old omens and *patang*s that most people were pleased to cease observing, particularly with the blessing and protection of the church.

Less common, but nonetheless significant, were efforts to work out what was "good" about the old ways. As the next section reveals, these were given shape and legitimization from about the mid-1970s by official liturgical "inculturation" policies. Even before that, however, a tendency toward "vernacularization" and making Christianity relevant to local conditions was shaping the work of the Sarawak missions. Many church workers, for example, picked up on the close enmeshment of morality and sociality within Bidayuh communities as a trait to be encouraged and developed within a Christian framework—a point on which the next chapter expands. More concrete were the efforts by priests and others to reuse old *gawai* artifacts in spreading and consolidating Christianity. While handing out crosses and medallions to *adat gawai* practitioners who requested them, priests were also dipping old leopard tooth necklaces (*sitagan*) in holy water and using them to sprinkle their congregations, in almost direct replication of *gawai* ceremonies. These and similar actions, more of which we shall see later, ensured that many "old" entities were reappropriated and rendered Christian rather than discarded entirely.

In order to prune the past, then, missionaries, catechists, and converts also had to define it (Engelke 2004, 2010; Meyer 1998): to reify certain entities and tendencies as either disposable or worthy of inclusion in the Christian present. In this regard, mission strategy in the 1960s and 1970s often constituted one lengthy "exercise in boundary drawing—in being able to say what count[ed] as Christian or ["bad"] traditional and on what grounds" (Engelke 2010: 184). However, this did not mean that everybody knew or agreed upon what that boundary looked like or where it lay. The fate of the old spirits constitutes a case in point. Realizing the futility of suggesting to Bidayuhs that the spirits that inhabited their world, and with which they had engaged through *adat gawai*, were fictional or irrelevant, the missionaries opted to tackle the problem head on. Consequently, when new converts complained (as they often did) of being harassed by the old spirits who were angry at being neglected or ignored, priests and catechists would give them the means by which to fight back. They might, for example, dole out bottles of holy water and crosses to those in need, or teach them specific prayers through which to call Jesus and God that would then chase away the bad spirits and stop them from feeling afraid. At the same time, they began depicting such troublesome spirits as "Satan," or as coming under the power of Satan ("*kuasa Satan*")—having earlier defined Satan as the most powerful *umot*, or demon, of all. The effectiveness of this strategy is widely discernible today, for "Satan" is now a common byword, used by both Christians and *nyamba gawai*, for all malicious spirit entities.

The "diabolisation" (Meyer 1999) of the old spirits, however, was never more than a partial enterprise. As Chapter 2 revealed, most spirit entities associated with *adat gawai* are fundamentally amoral rather than unremittingly benevolent or malevolent; consequently, a whole range of them, including village guardians, ancestors, and the rice spirit, do not slide easily into the category of "Satan." To complicate matters, some of these have also been embraced by the Anglican and Catholic churches as acceptable to Bidayuh Christianity. Both churches, for example, identify the Christian God as *Tăpa*—the name of the "supreme deity" in *adat gawai*. This is not merely a conceit of translation but an acknowledgement of the widespread understanding that both *adat*s share the same god (Chapter 2). Although *Tăpa*'s relationship with humans has been reconfigured under Christianity (Chapter 6), He thus remains a consistent node of continuity for Bidayuh converts. Second, the remit of Christianity now extends to include the well-being of those ancestral spirits who are also invoked and given offerings during *adat gawai* rituals. Although the status of non-Christian ancestors is seldom explicitly addressed by the church, there exists a pervasive lay understanding that they can also be prayed for and to during All Souls' Day and through regular incantations. A third example of an incorporated entity is the rice spirit, the well-being and "coolness" of which, as I explain later, is addressed in special Anglican and Catholic services held during the agricultural cycle. While such sessions leave open the question of whether people are praying for a generic spirit (life force) of the rice or the rice spirit in an individualized soul form, they have contributed to a widespread understanding that, rather like the saints and the Holy Spirit, some old spirits are basically "good" and worth having around.

By finding ways to Christianize rather than completely abandon the old spirits, the missionaries thus ended up reinforcing their reality and relevance—not only by treating them as genuine threats to be dealt with but also by making them legible within a specific Christian framework. Rather than holding the old world and Christianity at bay, then, their actions and teachings collapsed them into a single temporal, social, and causal framework. In the process, I suggest, they foreclosed the possibility of enacting a complete break with the past, transforming Christianity from an *adat* that demanded full rupture into one that kept open the channels between old and new, past and present. Not all aspects of the past or the old ways, it had been shown, were bad; indeed, some were still relevant and desirable in the present, and thus could be "returned to" if necessary. From here on, conversion would no longer be a straightforward "before" and "after" phenomenon, but a matter for constant negotiation.

The converts' own awareness of this fact is nicely encapsulated in another anecdote told to me by Father Meehan, this time of his own experiences in the Padawan area in the 1970s. When visiting villages around harvest time, priests were often asked to bless the new rice crop, which would be laid out across the longhouse veranda for the purpose. One day, having performed the usual Catholic prayers and sprinkled holy water over the stalks, he was invited by some elderly ladies to wave a chicken (*pisen*) over the same crop, as the Tua Gawai customarily did during rituals. "No, I can't do that," he recalled telling them, "that's a pagan practice; you're not supposed to follow it anymore." "But it's our tradition (*tradisi*)," they persisted slyly, "We want to do it because it's the old way, but we don't believe in it now that we're Christian." Unmoved, Father Meehan asked, "Well, why don't you ask one of your ritual specialists to do it?" "Ah, but Father," came the instantaneous reply, "that's because you always bring us good harvests!"

If Christianization entailed boundary drawing, then, missionaries and catechists were not the only ones involved in it. Here was not a "simple contest between missionaries and natives" (Barker 1992: 154), for as this episode reveals, the "goodness" or "badness" of the old ways could be ambiguated by converts themselves—in this case, some women who cannily deployed a valorized notion of "tradition" (more on which later) in defense of a particular practice. Like people in Benuk, they seem to have become aware that there were now debates to be had about the past, the present, and the relationship between them—and that they were enrolled in these debates as active participants. Most of these negotiations took place within a large gray area that defied clear compartmentalization into either "good" or "bad" fields. Within this space, missionaries, catechists, local converts, and *gawai* followers had ample room for discussion, compromise, innovation, and improvisation, while generally avoiding outright confrontation or conflict. In this situation, becoming Christian thus did not entail entering an entirely new world, because it was simply not necessary, and indeed impossible, for converts to entirely disassociate themselves from what was already there. The crucial point is that their inability—and unwillingness—to leave the old world behind was encouraged, endorsed, and lent definition by the missionaries and local catechists themselves.

The Anglican and Catholic churches, however, did more than keep certain elements of the past—both actual and objectified—in the lives and thoughts of their new flocks. Intentionally or otherwise, they also ended up shaping Bidayuh Christians' views of and attitudes toward *adat gawai* and its practitioners. Apart from demonstrating through their accommodatory efforts that the old ways were not thoroughly "bad," many of them went a step further by actively encouraging converts to treat their *gawai*-following elders with courtesy and respect. In some ways, this was a move born out of necessity and pragmatism, particularly in the early years of large-scale conversion, when Christians were the minority in most villages. Aware of the need to avoid alienating *gawai*-practicing village leaders on whose cooperation their presence in rural areas depended, church representatives were often scrupulous about keeping the peace with *gawai* followers. Such exhortations, moreover, may have reflected a genuine conviction, explored in the next chapter, that the new Christians ought to be good social beings by living peaceably with their neighbors, and showing them love and kindness rather than hatred and hostility. Consequently, as we saw in Denis Sembus's story (Chapter 3), the early converts were sometimes allowed and even encouraged to respect the authority of the village leaders and *gawai* elders, and to adhere to communal *patang*s even if it meant missing prayer sessions.

These efforts to structure intravillage interactions set the tone for relations between Christians and *nyamba gawai* for years to come, and in the process, prevented large-scale conversion from turning into complete rupture. Their effects, however, were boosted and given shape from about the mid-1970s by another phenomenon: official church policies and missionizing strategies known throughout the world as "inculturation."

Making "Culture": The Christianization of *Adat Gawai*

The term "inculturation" is believed to have been coined in 1973 by G. L. Barney, a Protestant missionary in New York (Chupungco 1992: 25). It quickly gained popularity among various Christian bodies, notably the Jesuits, who began using the Latin "inculturatio" from 1975, and the Vatican, which first officially used the term in 1979 (ibid.: 25–26). The vernacularizing impulse that underpinned the concept, however, had already been evident within institutional Christianity throughout the previous decade. At the Second Vatican Council (1962–1965), for example, it was stated explicitly that

> [T]he Church, sent to all peoples of every time and place, is not bound exclusively and indissolubly to any race or nation, nor to any particular way of life or any customary pattern of living, ancient or recent. Faithful to her own tradition and at the same time conscious of her universal mission, she can enter into communion with various cultural modes, to her own enrichment and theirs too. (Abbott 1966: 264, cited in Stewart 1999: 51)

In keeping with such antecedents, "inculturation" formally acknowledged that "a certain amount of cultural adaptation might not affect the content of the Christian message" (Stewart 1999: 53). As Christianity spread across the world, it could thus afford to "make the Gospel incarnate in different cultures" while simultaneously "introduc[ing] peoples, together with their cultures, into her own community" (John Paul II 1990: article 52; see also Paul VI 1965). In practical terms, this meant that missionaries and other Church representatives had to "immerse themselves in the cultural milieu of those to whom they are sent...understanding, appreciating, fostering and evangelizing the culture of the environment in which they are working, and...equipping themselves to communicate effectively with it" (John Paul II 1990: article 53). Allied to these efforts was "liturgical inculturation": a process of "inserting the texts and rites of the liturgy into the framework of the local culture" such that they would "assimilate people's thought, language, value, ritual, symbolic and artistic pattern" (Chupungco 1992: 30).

In theory, then, inculturation is a profoundly equalizing concept, seeking to translate Christian values and modes of thought into their local equivalents, while integrating and sacralizing other aspects of local society within Christian frameworks (Angrosino 1994: 825–826). Bearing in mind that "culture is a human creation and is therefore marked by sin," however, its advocates warn that only the "good elements" of each culture should be appropriated as such (John Paul II 1990: article 52). Through this process of "editing" (Volkman 1990: 92), Christian institutions can thus reprise their centuries-old role as arbiters of commensurability, exalting acceptable local practices as "culture" or "custom" and discarding others as "paganism" or "superstition."

In the last few decades, inculturation and its equivalents have become well-established policies in many churches' efforts to evangelize and minister to non-Western communities worldwide (e.g., Chupungco 1992; Schineller 1990; Schreiter 1985; Shorter 1989; Tovey 2004). As we have seen, its underlying principles were already being embraced and deployed by Anglican and Catholic missionaries in Sarawak (e.g., Varney 1968)—and indeed throughout Southeast Asia (Keyes 1996: 286)—well before the label entered official usage. The introduction of the concept, however, brought added clarity—or simplification—to the question of how to deal with the old ways. If previous accommodatory efforts had suspended *adat gawai* in that usefully vague gray area mentioned earlier, "inculturation" now positively extolled it by defining it as "culture." In the process, it also (theoretically, at least) neutralized it, dissolving the previously competitive relationship between *gawai* and Christianity by treating them as fundamentally different phenomena. Consequently, aspects of *adat gawai* could be safely incorporated into Anglican and Catholic prayer services as symbolic "cultural" touches rather than as actually efficacious modes of producing effects.

Since about the late-1970s, a very specific model of "Bidayuh culture" has come to feature in Anglican and Catholic practice: one that consists primarily of *gawai* hats, clothing, paraphernalia, baskets, gongs, blue-and-white offering bowls, and *baruk*s. In short, this is an object-centered, aesthetic, model of "culture" not far removed from—and in many ways deriving from—the officially sanctioned version (*budaya*) that we examined in Chapter 1. This pattern is not confined to Bidayuh areas, but can be discerned throughout Sarawak, where "inculturation" is a pervasive facet of many Christian establishments. Indeed, in urban churches there has even developed a generic template of "Borneo culture," consisting primarily of Iban warp-ikat (*pua*) print clothing, Bidayuh baskets, brass gongs, and swirling, geometric paintings reminiscent of Kayan and Kenyah artwork. This sort of "culture" also routinely features on major church occasions, such as during the 150th-anniversary celebrations of the Anglican Diocese of Sarawak and Brunei in St Thomas' Cathedral, Kuching (2005), when "[a] Dayak cultural group comprising parishioners in native costumes and with the beat of native instruments, greeted the Procession as it made its way...through the West Door of the Cathedral at the start of the Service" (Ang 2005: 1). Resolutely a-contextual (Angrosino 1994: 827–828), such manifestations of "culture" require no explanation and elaboration but are largely taken for granted as part of contemporary Sarawakian Christianity.

While not as lavish as those in the capital, similar performances of inculturation occasionally take place in Bidayuh villages. An excerpt from a description of a Catholic Gawai Dayak mass held in Kampung Gayu on June 1, 1998, offers a vivid example of what such efforts can entail:

> The church is decorated with palm leaves...Some of these decorations are in keeping with earlier traditions of what is sacred. For example, bamboo posts split at the top to form fonts (*kerah*)—which were used to hold spirit offerings [—] now become candleholders. Other items used for spirits offerings in the past are in evidence, a small bamboo altar (*sangan*), a plate (*tayan*), are in the church decorations yet are in keeping with the theme of offering and self-giving. (Mashman and Nayoi 2000: 235–236).

Later, during the Offertory,

> Women dressed in ethnic costume, wearing hats and red baskets, waving shawls of red or white cloth, dance around the altar to the beat of the gongs in a manner reminiscent of the ritual dance of the padi-cult (*bijaro*)...[T]his dance is performed by priestesses to entertain the spirits of the rice whose presence have [sic] been summoned by the offering of animal sacrifices...(ibid.: 238–239).

Here, then, is the very embodiment of the inculturation ideal: Old (*gawai*) ritual practices are transformed into, then sanctified as, "culture" under the auspices of the church. Or, as the authors put it,

> Today the Roman Catholic church provides a venue for expression of *Pinyawa'a*[8] culture. Christian worship is expressed through cultural components which have held sacred meaning to the community in the past. (2000: 235)

Broadly similar occurrences can sometimes be found in Kampung Benuk's Anglican and Catholic churches. Both, for example, hold special services to mark the two major stages of the rice-planting cycle that are still the object of annual *gawai* rituals: *gawai nyipa'an* (blessing of the new rice crop) and *gawai sawa* (the postharvest festival). During these services, members of the congregation bring rice plants from their farms, often in small rattan baskets, and place them at the altar to be blessed by the priests or prayer leaders. The same receptacles—viewed and marketed throughout Sarawak as distinctly Bidayuh crafts (Chua 2006b: 1; see also Chin 1980: 70–71; Munan 1989: 44)—are also frequently used to hold fundraising ribbons, cash donations, and small items involved in prayer services. Meanwhile, older *gawai* paraphernalia such as beads, leaf-bundles, and blue-and-white offering bowls, as well as more recent "cultural" products such as "Sarawak"-themed ceramic candleholders and vests bearing prints of Iban motifs, have become regular components of the prayer packages discussed in Chapter 3, sitting comfortably alongside more traditionally Christian artifacts such as medallions, rosaries, and pictures of Jesus and Mary. Finally, at community events such as church fundraisers, the teenage "cultural dance" troupe members mentioned in Chapter 1 can be found resplendent in their "traditional costumes," handing out tokens and collecting donations.

Over the last few decades, these "cultural" touches appear to have become an essential and unquestioned part of Bidayuh Christianity. Most of my acquaintances devote little thought to them, describing them matter-of-factly as "our culture" (*budaya mi*). Their nonchalant acceptance of such elements, however, belies the fact that Christianity has wrought an important conceptual shift in people's lives. Like the dream-interpreting schoolteacher, inculturation at the village level has essentially pulled apart what was previously the irreducible whole of *adat* into "religion" and "culture." A few decades ago, Pope John Paul's pronouncement that "[t]he church comes to bring Christ; she does not come to bring the culture of another race" (Pope John

Paul II, cited in Angrosino 1994: 824) would not have made a great deal of sense in Bidayuh villages. Today, however, it would strike many chords with my acquaintances, for by professing to unite "religion" and "culture," inculturation policies have in fact helped to create and delineate them as conceptual entities—as *agama* and *budaya*.

As we saw in chapters 1 and 4, a similar process of disassociation was set in motion at roughly the same time by postindependence politics, which elevated *bangsa* and *agama*, and later, *budaya*, into key categories of Malaysian citizenship. Cumulatively, these two processes appear to have dovetailed from around the 1980s, resulting in the conceptual transformation of *adat gawai* into a very specific, predominantly aesthetic, model of "Bidayuh culture." Propagated simultaneously by institutional churches, the Sarawakian state, and a large pool of mobile, urbanized Bidayuhs with connections to both these sources, this model of "culture" has given Christians a legitimate and positively valued idiom through which to conceive of and articulate their ongoing connections with the past and *adat gawai*. Rather than treating *adat gawai* and Christianity as competing *adats* of the same ilk, Bidayuhs can now, with the blessing of church and state, depict them as different but commensurate phenomena. While this does not detract from their functions as *adats* within the village, it thus gives them an additional set of identities that can be called into service when the need arises. In this framework, Christianity has not completely displaced *adat gawai* but simply nudged it into a different niche.

For the majority of my acquaintances, such conceptual maneuverings have been very useful means of justifying, and indeed celebrating, their continued support of *adat gawai* rituals. Many of them—particularly the *gawai* helpers—are aware of the institutional churches' ambivalence about their involvement in such ceremonies. While not condemning them outright, the missions and parish churches do not condone their actions either, thus preserving some of that gray area that was so central to early waves of conversion. One way for my acquaintances to avoid censure, then, has been to extend the positive overtones of the trope of "culture" to the *gawai* rituals themselves. In these instances, they valorize *gawai* not in order to incorporate it into the Christian liturgy or practice but in order to legitimate their own complicity in sustaining, and in many ways perpetuating, it. During *gawai* rituals, I would thus be told by attendees of all ages that they did not really know what was going on (Chua 2009b) and that Christians were not allowed to participate in the ritual dances—but that it was fundamentally all right to be there and to help their elders because this was their "culture." Always chary of the potential dangers posed by the invisible entities involved in such affairs, however, they added that they themselves did not pray to the *gawai* spirits—only Jesus, since their *agama* was now Christianity. In this way, they justified their interest in the old *adat* by invoking its status as *budaya*, while simultaneously affirming their affiliation with a different *agama*, whose deity would protect them on the off-chance that an old spirit caused them trouble.

Such deft conceptual criss-crossing is a common feature of life in this "not yet pure" Christian village, reflecting both the prevalence of *budaya* and *agama* and the impossibility of pinning them down to any one manifestation. However, there remains one prominent exception to this pattern: the SIB congregation, to which we must finally turn. As Chapter 3 revealed, SIB adherents in Kampung Benuk are not converted *gawai* practitioners, but mostly former Anglicans, many of whom would have been party to the same ruptures, realignments, and "cultural" exercises described earlier. On this point, it is worth noting that SIBs, by and large, also subscribe to the model of "Bidayuh culture" that we have just examined. While not interested in incorporating its artifacts and practices into their services, they are nonetheless willing to don certain items of "cultural" clothing at official functions, watch "traditional dances," and generally support similar "culture"-making exercises. In short, they are prepared to embrace a relatively secular, deritualized notion of "culture" that is categorically different from "religion"—the differentiation between which was earlier set in train by inculturation policies. However, unlike their Anglican and Catholic counterparts, they draw the line at *adat gawai* rituals, which they see as anathema to their lives as Christians. As such, they generally avoid and actively shun anything *gawai*-related, such as the annual *nawar*.

In sum, the effects of inculturation policies have been somewhat uneven. While they have helped to carve a specific, a-religious conceptual niche for a notion of "culture" that is acceptable to all Christians—Anglican, Catholic, and SIB alike—they have nonetheless failed to convince the latter of the desirability of seeking rapprochement with rather than rupture from *adat gawai*. While everyone thus agrees that having a "culture" is a good thing, they remain divided over the extent to which this "culture" and the rituals from which it derives can and should feature in the Christian present. Such polarity of opinion, however, raises a pressing question: Why, despite earlier going through the same conversion experiences as their Anglican and

Catholic counterparts, have the SIBs not pursued a similar relationship of continuity and contiguity with the old ways? To answer this, we need to examine the discourses of rupture—and alignment—that feature so strongly in SIB Christianity, and shape its adherents' lives and attitudes toward the past.

Rupture, Repentance, and Renewal: SIB Christianity and Questions of (Dis)continuity

SIB Christianity first arrived in Kampung Benuk in 1992, when four households left the Anglican fold and established their own congregation in the village. Initially based in individual houses, the nascent group raised enough funds to construct its own building in 1995, on a piece of land on the outskirts of the village donated by Nimo, one of the church elders. In the intervening years, the SIB congregation has grown to about 25 households—still a distinct minority in the village—most of whose members are former Anglicans. In this respect, many SIBs are acutely conscious of having made a double break from two old orders—first, *adat gawai*, then the Anglican church. But why did they choose to become SIB in the first place?

When I posed this question to Anglicans and Catholics, I would usually be greeted with bemused shrugs. Conversion narratives are not commonplace among members of the two older churches, and I usually had to feed them endless prompts and questions to elicit their reasons for "entering" Christianity. Their disinterest in reflecting on conversion extended to the SIBs: If the latter wanted to join a different congregation, who were they to question their motives? Of the answers that I garnered, however, two main factors seemed to have stuck in collective memory. First, a number of people suggested that SIBs left the Anglican church because "they wanted to be their own priests" (*jadi padri adŭp*) rather than follow an authority or older protocol—a notion on which I shall explicate later. Second, it was widely rumored that the father of one of the original households had converted to Islam when he was serving in the Malaysian army, possibly to get a promotion. When he retired and he and his family returned to the village, they tried to reenter the Anglican church but were rebuffed. Unable to officially change their religions and names, they turned to the self-consciously nondenominational, nonexclusive SIB as a more welcoming alternative, and had since remained stalwarts.

My aim here is not to substantiate or dismiss these speculations, nor to suggest that they be treated as somehow more real or revealing than the SIBs' own accounts of why they switched churches. My interest, rather, is in taking seriously SIBs' narratives, discourses, and models of conversion and Christianity—as Robbins (2007) argues anthropologists should—and trying to understand how these have molded their attitudes toward the past and *adat gawai*. As we shall see, their concerns about (dis)continuity are not dissimilar to those with which the earlier waves of converts had to deal. These, however, have resulted in the establishment of a markedly different set of social, moral, and temporal models to which the notional ideal of breaking with the past is utterly central.

Unlike Anglicans and Catholics, but like fundamentalist Christians the world over, many SIBs do have well-developed conversion narratives. These are often carefully and consciously honed, with the retrospective construction of a past being a prerequisite for its rejection in the present (Meyer 1998: 339–340; see also Engelke 2004, 2010). Crucially for my SIB acquaintances, however, this past does not only consist of *adat gawai* but also of what they perceive—and in some ways reify—as the shortcomings and problems faced by the "old" churches. When I asked one of the village's church elders why he became SIB, he highlighted two main reasons: repentance and Bible knowledge, both of which, in his opinion, the Anglican church lacked. Anglicans, he said, were often promised Heaven even if they did not repent properly and kept lapsing or behaving inconsistently. However, SIBs knew that the road to Heaven was narrow and that only a few were able to follow it (Matt. 7: 13–14). To do so, they had to be "righteous" and live carefully, and to truly know the meaning of repentance. (This was also why the *gawai* practitioners would not go to Heaven, although he prevaricated on where they *would* go—not to Hell, but their "own place," perhaps.)

Connected with this was the conviction that serious Christians had to "know the work of God in the Bible." Lots of Anglicans, he said, did not follow the Bible, and therefore smoked, drank, gambled, got tattoos, and pursued other worldly vices. This lack of Bible knowledge was a key reason that he and others chose to leave the old church and join the SIB congregation. The SIBs, he said, really knew the Bible; they read it all the time and repeatedly so that they could "absorb" its message. In doing so, they had to bring about "inner change" (*perubahan dalam*) in themselves and live cleanly, avoiding all vices and bad thoughts, since they had the Holy Spirit in them. He added that when he was an Anglican, he was always drunk and misbehaving because he did not understand the message of the Bible. Now that he had changed, he had to stay changed and not lapse, because repentance meant "not doing it again." In this regard, SIB Christianity promoted "*tanggungjawab individu*" (Malay)—individual responsibility. "You yourself are the cross," he argued, which meant that there was no need for crosses, pictures, candles, incense, and other paraphernalia in SIB services—because what mattered was the individual Christian and his or her relationship with God (see Chapter 6).

These reflections outline a model of Christianity that pivots on ruptures and breakages—on drawing a clear line between a sinful, ignorant past and a salvific (SIB) Christian present. Like Robbins's Urapmin informants (2001b, 2004, 2007), my SIB acquaintances orientate themselves, often in very quotidian ways, toward the future and the Second Coming—the point when all those who are truly penitent will be taken to Heaven. To be ready for this, however, they must also divest themselves of the "bad" aspects of the past that may distract them, or worse, knock them off-course. Leaving the Anglican church was, of course, the most proximate step toward this ideal future; but to be fully certain of salvation, they have also had to steer well clear of the old, pre-Christian world—one that, problematically, continues to be embodied by *adat gawai* today. SIBs portray *adat gawai* as the work of Satan: as a "pagan" relic from a dark, unknowing past. While they thus engage in daily interaction with *gawai* practitioners and would be unwilling to condemn them as inherently bad, they do assert that such people pray to Satan and will not be saved. Consequently, while they are technically able to watch *gawai* rituals, they are categorically forbidden from participating in or even showing any respect toward them, because, as the church elder pointed out, this would be akin to serving two masters (Luke 16: 13; Matt. 6: 24). Even being in the vicinity of those rituals is deemed to be risky, because if people's faith is insufficiently strong and their knowledge of God insufficiently deep, they risk getting misled by Satan.

Like the Anglican and Catholic churches in the 1960s and 1970s, then, SIBs have "diabolised" (Meyer 1999) a large portion of the old ways, extending their scope to effectively include *adat gawai* as a whole. Their depictions of it have been influenced not only by fundamentalist Christian ideas but also, I suggest, by earlier missionary efforts to delineate "bad" aspects of Bidayuh sociality that had to be discarded. These include the arguments that "pagans" are quick to anger, ignorant of fear and forgiveness, and unacquainted with the notion of sin—more of which we shall see in Chapter 6. All these characteristics provide important foils against which SIBs can measure their progress as born-again Christians, and their concomitant alignment with "an extant and imagined Christian history" (Engelke 2010: 179) and future. Yet, the irony is that in trying to accomplish this break from the past, they have enhanced its perceived power by attributing to it the capacity to derail their entire soteriological project. And it is this fear of derailment—of falling prey to Satan—that, I would argue, sets SIBs in such apparently diametric opposition to Anglicans and Catholics over the *adat gawai* question.

The SIBs' attitude toward the old ways indexes a fundamental insecurity about conversion that, I suggest, is not shared by adherents of the other two churches. As the SIB prayer leader's remarks reveal, conversion (whether from *adat gawai* or from a different denomination) is never a straightforward, one-off matter. The line between repentance and lapsing into old, sinful habits is dangerously fine; and true Christians cannot afford to rest on their laurels. This sense of precariousness is felt not only by older SIB adherents, many of whom spent part of their lives in a *gawai*-practicing environment, but also by teenagers and young adults, who, while not personally acquainted with this dark past (except from a distance, through contemporary *gawai* rituals), seem to have acquired their elders' fear of being tainted by it. This collective attitude is regularly bolstered during prayer services and gatherings, as is encapsulated in the curious but nonetheless apt injunction, which I heard during a sermon, for Christians to be "single-eye[d]," focusing solely on God and Jesus rather than "branching here and there." Failure to do so could mean slipping; falling back into sin and "pagan" (or indeed Anglican) wretchedness. Consequently, unlike most Anglicans and Catholics, for whom "conversion implies crossing the boundary between 'heathendom' and Christianity once and for all" (Meyer 1998: 321–322), SIB adherents "continuously dwell on this boundary" (ibid.: 322). Staying on the right side of it does not only mean living a good Christian life but also constantly, punctiliously, reinscribing it by showing how different that life is from what came before.

In this respect, what the SIBs' strident discourses about rupture reflect is not a conviction that they truly have moved on from the past, but the very real fear of their inability to make that break. This gives rise to a curious paradox. One of the reasons that SIB Christianity has largely been unattractive to most of my Anglican and Catholic informants, I suggest, is that it appears to enact the sort of rupture that they associate with conversion to Islam: a one-way movement into a strict, fixed *adat* that permits no further movement or return. Yet, as we have just seen, SIBs place so much emphasis on breaking with the past precisely because they are all too aware of the possibility of backsliding: of lapsing and slipping across that boundary. The past is dangerous for SIBs because there is still too much of a connection between it and the present. In this respect, their projects of rupture may be seen as reactions to a highly problematic, persistent situation in which *continuity* is presumed to be the norm.

The converse, however, appears to be true for Anglicans and Catholics, for whom the shift, once made, has been made. Satan may of course tempt them to do wrong, and there is always the (theoretical, but highly implausible) possibility of moving on from Christianity into something else. Yet, even if they sin or fall short of their ideals, their status as Christians remains secure. They thus do not have to linger worriedly at the boundary of the pre-Christian past and Christian present; what matters most (as we shall see in the next chapter) is "doing" Christianity properly in the here and now. The upshot of all this is that rather than fretting about the threat of being pulled back into heathendom through association with *adat gawai*, most Anglicans and Catholics have had the liberty to cultivate generally positive, contiguous relations with the old practitioners. For them, continuity is not an ongoing threat, but, in keeping with the theory of translatability outlined in the last chapter, a laudable connection that needs to be crafted and maintained.

Complicating Continuity and Rupture

By fleshing out the "processes and projects of both continuity and discontinuity" (Robbins 2007: 31) at work in one village, this chapter has sought to highlight the sheer complexity and even contradiction involved in converting to Christianity. For Bidayuhs, becoming Christian did not simply involve moving from one *adat* to another, but developing new modes of conceptualizing temporality, the past, the old ways, and the future. These were inspired not only by their own concerns about movement and translatability (Chapter 4) but also by the twists and turns of the conversion process, and various distinctive features of Christian theology and practice—more of which we shall see in the next chapter. For most of my acquaintances, continuity and discontinuity are thus not foregone conclusions or unproblematic developments, but open-ended questions. My aim in this chapter, then, has been to think through and interrogate some of these questions rather than to impose analytical models of continuity or discontinuity on their words, thoughts, and experiences.

As will have become clear in the preceding pages, it would be far too simplistic to draw clear lines between continuity-seeking

Anglicans and Catholics and rupture-oriented SIBs, discourse and lived experience, or past and present. Neither is it possible to subsume the past, depictions of the past, *adat gawai*, "culture," and *nyamba gawai* within a single category, or to treat all branches of Christianity as sharing the same attitudes toward continuity and rupture. While most SIBs, for example, eschew *adat gawai* rituals, they still interact socially with the old practitioners in the village, and will usually accommodate "cultural" displays and performances. Most Anglicans and Catholics, meanwhile, are broadly supportive of both *gawai* rituals and "cultural" events—but the degree to which individuals are willing to embrace or distance themselves from other aspects of the past, such as omens and *patang*s (Chua 2009b), varies greatly. If there is an analytical conclusion to be drawn from all this, then, it is that both discursive and analytical models of continuity and discontinuity cannot be taken for granted, but always warrant critical examination. Crucially, the normative value of tropes such as "freedom," "throwing away" the past, and "culture" must be assessed in relation to the lived realities in which they play out, for these reveal how both continuity and discontinuity need to be "configured at the micro-level as something to be enacted...relative to person and place" (Engelke 2010: 191).

If Christianity has encouraged Bidayuhs to think about the past and *adat gawai* in certain ways, however, it has also affected their relations with the old practitioners. In the next chapter, we move from temporal considerations of (dis)continuity to the more "horizontal" theme of social relations within the community. As will have become obvious in the preceding pages, questions of continuity and rupture are tightly entangled with notions of personhood, social relations, morality, and responsibility. These are no less contentious than those issues we have just examined; and they are certainly no less important in shaping Bidayuhs' responses to the *adat gawai* "question."

Chapter 6

"We Are One in Jesus"? Sociality, Salvation, and Moral Dilemmas

Several Sundays a year, the vernacularized version of a modern English hymn used in churches across Malaysia, *We are One in Jesus*, is sung to the accompaniment of guitars by the congregation of St Matthew's Chapel. It begins with the lines, "*Bara ta ndi rawang, ndi darum Jesus*," which, literally translated, gives its English counterpart a rather more specific gloss, because *rawang* actually means "household," the core unit of belonging, ownership, and obligation in Bidayuh society. What my acquaintances are singing, in other words, is "We are one household, one household in Jesus."

I begin this chapter with this refrain, because, as will become clear later, it encapsulates not only an important facet of Bidayuh Christianity but also the sorts of dilemmas that have emerged in the process of converting to it. As earlier chapters have shown, the notion that Anglicans, Catholics, and members of the Sidang Injil Borneo ("SIB"s) constitute one big, cohesive Christian whole is generally upheld and idealized in the village. Yet, this claim is not free from irony, for the unity it implies has limits—particularly when it comes to the *adat gawai* question. In this chapter, I shall argue that the three congregations' divergent attitudes toward the old ways stem not only from the debates over temporality, rupture, and continuity that we examined in the previous chapter but also from the (re)molding of social relations, modes of personhood, and frameworks of morality that has taken place through Christianization.

Running through this chapter will be an implicit, and by no means uncomplicated, analytical question: To what extent has Christianity created new modes of personhood and relationality among its Bidayuh adherents? Similar queries were in fact being raised as far back as the

1950s by anthropologists and missionaries who wondered about the dual impact of individualism and Christianity on traditional Bidayuh societies (e.g., Geddes 1954: 54; Howes 1960: 494; Sidaway 1969: 143–144). In this, they were in good scholarly company. The notion that Christianity situates its adherents as "individuals, qua individuals, in a vast, abstract community of faith constituted by the Church" (Schneider and Lindenbaum 1987: 2) is a long-running theme in the study of religion (e.g., Dumont 1986; Foucault 1978; Mauss 1985; Weber 1956 but cf. Durkheim 2001) and has been recently revived by certain anthropologists of Christianity as one of its key defining characteristics. Bialecki, Haynes, and Robbins, for example, state categorically that

> Christian conversion shifts the primary locus of obligation away from lateral social bonds among consociates toward dyadic bonds between an individual and a divine alter. Once this shift takes place, relationships with both human peers and superiors become less important than an individual's relationship with God, and are therefore subject to the tenets of Christianity over against [sic] the obligations of social relationships. (2008: 1147–1148)

As will become clear later, Christianity has indubitably introduced important individualist strains into Bidayuh life; indeed, it might even be argued that Bidayuh Christians have become different persons though conversion. However, this chapter also serves as a "thick" ethnographic caution against allowing "universalising theses about Christianity . . . [to] turn into *a priori* assumptions" (Scott 2005: 104). If my acquaintances have become Christian individuals, they have also, through the same processes, become quintessentially Christian social beings. Yet, as we shall later see, reconciling these two facets of their contemporary religiosity has not always been straightforward. To lay the groundwork for this exploration, then, we need to examine what might be described as an indigenous model of sociality and morality—one that predated Christianity and has remained instrumental in village life up to the present.

How to be a Proper Person: Sociality and Morality in Bidayuh Life

Perhaps the closest thing that we have to an analysis of pre-Christian Bidayuh morality can be found in the writings of the anthropologist William Geddes. Apart from his social scientific survey of Mentu

Tapuh in the 1950s (1954), Geddes published a popular account of Land Dayak life (1961) in which he recounted the story of Kichapi, told to him over nine nights by his informant, Raseh. Through this action-packed tale filled with adventure, strife, gore, sex, and endless plot twists, we follow the protagonist through a series of encounters with the woman who eventually becomes his wife, a number of superhuman enemies, and various other characters and communities. Raseh's story, however, is not a morality tale in the Western sense (Geddes 1961: 74). Here, there are no clear rights or wrongs, no obvious heroes and villains, and "small concern for 'character,' either psychologically or morally" (ibid.: 74). Kichapi himself is "hardly a shining exemplar to the Dayak young.... He seduced maidens [including his beloved's sister]...He raged, he sulked, he tricked his benefactors and he stole from them," (ibid.: 75) and ultimately killed many of them.

In short, Kichapi repeatedly and deliberately "def[ies] the laws of man and gods" (ibid.), breaking every social convention in the rulebook while performing his great deeds. Yet, unlike ordinary humans who rightly meet sticky ends for such behavior, Kichapi escapes unscathed because he possesses magical, superhuman potency: a "boldness and power...beyond the dreams of ordinary men" (ibid.: 75). Consequently, Geddes suggests, rather than encouraging its listeners to imitate Kichapi's herculean deeds, the tale actually reinforces the difficulty and undesirability of doing so: "The things at which so strong a man tilts cannot be windmills. And so the standards of society are enhanced, or at least protected, by the extraordinary power shown to be necessary to disrespect them" (ibid.: 76). In view of this,

> [w]hereas under our Christian ideology the supernatural holds the human heart responsible to it, under the Dayak ideology it exercises its power more directly. The Dayaks therefore rely less on personal condemnation and have a greater regard for the ordained law. This attitude the Story supports. (ibid.: 76)

Rather than explicitly prescribing good behavior, the Kichapi story encapsulates the foundational principles of what we might call an indigenous Bidayuh model of morality—one that underpinned the practice of *adat gawai* in the past and continues to regulate village life in the present. Crucially, this model decouples morality from the individual self—Kichapi's personal character and motivations are of no interest here—and tightly entwines it with "the standards of society" and "the ordained law." In this framework, persons are not inherently "good" or "wicked"; rather, what matters are their actions and behavior vis-à-vis other persons and social conventions. But who or what determines those norms? The answer, I suggest, lies in the concept of *adat* that we examined in Chapter 2.

As explained earlier, *adat* may be described as a science of ideals: a collection of models and principles that, in its prescriptive capacity, can structure the lives and actions of humans. Its ultimate goal is to establish and maintain a state of "coolness": of communal peace, stability, health, and prosperity. This is often manifested in an ideal image of social cohesion and equilibrium, whereby individuals live as part of a wider collective without upheaval, conflict, or other "hot" influences. In this framework, following *adat* is tantamount to doing things that will contribute to, maintain, or restore a vague notion of "the social good." The incentive to do so is bolstered by the widespread understanding that a generalized state of "heatiness" and social disorder benefits no one and that individual units—households, communities, or persons—live best when the collective is working smoothly and peacefully.

This perceived interdependence of parts and wholes is summed up in what Zainal Kling calls the "general altruistic principle" of *adat:* "Good for others, good for me" (1997: 50). In this respect, *adat* acts as an important yardstick against which moral or "proper" (*patut*) behavior—defined, by default, as that which contributes to the social good—can be gauged and interpreted. It is here, I suggest, that we may locate what Caroline Humphrey calls an "arena of morality": one forged not in rules but in the "relation between persons and exemplars or precedents" (1997: 25). Within this arena, individuals are not slavishly bound to regulations but have the freedom and capacity to make ethical choices (Laidlaw 2002) in relation to *adat* and other persons. Accordingly, their actions and behavior are judged by their social peers on the basis of how well or badly they have followed *adat*. This mode of morality is thus located not in individual persons or inner characters but at the interface between them, exemplary models of *adat*, and their social others. In the *adat gawai*-following past, this notion was regularly embodied in the ritual transactions that existed between humans and spirits. As Chapter 2 explained, most of these spirits were, like Kichapi, neither implacably malevolent nor unconditionally benevolent; what mattered, rather, were those reciprocal exchanges of gifts and obligations that they shared with humans. If there was a morality to these relations, it thus lay in those transactions themselves, which, if performed properly, would engender beneficial outcomes.

While this model of *gawai* ritual morality has diminished in recent decades, the principles underlying it continue to feature strongly in contemporary village life. This is illustrated in an incident that a young Anglican man, "Andrew," recounted to me in 2005. Andrew said that his cousin "Felicia" had recently started acting very strangely—wandering around the village late at night, "just like a mental patient, or a pontianak [female vampire]." Andrew and his family suspected that she had been hexed by her Malay boss at the city hospital in retaliation for her slapping him when he said to her, "You're so pretty; what would you say if I raped you?" While agreeing that her boss was in the wrong, Andrew nevertheless acknowledged that Felicia had also behaved improperly. Of course, he said, her anger was understandable—but then she should have stayed calm and gone to the police, rather than let her feelings get the better of her and lash out in public. Such behavior, the family agreed, was not *patut* because it exacerbated social unrest rather than alleviating it. For them, Felicia's fault thus lay not in her response to her boss but in what she did in relation to an *adat*-based exemplar of proper, considerate behavior. With that slap, she had effectively assaulted an ideal of social harmony and cohesion enshrined in *adat*, behaving as a reckless individual rather than a good social being.

These deliberations over Felicia's action and fate bring to light an important point. If *adat* is organized around an ideal image of the social whole, it is also interpreted, regulated, and often enforced in reality by other social entities, including kin, neighbors, and a whole set of mechanisms designed for the purpose, such as fines and village sanctions. In poor Felicia's case, there was little that the family could do. Having ascertained that she had behaved improperly, they took her to both a Malay *bomoh* (medicine man/healer) and several Anglican prayer sessions in the hope of ridding her of the curse. However, there are other cases in which the strength of the social collective in enforcing *adat* is more clearly demonstrated. This happened, for example, in the aftermath of the incident mentioned in Chapter 3, when a drunken man tried breaking into my house late one night. Over the next week, the culprit experienced the full force of village fury as one person after another laid into him for what he had done. Yet, rather than slating his character, they only castigated his behavior—he was drunk, they said, and had lost his sense of *adat*. While his actions were wrong, they thus did not make him an intrinsically "bad" person. Instead, the villagers largely couched their criticisms in the idiom of *mangŭh*, or shame: Was he not *mangŭh* about what he did? Did he not realize that his actions had also made the entire village *mangŭh*?

Such charges underscore the crucial fact that in much of Bidayuh life, from the pre-Christian past to the Christian present, the most potent mechanism for instilling a sense of *adat* and redressing its breaches is communal opinion. *Mangŭh*—a deeply unpleasant sensation, by all accounts—is described as a feeling of being watched and disapproved of by one's peers for having done something wrong. In this regard, it is closer to a sense of social ignominy—or what Geddes called "the felt pressure of convention upon the individual person" (1954: 54)—rather than personal guilt. Within a *mangŭh*-based framework, one does the right thing not because of one's own conscience but because of the lateral pressure exerted by social others. If the villagers were trying to bring about a shift in the drunkard's behavior, it was by appealing to his actions and responsibilities as a member of a collective—particularly through the cultivation of a sense of shame that, they hoped, would deter him from replicating his mistake.

These three examples bring to light a model of morality that centers not on individual characters per se but on individuals as social beings. Here, the relationship between *adat* and the social is cyclical: If *adat*'s professed aim is to keep an ideal social whole "cool," cohesive, and balanced, a vital mechanism that enables it to do so is the social itself, in the form of persons and collective action and judgment. Within this framework, morality is thus eminently and inescapably social: located not on the "inside" of individual selves, but out there, in their connections with the wider world. As we shall later see, this model of morality has not completely vanished as a result of Christianization, but continued to exist, evolve, and influence life in Bidayuh villages. In the last few decades, however, it has been joined, and in some ways transformed, by various Christian precepts, directives, and relational frameworks. It is to these recent additions that the next section turns.

On Sin and Salvation: The Ethnotheology of Bidayuh Christianity

Like other types of *adat*, Christianity has its own foundational "story" (*dundan/cerita*), with which its followers are all familiar. While not conventionally narrated in a single sitting, one can glean a fairly consistent account of it from fieldwork conversations, sermons, catechism booklets, and other pedagogical materials. The story begins, as do Islam, Buddhism, Hinduism, *adat gawai*, and other "ways" (Geddes 1954: 25), with *Tăpa*—the one true God.[1] *Tăpa* was not made by anyone; from the beginning He simply was (Gereja Katolik St Ann

2004: 4). *Tăpa* made everything in the world and created humans so that they could know (*pu'an*) and love (*rindu*) Him, follow His words, and do His work on earth (ibid.: 5). The first humans on earth were Adam and Eve. They helped *Tăpa* bring forth children and are therefore the parents of all humankind—although *Tăpa*, in his creative role, is also our Father in a general sense. One day, Adam and Eve came under the influence of a demon (*umot*) called Satan, who has great power and can cause sickness, poor crops, disputes, and other undesirable effects in the world. Satan was unhappy at seeing Adam and Eve so close (*bimadis*; "related to") to God, and thus bewitched (*nyirasun*; literally, "poisoned") them into following him and quarrelling (*rawan*) with God (ibid.: 5).

Because of what Adam and Eve did, life became, and remains, difficult and unhappy (*susah*) for humans. To help them—and here the narrative ploughs forward rapidly—*Tăpa* sent his only Son Jesus to the world. My informants concur that Jesus probably came from white people's land (*rais branda*), where he was born the child of Mary (Sante Maria). Malicious people[2] put him to death on a cross; he was then buried in a grave, but he came back to life three days later and went to Heaven. Jesus died so that we could once again be part of God's family or household (*rawang*), of which He is now the head. His death enabled humans to reinstate their relations (*bimadis dinge*) with God, which were lost when Adam and Eve fought with him. Today, Christians should do good things, follow *Tăpa*'s will, and not sin (*nai dosa*), so that when they die, they will go to Heaven (*sorga*; sometimes known as *rais Jesus*, or Jesus' village). While on earth, they must avoid the power of Satan, who remains responsible for most bad things. The best way to do all this is to pray (*simayang*) diligently to *Tăpa*, Jesus, the Holy Spirit (Roh Kudus), and in the case of Catholics, Mary and the saints, and to go to church and to ask for their help and mercy (*masi*). In this way, life will be *sănang* (healthy, safe, smooth) and *madud* (cool)—or at least marginally less difficult.

This basic narrative is one to which Anglicans, Catholics, and SIBs alike subscribe—although the latter, with their extensive Bible knowledge, are more adept at filling in the blanks between the Fall and the coming of Jesus. Embedded within it is a whole set of principles, concepts, and relations that form the foundations of what, following Michael Scott (2005, 2007), I call my acquaintances' "ethnotheology"—that is, "the indigenous theological speculations and constructions of both laypersons and clergy" (Scott 2005: 102). Taking their models, discourses, and actions seriously can reveal how converts often "attend selectively to their authorities and privilege portions of the Bible that, in culturally meaningful ways, become imbricated with their material, social, and philosophical undertakings" (ibid.: 106). The notion of "ethnotheology" thus entails the recognition that in the process of converting, people often neither absorb Christianity wholesale nor fragment it into oblivion.

The ethnotheology developed by my Bidayuh acquaintances over the last half-century consists of a peculiar combination of Christian doctrine, institutional policy, missionary effort, and converts' own sociocultural assumptions, principles, and relational frameworks. In the following pages, we shall take a closer look at some of its key features, particularly at how the themes in the narrative outlined earlier have shaped social relations and models of personhood in Bidayuh communities. These will reveal how my acquaintances have found ways not to "hybridize" or "syncretize" Christianity but to fashion parts of their lives according to its terms and idioms. At the same time, however, it is instructive to note which features of the narrative and other Christian precepts have been downplayed or even omitted by Bidayuhs. Such selective maneuvers, as will later become clear, have had important implications for their understandings of Christian personhood, morality, relationality—and their interactions with the *gawai* elders.

From Exchange to Hierarchy: Relations with Christian Personages

Like *adat gawai*, Christianity is distinguished from other *adat*s by the fact that it revolves around relations with various spirit entities. However, the nature of the relationship between humans and Christian personages is fundamentally different to that between humans and *gawai* spirits. As Chapter 2 revealed, the old rituals frequently involve attempts to cajole, berate, and trick spirit entities into helping humans to achieve specific ends. Although they possess capabilities that humans do not, such spirits are thus not unassailably superior to them; instead, they are eminently manipulable social others, responding to baits and offers with mercenary ease.

By contrast, the tutelary entities that Christianity has introduced to Bidayuh life are far removed from this largely equal relationship of exchange. Most of my acquaintances concur that personages such as God, Jesus, Mary, the Holy Spirit, and the saints have existed for time immemorial and that Bidayuhs have got to know and interact with them only relatively recently. Such ties, however, are marked by a fundamental unevenness. Unlike *gawai* spirits, Christian personages are beyond human control; they cannot be beguiled or scolded into doing things. Instead, what people need to seek, through prayer and church attendance, are their benevolence, mercy, gifts, and help—all of which, my acquaintances hope, will directly or indirectly engender beneficial results. While Christianity is thus treated, like other *adat*s, as a technical resource (Chapter 2), it is fundamentally a power-displacing one, fixing human adherents in a position of supplication vis-à-vis an indisputably greater set of powers.

At either end of this set, as we might expect, are God and Satan. In addition to being the creator-father of Christians, the former is understood to be an omnipotent, omniscient entity. More important, unlike the remote *Tăpa* or the amoral spirits of *adat gawai*, He is known to be inherently "good" (*kănà*) and "kind" (*măndis*). These traits are commonly expressed within a framework of *rindu*, which is the closest thing that Bidayuhs have to a linguistic concept of "love."[3] As the narrative earlier implied, God created the world because He loved us, and so that we would love Him and our fellow human beings. In this respect, *rindu* may be seen as the fuel of humans' bond with God and with each other—a relationship that all three churches in Benuk seek to cultivate. However, while the organizational structures of the Anglican and Catholic churches include an extra layer of mediation between their adherents and God in the form of priests, prayer leaders, and other knowledgeable, respected figures, the SIBs tend to emphasize "live and direct" connections with the divine—a point to which we shall later return.

In diametric opposition to *Tapă*, Satan is depicted as an inherently bad (*arap*) agent who will do anything to harm humankind and threaten their relationship with God. While described with the familiar term *umot*, a blanket term for dangerous demons, Satan is a fairly novel addition to the Bidayuh pantheon. Unlike the average malicious spirit, he is an entity of great power, almost on a par with *Tăpa*, whom he is said to constantly antagonize (*kisi'is*). In the last few decades, his name has become a byword for anything undesirable, detrimental, difficult, and generally "hot"[4]—such as the excessive spate of deaths for which the joint prayer procession described in Chapter 3 was held. Consequently, when things go wrong or misdeeds are committed, they are often attributed by Christians, and increasingly, *gawai* people, to "*kuasa Satan*"—Satan's power—protection from which people seek by praying to *Tăpa*.

As we shall see, the consciousness of human frailty and powerlessness vis-à-vis these two unutterably powerful absolutes of good and evil has important ramifications for my acquaintances' soteriological understandings and expectations. This recognition of their relative helplessness, however, has not left them bereft of resources or a sense of agency. As I later explain, the notion of living as part of God's household is inherently performative, implying the need to constantly "do" things well in order to get to Heaven. And a critical concept around which their efforts revolve is that of sin (*dosa*), as well as its attendant salves, mercy (*masi*) and forgiveness (*pingapun*).

Sin, Retribution, and New Models of Moral Personhood

Earlier on, we looked briefly at what might be described as an indigenous Bidayuh model of morality: one characterized by lateral pressures and relations and built around an ideal image of social cohesiveness. Within this model, the closest thing to a notion of wrongdoing is the idea of *mangŭh*, the invocation and avoidance of which serves as a potent regulator of proper social behavior. In recent decades, however, this mechanism has been joined by a new and equally potent concept: sin (*dosa*).

Sin, my acquaintances acknowledge, is a novel and specifically Christian addition to their lives. In many ways, it is an important marker of their new status as Christians—a form of self-knowledge that, they argue, distinguishes them from the *adat gawai* practitioners and other non-Christians. This was made clear, for example, during a conversation about headhunting with friends in Rejoi (Chapter 5), when I asked my interlocutors whether people were often afraid in the distant past, when warfare was still rife. At this, the wife of the Anglican prayer leader immediately responded, "No—people then did not know God (*Tăpa*); they had no mercy, and they did not know sin." By this, she meant that although her forebears were afraid of being attacked and beheaded (the point of my original question), they had no knowledge of fear in the Christian sense—of God, or of being punished for what they did. And if they did not know God, they would not know what it meant to sin, or to show or be shown mercy.

Entrenched in this remark is a notion of wrongdoing that differs fundamentally from that of the *mangŭh*-based model examined earlier. More than extending the pre-Christian "moral logic" (Aragon 1996: 352) of what it means to contravene *adat*, sin is depicted as a function of knowing God and being in a relationship with Him. (This is why headhunters of days past cannot be described as sinners in the same sense.) Crucially, sinning does not only engender damaging social consequences but also entails repudiating or betraying God's love (*rindu*)—a vital trope that frames relations between Him and humans—and a rejection of the ties that link individual Christians to His household. In this respect, it does not only produce diffuse relational effects but also highly personal, affective ones—sinning, people say, makes God sad or distressed (*susah ashŭng*; Gereja Katolik St Ann 2004: 3). Such effects cannot be rectified simply by righting the social imbalance but must be addressed on an individual level through self-improvement and the conscious avoidance of one's earlier mistakes—all of which will hopefully lead to forgiveness from God.

In this regard, the Christian concept of sin entails new kinds of self-knowledge and relations that would have been largely absent in the *mangŭh*-based model of morality. If Bidayuhs were once "horizontally" responsible to their social peers, Christianity has now entrenched them in a set of "vertical" relationships: with God on the one hand and Satan on the other. Moreover, because God (and, to a lesser degree, Satan) is said to know and to see what social others cannot, this relationship extends beyond "outer" relations and actions and into the newly forged realm of private, "inner" thoughts and desires. With their social peers unable to monitor this realm, individuals must thus fall back on themselves to continue being good Christians. Torn between the love of God and the wiles of Satan—whose power (*kuasa*) can lead people to sin and away from Heaven—individual Christians must thus also pursue a careful program of constant self-regulation.

Although a similar tendency toward reflexivity appears to have existed in the *gawai*-following past—as it certainly does in day-to-day village sociality—I would argue that Christianity has trebled its importance to Bidayuhs' lives by making it a central tenet of religiosity. In the process, I suggest, it has also presented them with a new model of moral personhood, in which one's personal thoughts, desires, and actions have salvific consequences even if they are not directly manifested in social effects. Put differently, the lateral pressures and (dis)incentives associated with the pre-Christian model of "proper" behavior examined earlier are far less important in this model than the personal, dyadic relation of love between Christians and God—a bond that, ideally, turns them into conscientious, self-regulating individuals. If this model has a locus of morality, then, it is not the individual as a social being, but more akin to what Mauss calls the individual self (*le moi*; Mauss 1985)—an autonomous, reflexive moral agent highly aware of his or her capacities and culpabilities vis-à-vis social others (Carrithers 1985: 236).

The cultivation of this self and the "vertical" relations associated with it are emphasized to different degrees in the three churches. Anglican and Catholic liturgies and prayer services usually feature significant "quiet" pauses in which attendees are encouraged to reflect on their sins and wrongdoings, to "pray within their own hearts/ spirits" (*bidoa darŭm asŭng-adŭp-i*; Diocese of Kuching 2009: 29), and to ask God for His help, mercy, and forgiveness. Congregation members, moreover, are encouraged to reflect on their failings and faults when they pray directly to God on their own, at home, before meals, and before going to sleep. The results of such dyadic interactions are often registered on individual rather than on social scales: one may, for instance, be healed from an illness or become a better Christian as a result of nurturing that relationship with God, Jesus, and other personages (see also Barker 2003: 289). On the whole, however, such confessional modes of religiosity do not tend to dominate Anglican and Catholic experiences but coexist alongside the "ritually doctrinal" mode of religiosity (Howe 2004: 137) mentioned in Chapter 3, in which the emphasis is very much on getting things right. In this regard, as I shall later explain, while sin and inner reflection are important parts of Anglican and Catholic ethnotheology, they do not govern their religious practices but are taken as components of a larger package of religiosity and relations.

For SIBs, by contrast, individual connections with God are the very crux of religiosity. As the previous chapter revealed, what truly matters for them are inner change and repentance; these are the ideals and impulses that guide its adherents' thoughts and actions. In this regard, SIBs have become sinners (Robbins 2004) in a far more pronounced and urgent manner than their Anglican and Catholic counterparts. Like the fundamentalist Christians studied by Engelke (2010) and Meyer (1998), SIBs are encouraged to constantly reflect on their past failings, which are depicted as the source of their troubles in the present day, and to purge themselves of them through prayer, Bible knowledge, and repentance. In this enterprise, they may be supported and guided by their fellow congregation members—but ultimately, repentance is a matter between them and God, and no one else. Apropos of this, many SIBs also play down the importance of denominational identity and ritual protocol in enacting salvation. As part of a self-consciously nondenominational congregation, they often accuse the Anglican church (from which their founding members came) of being too rigid and hierarchical—of telling people, as an SIB elder who was also heavily involved in village administration, put it, that they could not go to Heaven unless they were Anglican.

"It's like 'One Malaysia' (*Satu Malaysia*)," he explained, referring to the latest slogan on Malaysian national unity[5]: just as all Malaysians should be united regardless of their *bangsa* (ethnicity), all Christians should be united without being divided by denominational barriers.

The difference between the older churches and the SIB, however, raises an important question: To what extent *does* this model of individual, self-regulating personhood get translated into real life? Although the SIB differs from the other two churches in placing the conscientious individual at its core, the model on which it draws is not new, for concepts of sin and individual self-formation were already linchpins of Bidayuh Christian ethnotheology by the time of its arrival. Moreover, as mentioned earlier, the notion that Bidayuh have become individuals through conversion would seem to gel nicely with the widespread scholarly portrayal of Christianity as an "unrelentingly individualist" religion (Robbins 2004: 293). In light of such considerations, one might thus be tempted to conclude that Christianity really has turned Bidayuhs into different persons—into individuals of the same ilk as the predominantly Protestant subjects of much anthropological theory (Scott 2005: 104–106). However, it is here that the previous chapter's admonition against incautiously mapping discourse onto reality must be rehashed. As I shall now explain, individual modalities have not been the only things that Bidayuhs have acquired in the course of becoming Christian. Consequently, these modalities must be viewed in their wider historical and social context, as existing alongside other models and facets of personhood, morality, and relationality. In the next section, then, we turn from "verticality" back to "horizontality" and to the lateral relations that Christianity has also fostered among its adherents.

Relatedness and Responsibility in God's Household

As the last chapter explained, a major challenge for missionaries in the 1960s and 1970s was to make Christianity resonate with their new flocks. The strong moral influence of social ties in Bidayuh communities did not escape their notice; indeed, many of them saw it as a positive trait that could be encouraged and incorporated into Christian practice. Some, however, took things a step further by treating pre-Christian modes of morality as fundamentally "isomorphic" with Christianity (Aragon 1996: 371; see also Scott 2007), rather than merely analogous to or commensurate with them. This was the view adopted by Father Meehan, for example, who told me that the non-Christian Sarawakians he met in the 1960s were already acquainted with Christian moral precepts in principle, if not in name: They were aware, for example, that killing, stealing, and committing adultery, among other things, were not acceptable. Consequently, he reflected, "from a morality point of view, we hardly taught them anything." All that remained was for the church to pull these moral understandings—entangled as they were in social norms and regulations—into a Christian theological framework.

Among these was the concept of *rawang* (household), the basic corporate and residential unit of Bidayuh village life. Like the Iban *"bilek-families"* identified by Derek Freeman (1970: 2), *rawang*s are often built around nuclear families and possess their own land, fruit trees, farms, and property.[6] Every member of the *rawang*, regardless of age, sex, or genealogy, has equal rights to inheritance and other resources within it—on the condition that they regularly contribute to it through work, income, or other means. Conversely, when individuals leave a *rawang*, they relinquish their claim to its crops, land, and property, but they often acquire new rights when they become part of a different *rawang*, such as through marriage. In this way, it is possible for adopted children, affines, carers of elderly people, and others with no genealogical link to the core family of the *rawang* to belong to it and to have both rights and responsibilities within it.

Viewed against this backdrop, the line *"bara ta ndi rawang"* is more than just a turn of phrase, for it has very specific moral and social ramifications. While *rawang* is not the only corporate idiom used in Bidayuh Christianity—other common tropes include sitting at God's table (i.e., eating together) and being part of His kingdom (*pritah*)—it has played a critical conceptual and organizational role in shaping my acquaintances' sense of Christian belonging and sociality. By depicting the nascent converts as one big *rawang*, the missionaries and catechists were arguably able to exploit its moral and affective dimensions in order to reinforce various tenets of Christian life and behavior. (An example I sometimes heard was the admonition that if stealing was bad, stealing from one's own *rawang* was even worse—so one should obey the Ten Commandments and not steal.) In the intervening years, this sense of relatedness and mutual obligation has not diminished and is regularly reiterated through sermons, songs such as *Bara Ta Ndi Rawang*, and communal meals, many based in actual households, which are intrinsic to church gatherings. Within this *rawang*, people are ensconced in a largely "horizontal" set of relations with their peers,[7] who, in keeping with Christian imagery, are depicted as *bimadis* (kin/siblings), or *sudek madis darum Kristus* (brothers and sisters in Christ). In this fraternal framework, being a good Christian does not necessarily mean behaving as a good child of the Father, but being a proper participant in His *rawang*, of which the parental (rather than specifically paternal) bond is a cornerstone.

In accordance with Bidayuh understandings, however, one's rights and position within that *rawang* are not a given but must be constantly acquired and justified through good behavior. Just as members of a *rawang* who fail to contribute to it can lose their inheritance, my acquaintances are aware that their place in Heaven is contingent on their repeated efforts to "do" Christianity correctly on earth. This awareness is particularly stark among SIB members, who, as the last chapter revealed, fear that the slightest misstep might cause them to slide back into heathendom. However, it is also shared by my Anglican and Catholic acquaintances, who, while less concerned about falling off that edge, are nonetheless cognizant of the need to keep working at being good Christians. As the narrative examined earlier suggests, doing wrong can sometimes be portrayed as breaking off or repudiating relations with God and His household—a prospect that, examined in the context of the rules of *rawang* membership, can also mean losing one's claim to the benefits of Christianity. In this way, I suggest, the moral and social imperatives of *rawang* membership have generated a model of Christian belonging and obligation that emphasizes continual performativity and improvement. Rather like being Dayak (Chapter 4) or a member of a *rawang*, being a good Christian is not a given but must be constantly rehashed and reinforced.

The transformation of the concept of *rawang* into a central tenet of Christianity exemplifies a broader trend that took place during the height of conversion. At the time that they were introducing new dyadic relations and models of self-regulation to their flock, the Anglican and Catholic churches were simultaneously fostering certain kinds of lateral ties and modes of organization as intrinsic to Christianity, emphasizing "horizontal" bonds of obligation and responsibility as much as they did those new "vertical" relations with God and Satan. To do so, they seem to have legitimated and indeed elaborated upon certain features of the pre-Christian model of morality that we examined earlier, notably those that, like *rawang*, emphasized cohesion, peaceability, and cooperation. In the process, however, they also redefined those features, incorporating them into a distinctly Christian framework of love, mercy, kindness, and generosity. If stealing was once depicted as objectionable because it would upset the social balance and generate collective censure and *mangŭh*, it was now depicted as sinful and a personal betrayal of God's love. If people were once discouraged from disturbing the peace because of the "hot" social consequences that might follow, they were now advised to love their neighbors (Gal. 5: 14; James 2: 8; Lev. 22: 39; Luke 19: 18; Rom. 13: 9) and to "do unto others what you would have them do to you" (Matt. 7: 12).

In short, an important upshot of Christianization has been the convergence, rather than mere "parallelism" (Aragon 1996: 370; cf. Robbins 2004), of two distinct, "horizontal" models of morality: one, the *adat*-based indigenous model examined earlier, and the other, a largely New Testament-based model of brotherly love, peaceful behavior, and kindness. Although each has a different locus and impetus, their outcomes are essentially the same: the establishment and maintenance of social harmony, cohesion, and equilibrium. Cumulatively, these have generated the deep-seated understanding that being a good Christian fundamentally involves being a good social being, for it is by loving one's neighbor and living in harmony with the rest of society that one reciprocates God's love. Here, "vertical" and the "horizontal" modes of relationality are thus not mutually exclusive, but imply each other, for fulfilling one's personal responsibilities toward God also entails fulfilling responsibilities toward one's fellow Christians and vice versa. This, at least, is a point on which members of both the old churches and the SIB concur. However, when we follow their understandings to their soteriological end, we find that they reach rather different conclusions about the place of such "horizontal" ties in their salvific projects.

The Point of Christianity:
Soteriological Models and Practices

As the preceding pages have shown, the ethnotheology of Bidayuh Christianity is a complex tapestry comprising many strands of morality, personhood, agency, and relationality. Here, I deliberately use the singular "ethnotheology" rather than "ethnotheologies" because, as we have seen, Anglicans, Catholics, and SIBs all share certain core Christian understandings, concepts, and frameworks. What differs, however, is the extent to which certain impulses and models within this basic template are prioritized, downplayed, or elaborated. Earlier in this chapter, we examined how both "vertical," dyadic relations and "horizontal," fraternal ones have been cultivated in and remain intrinsic to contemporary Bidayuh Christianity. In this section, we turn to how these impulses have influenced the soteriological enterprises of the Anglicans and Catholics, on the one hand, and the SIBs on the other, generating two distinct models of salvation and salvific action.

The differences between them can be discerned in two sermons, both on the popular theme of light, which I recorded in 2010.

The first took place on the evening of Holy Saturday, which (in keeping with worldwide liturgical practice) began with the Service of Light on the grass slope beside St Matthew's Chapel. At its commencement, a Paschal candle was lit from a bonfire and its flame passed from one individual to another (figure 6.1). This culminated in a beautiful candlelit procession in the darkness, back up the hill and into the church for the service. During his sermon, the prayer leader reiterated several times that just as we had followed the Paschal candle back into the church, we had to follow *jawa Kristus* (the light of Christ), which would lead us out of darkness (*karŭm*) and free us from suffering (*susah*) and fear (*tăru*). He further implied that Christians should do so in togetherness, as one—a notion repeatedly enacted by the care that congregation members took to keep their neighbors' flames alight, reaching over to rekindle them if they were extinguished during the proceedings.

A few months later, I attended an SIB service, where a passage from the Gospel of Matthew, in which Jesus describes His followers as "the salt of the earth" and "the light of the world" (Matt. 5: 13–16), was read aloud. This was linked during the sermon to a passage from John 1: 1–5 ("In the beginning was the Word…"), in which Jesus

Figure 6.1   Lighting the Paschal Candle at St Matthew's Catholic Chapel on Holy Saturday, Kampung Benuk, 2010.

is depicted as "the light [that] shines in the darkness" (John 1: 5). Drawing on these two images, the pastor crafted a striking analogy: Christians, he said, were like light bulbs on a ceiling, all connected to a single "generator,"[8] Jesus. We are all thus auxiliary lights of Christ and cannot escape from the power and light at the source. As the sermon progressed, the ramifications of this image became clear: Having got connected to Jesus, one could not remain idle but had to work consistently at cultivating one's inner life and being a good Christian. The sermon ended with a prayer for strength, protection, and wisdom for the capacity to take on the heavy responsibility that God had given us and to keep following Him.

While the two sermons were more complex, carefully contextualized sets of ruminations than these brief notes suggest, their juxtaposition reveals an important point of divergence between the older churches and the SIB. While the first sermon encapsulates a soteriological model of deliverance and patronage, the second invokes a model of self-empowerment. For many Anglicans and Catholics, the ultimate point of Christianity is to "free" them from suffering, sadness, and fear. Within this model, the supplicatory position of Christians vis-à-vis God and other Christian personages is underscored: Good outcomes are generated because these greater powers have felt sufficiently *rindu*, merciful, and benevolent toward humans to answer their entreaties and to give (*ngyen*) them what they need. Accordingly, many of their prayers and practices are explicitly oriented toward eliciting a sense of *rindu* in God and other potential spiritual patrons.

This prospect of deliverance plays an important explanatory and organizational role in many Anglicans' and Catholics' lives. In 2009, for example, tragedy befell one of the rural villages in Padawan where I also work, when one of its residents, a pillar of the community, was killed in mysterious circumstances—shot from a distance while hunting near the Indonesian border. For days, the village was saturated in shock and disbelief, as people tried to work out what had happened. Amid the speculation, however, there was one consistent node of support to which they could all turn: Christianity. Several days after the incident, the entire community attended an Anglican fellowship gathering, held at the house of the dead man's neighbors, at which they prayed to God to free them from fear and sadness over the event. Reflecting on the event the next day, my host suggested that perhaps this was all God's plan: that maybe God loved the man so much that He decided to take him out of a life of hardship earlier than everyone else. In this manner, she, like others, attempted to rationalize this horrible, apparently senseless, incident, reframing it in accordance with her own ethnotheological understandings. Her friend may have been killed by an unknown perpetrator, but there was great solace to be found in the proposition that God had brought him to a better place.

As my host's reflections suggest, the ultimate release from the hardships of this life is seen to take place when Christians go to Heaven—to God's village (*rais*). Although few Anglicans and Catholics have a clear conception of what Heaven is like, they largely agree that it is a place where there is no more pain or fear—a place, in short, of perfect "coolness" in which they all want to live. Yet, it is important to note that despite their desire to get there, they do not structure their lives and thoughts around their transition from this life into the next. Instead, I suggest, they largely channel their efforts into creating an image of Heaven on earth: on relieving suffering, sadness, and fear in their own lives and the lives of others, and acting as part of a single, unified Christian *rawang*.[9] More than beseeching God and other Christian personages for their help, kindness, and mercy, then, my Anglican and Catholic acquaintances are keenly aware of their own obligation to keep "doing" Christianity properly in the here and now, acting together, and taking care of each other.

This was brought home to me during a conversation with a young Catholic mother about the *adat* of Lent shortly after I began fieldwork. As Chapter 2 revealed, Lent is depicted by the Catholic establishment as one long, 40-day *patang* on being *rami* (having fun, socializing). My friend explained that apart from not being allowed to hold birthday parties, weddings, and other festive events during this time, Catholics also had to go about doing good deeds, such as visiting and bringing food to poor and sick people. She was surprised to hear that a similarly strict *patang* did not exist in Singapore or Britain, and bemused by the idea, which I tried explicating, of giving up something for Lent, such as certain foods or items. "You mean they give up those things *to* poor or sick people?" she immediately asked. The notion of self-denial underlying such personal sacrifices struck her as odd: Why refrain from eating certain foods or doing certain things when this would benefit no one else? For her, as for many others, every act and prayer performed in the observance of *adat Kristen* does not take place in isolation but must—and will— have tangible repercussions in the world. By contrast, practices such as self-denial are seen to be of only the vaguest benefit to one's own soul, eliciting neither concrete outcomes nor wider advantages for the community.

These deliberations clearly reveal how my Anglican and Catholic acquaintances' particular economy of salvation emphasizes doing things properly and acting in tandem with other Christians as one household on earth. It is in this context, they understand, that God will "give" (*ngyen*) His followers freedom, safety, deliverance, and ultimately, a place in Heaven. In this regard, it is instructive that Anglicans and Catholics sometimes criticize the SIBs for always thinking about the end of the world, and for constantly distancing themselves from it by avoiding alcohol, excessive feasting, smoking, and other activities that are so central to village sociality. For the former, the SIBs' worldly rejection effectively entails a rejection of the social ties that exist in the here and now; it is a kind of relational rupture that, like that demanded by Islam (Chapter 4), contravenes the love-thy-neighbor principle that they see as intrinsic to being Christian. Indeed, Anglicans and Catholics arguably construe salvation and Heaven as "their world's development, not as its opposite" (Cannell 2005: 336); for them, relatedness and material conditions in the here and now are "coextensive [with], not contradictory" (ibid.: 337) to life after death.

On this note, it is worth turning to the SIB sermon. In it, we also find intimations of supplication—particularly in the depiction of Christ as the source of power and light, without which humans are nothing. However, what this sermon seeks is not deliverance in the Anglican and Catholic sense,[10] but self-empowerment. Here, God and Jesus do not only give good things to people and free them from wretchedness; more importantly, they equip Christians with the strength and wisdom with which to help themselves. The recipient of such blessings, moreover, is not a generic community but individual Christians—a notion compellingly illustrated by the image of discrete light bulbs on a ceiling. The connection between Christ and His followers is direct and unmediated; the responsibility for being saved and getting to Heaven lies with the individual, and no one and nothing else.

As we saw in the last chapter, the end point to which these SIB efforts are directed is an anticipated Second Coming. Like Robbins' Urapmin informants, the SIBs organize their thoughts and actions around this expectation; in ideal terms, at least, they exist in a "sloping temporal order in which people are forever pitched forward, placing their best attention on the future and their best energy on their efforts to be ready for that future" (Robbins 2004: 164). In concrete terms, such millenarianism has a much more "everyday" (Robbins 2001b) character, with people concentrating on leading good lives while paying special attention to things that increase their chances of being saved when the end does come: repentance, scriptural knowledge, and resisting the temptations and power of Satan. All these center on a specific concept of the self-regulating, self-aware Christian individual, which, in SIB thought, is "the sole unit of divine judgment"; after all, "families, churches, denominations, and towns do not get saved, only individuals do" (Robbins 2004: 293). The upshot of this is that SIBs largely view and portray themselves as Christians who "owe their salvation to no one but themselves and God" (Bialecki, Haynes, and Robbins 2008: 1147).

This is not to suggest, of course, that the SIBs ride roughshod over the "love thy neighbor" ideal, which they share with Anglicans and Catholics. Like the members of the two old churches, SIBs acknowledge themselves to be members of a wider collective—the village—in addition to being members of a worldwide Christian community. Indeed, on a day-to-day basis, it is this fraternal principle that is most evident in Christian practice and interaction within Kampung Benuk. However, as this exposition has revealed, members of the three churches construe such good social conduct through varying lenses. For SIBs, "proper" social behavior is both an offshoot of and disciplinary technique for cultivating inner, Christian selfhood. At the end of the day, they must love each other *because* they are Christian individuals who share a dyadic bond of love with God, and are on a trajectory toward salvation. Conversely, while Anglicans and Catholics also recognize this principle, I would argue that they view it in a different light. For them, getting to Heaven is more like the *corollary* to the conscientious, collective performance of Christianity on earth—one of its many beneficial outcomes, such as large harvests, prosperity, and health—rather than an a priori incentive to do so. Salvation for them is thus a profoundly collective project: The individual may well be "the sole unit of divine judgment" but individuals will get nowhere without the help and support of others in their *rawang*.

While models of self-regulation and individual modes of relationality are indubitably central to Anglican and Catholic experiences of Christianity, then, these have nevertheless been superseded by an overarching ethnotheological and praxiological emphasis on living and behaving well as part of a larger collective—a Christian *rawang*. In this respect, "[t]he Christian message of individual salvation" (Hefner 1993a: 5) has had only limited resonance for the members of the older churches, for whom lateral bonds with social others—whether Christian or non-Christian—matter a great deal. And this, as I shall now explain, has vital implications for their relations with the elderly *adat gawai* practitioners.

The Dilemma of Loving One's Neighbor: The *Adat Gawai* Question

Having examined how "vertical" and "horizontal" modes of relationality and personhood have been configured in the different churches, we are now in a better position to understand the shape of Christian-*gawai* relations in Kampung Benuk. As the last chapter revealed, the persistence of the old ways in the present has been a source of contention within Kampung Benuk, with Anglicans and Catholics tending to craft discourses of continuity with them and the SIBs doing quite the opposite. What complicates these efforts, however, is the presence of the elderly *adat gawai* practitioners themselves. Debating the past, "the old rituals," or even "culture" is one thing; debating them in relation to very real people is something else altogether. For far from being temporal and religious "Others," the *adat gawai* elders are full social and moral and members of the village community. Although everyone thus speaks of the village as "now Christian," these people's continued existence serves as a problematic reminder that this is not entirely the case.

In this respect, the Christians in my village are confronted with the same problem that Birgit Meyer identifies among pentecostalists in Ghana (see also Connolly 2009; Engelke 2010; Harris 2006). She points out that although the ideology of "breaking with the past" is encouraged and idealized in pentecostalist circles, "actually, this break is difficult to achieve fully and once and for all." The key problem, she suggests, is that discourses of rupture are not purely temporal but also relational, often demanding the severance of ties with "persons with whom one actually shares time and space" (Meyer 1998: 329). Yet, for many born-again Christians, "all those ties that have been relegated to 'the past' *actually still matter in the present*" (ibid.: 340; italics added). Consequently, Meyer points out, her subjects often find themselves in "a constant struggle to close themselves off from kin...[a struggle] which is experienced as problematic, not an accomplished reality" (ibid.: 336).

As the last chapter revealed, all Christians in Kampung Benuk are, to a greater or lesser degree, conscious of the fact that Christianity has "freed" them from the fears and problems of the past. However, the extent to which they have been able and willing to translate that temporal breakage into *relational* breakage varies considerably. And it is here, I suggest, that the differences between the two older churches and the SIB become clearest, and often, most problematic. As I have shown elsewhere (Chua 2009b), nearly all Christians are adamant about avoiding relations with most old *gawai* spirits. But relations with the *nyamba gawai* are a whole different matter, for the simple fact that these practitioners are also their parents, grandparents, kin, and neighbors. They live as part of the village, move within the same social networks, work on the same farms, and eat in the same households as Christians. In this sense, more than simply accommodating the old rituals, my Anglican and Catholic acquaintances are also trying their best to maintain healthy relations with people with whom they share many social, moral, and affective ties. Even though the *nyamba gawai* are not members of their Christian *rawang*, they are part of the wider moral community of the village—that *adat*-based ideal whole that, as I explained earlier, predates Christianity and remains central to Bidayuh life today.

It is in these moments, I suggest, that a fissure that largely remains invisible in contemporary Bidayuh Christianity briefly manifests itself. As we have seen, the cultivation of a generic "love thy neighbor" template through concepts such as the Christian *rawang* effectively collapsed, and thus elided, the differences between the indigenous model of morality and a New Testament model of fraternal love and kindness. For the most part, these distinctions remain invisible because they both lead to the same end: the maintenance of "cool" sociality, cohesion, and peaceability. It is only in situations where the moral collectives that these models regulate are shown to be discrepant—in this case, the village as a whole versus the Christian community within the village—that this fissure becomes problematic. In short, the *adat gawai* question presents Christians with an unfamiliar moral dilemma: to be a good social being, or to be a good Christian individual? Although these modes of morality are usually conflated in practice, their brief emergence in the context of *gawai* rituals can be the source of real and unexpected anxieties.

For all their discursive efforts at bridging the *adat gawai* past with the Christian present, then, my Anglican and Catholic acquaintances' efforts to maintain good relations with the *gawai* practitioners are not free from tension and unease. On the one hand, they are aware that church institutions do not officially condone their support of *adat gawai* rituals (Chapter 5). They also know how dangerous it can be to get too close to the proceedings and to the old spirits that inevitably show up (Chua 2009b). On the other hand, however, they share an abiding religious and moral conviction that by being good to their *gawai* elders, they are also being good Christians. For them,

I suggest, "loving thy neighbor" does not only entail loving one's fellow Christians but also those other villagers who are not members of the same religious *rawang*, with whom they nevertheless share moral and social connections. To do otherwise—to break the peace by causing a rift with the elders—would contradict *both* a village-based moral sensibility *and* a model of good Christian practice. Perhaps it is no surprise, then, that many of the Anglicans and Catholics I met at *gawai* rituals said quite simply that they were there to support their village elders, who were elderly and needed their help. Such statements required little justification or explanation; the close entwinement of sociality and morality that underpinned them was evident to all present.

At the end of the day, most Anglicans and Catholics thus appear to have resolved their moral dilemma by maintaining, rather than repudiating, links with the *nyamba gawai* and their rituals. Accordingly, they justify this not only by recourse to "culture" and notions of continuity (Chapter 5) but also by what may be described as a discourse of *contiguity*—implying, as Father Meehan and other missionaries did, that Christianity and *adat gawai* are fundamentally commensurate, or even "the same." It is not infrequently said, for example, that Christianity and *gawai* have the same basic aims (*rǎti*) and mechanisms (*gaya*)—keeping the village "cool" and safe, and calling (*bǎgan*) good spirits while throwing away (*tǎran*) bad ones,—that they permit Bidayuhs to consume the same substances, notably alcohol and pork, and that they share the same God (*Tǎpa*). Interestingly, this tendency does not appear to be confined to village populations. Clare Boulanger's interviews with urban Dayaks in Sarawak, for example, revealed how several of them "maintained that Christianity merely reinforced the values that people had previously held as non-Christians" (2009: 131). Similarly, one "Pagan" interviewee pointed out that there was no need for him to convert since he was already following "Biblical precepts" (ibid.), while a Christian noted that pre-Christian Bidayuhs "held that there 'must be a Great Being' no less fervently than Christians" (ibid.).

Here, the contrast between such assertions and those of the SIBs could not be starker. While the latter do try to behave as good village residents and certainly interact with the elderly *gawai* practitioners on a day-to-day basis, they differ from Anglicans and Catholics by drawing the line at the old rituals themselves. It is at this point, I suggest, that their *social* sensibilities give way to their *religious* convictions, and their overwhelming sense of responsibility—and fragility—as individual Christians. If the Anglicans and Catholics have responded to the fissure between different moral communities by trying to overcome it, SIBs have, conversely, tried to fortify the line between them. *Gawai* elders may well be part of the village, but they emphatically cannot be accommodated within or even by the *rawang* of Christianity; in this context, one set of relations must trump the other.

This recognition, however, appears to thrust SIBs into a different moral dilemma to that faced by Anglicans and Catholics. Should they cast aside the *nyamba gawai* as ignorant, sinful, pagans, or should they try to save their souls too? While genuinely fearful of the Satanic potency and danger posed by the old rituals, the SIBs are also cognizant of their evangelical duty to spread the Gospel to those who still dwell in darkness and sin. In practice, then, their responses take two forms. While brusquely rejecting the old ways, and consistently condemning them (often in front of the practitioners) as the work of Satan, some SIBs have also tried to persuade their *gawai*-following kin to become Christian. Although their success rate is limited— most *gawai* followers I know in Benuk and other villages find the SIBs' rupture-oriented attempts excessively harsh—such actions may well demonstrate their desire to love thy *gawai* neighbors by incorporating them into their Christian *rawang*. For them, however, as for Anglicans and Catholics, however, there is simply no easy solution to the problem.

Conclusion

This chapter reveals how the relational changes enacted by conversion and Christianity have impacted on my acquaintances' relations with the small, *gawai*-following minority in today's village. Viewed in conjunction with the concerns about temporality, continuity, and rupture that we examined in the previous chapter, such changes may account for why Anglicans and Catholics tend to speak of continuity and contiguity with the old ways, and why, conversely the SIBs have done the opposite. The point I wish to reiterate here, however, is that these divergent attitudes are not differences of *type* but of *degree*. As we have seen, Bidayuh Christianity contains modes of both individualism and social relationality and both "vertical" and "horizontal" ties. In real life, these elements constantly overlap and mingle: Individual reflexivity and responsibility, for example, are also important aspects of Anglican and Catholic understandings of sin and membership of a single *rawang*, while "Bible sharing," "fellowship" gatherings, and other forms of communal interaction are as central as individual modes of personhood to SIB Christianity. In this respect, it is vital not to dichotomize the relationship between the two old churches and the SIB, treating the former as purely concerned with "this worldly" issues and communality and the latter as "world reject[ers]" (Bellah 1964: 359) and bloody-minded individuals, for all these Christians have, at one point or another, had to grapple with elements of individual selfhood, communal responsibility, embeddedness in the world, and the impulse to transcend it.

This brings us to an important point that has also been raised by a number of anthropologists in response to a predominantly "culturalist" model of Christianity (e.g., Barker 2008; Englund 2007; Hann 2007; Hann and Goltz 2010; Scott 2005). While it is clearly important, as Robbins and others have argued (Introduction), for anthropologists to deal seriously with the content, sociotemporal models and monolithic "cultural logic" of Christianity, it is equally imperative that we attend to its particular and sometimes unexpected manifestations in ethnographic reality. Viewed through a certain theoretical lens, the ethnotheology that I have just described could easily be construed as proof of how Christianity retains its shape across cultural, social, and temporal boundaries, and in fact comes to reshape its adherents' lives in its very image (Bialecki, Haynes, and Robbins 2008; Robbins 2003, 2007). However, as Englund has argued,

> [w]hat the concept of an encompassing Christian culture is unlikely to discern...is the way in which...[Christian] engagement with the world produces relationships and events that no cultural scheme can govern. (2007: 482)

This, in a nutshell, captures what I have tried to demonstrate through my explorations. While recognizably Christian, my Bidayuh acquaintances cannot be pigeonholed as universal Christian individuals but must always be situated and understood within the context of their lived experiences. Insisting on this point does not mean denying the genuine novelty of many Christian introductions to their lives, or replicating the sin of "continuity thinking" (Introduction), but reasserting a "commitment to [ethnographic] thickness" (Ortner 1995: 174) by tracing the specificities of their engagements with "multiple interlocking micro and macro Christian logics" (Scott 2005: 102). Doing so reveals that scholars are not the only ones to be "think[ing] *with*" rather than just about religion (Robbins and Engelke 2010: 625; italics in original) but that people like the Bidayuh and countless other Christian converts around the world are also dealing with their own concerns, debates, and controversies.

Christianity, however, is not the only religion with which Bidayuhs are thinking. In the final chapter, we turn to another phenomenon that has hitherto remained occluded—*adat gawai* itself. I suggest that more than being an object to be debated, supported, or shunned by the Christian majority, *adat gawai* can also be good to think and work through for both Bidayuhs and anthropologists. To round off our exploration, then, the last chapter takes a closer look at how *adat gawai* itself is understood to "tick" and the implications of these understandings on my acquaintances' conceptions of "culture" and transformation.

Chapter 7

Thinking through *Adat Gawai*: "Culture," Transformation, and the Matter of Religiosity

As we have seen, many Christians' responses to the *adat gawai* question are tinged by ambivalence, with even the staunchest opponents and supporters of the old rituals occasionally finding themselves in moral, social, and religious quandaries. In many ways, this situation derives from the basic fact that *adat gawai* and its practitioners are still present and active within certain Bidayuh communities today. Even in villages where they no longer exist, the old rituals have not been reduced to caricatures of a distant past but remain fresh in collective memory and experience. Consequently, although most Christians lack detailed semantic and "doctrinal" knowledge of *adat gawai*, many of them will have at least some idea of its mechanisms, principles, and tutelary presences (see Chua 2009b). These ideas, I argue, continue to exert an agentive influence on villagers of all ages and must be taken seriously if we are to get to grips with contemporary manifestations of both *adat gawai* and "Bidayuh culture."

The present chapter thus brings this book full circle by returning to the very problem with which it opened: What should anthropologists make of the apparent politicization and commodification of indigenous ritual practices as "culture"? To address this question, I shall think through a number of explicitly "cultural" exercises in which *gawai*-based artifacts and performances feature heavily. Rather than interpreting them through an a priori analytical template as mere "cultural objectifications" or as cynical efforts to maximize political and economic benefits (Chapter 1), I shall attempt to capture my acquaintances' own exegeses and experiences of these affairs.

Doing so reveals a particular model of transformation inherent to *adat gawai:* one that conceptualizes the relationship between past and present in quite a different way to the discourses and policies of Christianity examined earlier (Chapter 5). To round off our exploration of the *adat gawai* question, then, we need to scrutinize this particular model of continuity and change and to apply its insights to the relationship between Christianity, *adat gawai*, and "culture."

Chasing Away Wind? A Cultural Dance Performance in Kampung Benuk

It was a warm, hazy Tuesday morning in March 2005, and Kampung Benuk's community hall was abuzz with activity. The occasion: a visit by a batch of conscripts to Malaysia's new National Service program (*Program Latihan Khidmat Negara*). Introduced in 2003, the *Khidmat Negara* scheme aims to foster "national integration" by bringing together 17-year-olds from different ethnic backgrounds for three months of community service, physical training, and nation- and character-building activities.[1] Today's 60-strong contingent was coming to Benuk in the name of cultural education—to see how one of Sarawak's indigenous communities lived. This was a major occasion for the village, and rumor had it that someone from the District Office in Siburan was going to read out an important letter (*surat*) from the government.

To mark the event, Nija, the Ketua Káum (village head), arranged a welcome reception to which all heads of household and elderly inhabitants were invited. As they awaited the visitors, village leaders and district councilors clad in their best clothes milled around making small talk, exchanging handshakes, and smoking. Nearby, Diyong, who ran the tourism hut, was busy putting the finishing touches on his miniature *pangah*, which would receive its first airing in a few hours. Knowing that tourists often came to Benuk wanting to see a "headhouse," he had decided to set one up at the entrance to the village, to "brief" them, he said, on what they could expect. "Do you think this would get thirty percent [in marks] in a model longhouse competition?"[2] he asked jovially, beaming at his creation, "What about fifty percent?"

Eventually, the *Khidmat Negara* party arrived in a string of buses, an hour late ("Malaysian time," griped Nija). The youth and their instructors filed into the florescent bulb-lit hall, greeted by handshakes from villagers flanking the entrance. Following speeches by the Ketua Kaum, government officials, and program instructors, we settled down in neat rows of plastic chairs to watch the highlight of the event: a series of "*tarian asal*" (original/authentic dances) performed onstage by a small group of teenage girls from the village's "cultural" troupe (Chapter 1). The costumes, accessories, music, and choreography of these dances were based loosely on *adat gawai* rituals, notably its offertory processions (*birăjang*). These were punctuated by a commentary in Malay on their "original" functions by the emcee for the day, the principal of the village kindergarten. The display marked the commencement of the "cultural education" program for the visitors, who later clambered onstage to dance with the girls and experiment with the gongs before being shown round the village.

During the performance, I took the opportunity to mingle with the villagers in the audience, including several *adat gawai* practitioners, to see what they thought of the dances. Most of them agreed that the gong tunes—played by regular *gawai* helpers—were *asar* (original/authentic), accurate reproductions of ritual refrains. The dances, however, were harder to pin down. A *gawai* woman, watching her granddaughter mimic the actions of the *birăjang*, declared that the dance was nice, but a *wayang*—a theatrical performance— because the girls were Christian and moving in a peculiarly exaggerated, coordinated fashion. Meanwhile, upon hearing the emcee describe a dance as originally being used to chase away evil spirits, an elderly Catholic leader leaned over and murmured conspiratorially, "Once they chased away ghosts, but now they are chasing away wind." The consensus among those with whom I spoke was that this was not *adat* but *budaya* (culture)—a point that the *gawai* elders, Paka's family, and several others had also made when explaining to me what tourists came to see in Benuk.

If the dances were viewed by most villagers present as light entertainment, the gongs that accompanied them generated some undercurrents of unease. Although nobody mentioned it at the time, I later found out from Sumuk Nyangŭ, the most senior female *gawai* practitioner, that the village committee usually arranged for a small bamboo altar—a miniature version of the *sangar* used in *gawai* rituals—bearing food, betel nut, and cigarette offerings to be erected in a corner at such cultural performances. This, she said, was because the unmodified *gawai* tunes played on the gongs could travel a long way into the environs, where they might be heard by spirits who would take them as invitations to a ritual. If they followed the sounds expecting to be fed and entertained, they might be disappointed and cause problems for the villagers. The altar was thus there to mollify any such un(for)seen visitors.

This episode contains a number of themes and puzzles that warrant unpacking. For a start, what did the audience at the cultural dance performance make of the whole affair? When the Catholic leader described the dance as "now...chasing away wind," was he implying that the old spirits were in fact fictional, or perhaps that they no longer existed? By distinguishing *adat* from *budaya*, were my interlocutors treating the latter as an entirely different phenomenon? If so, where did that leave the "original" gong tunes, which were deemed likely to attract the old *gawai* spirits? And finally, what did people think of the presence of government officials and the letter from the state?

Over the course of this chapter, I shall address these queries by thinking through my acquaintances' own exegeses on both *adat gawai* and "culture." The *Khidmat Negara* performance, I suggest, exemplified the apparent paradox at the heart of "Bidayuh culture": the fact that it is neither full-blown ritual nor completely shorn of ritual potency. This ambiguity appears to have been recognized by the audience of the dance performance, who, despite depicting the dance as a *wayang*—as not actually *gawai*—were sufficiently anxious about its effects to ensure that an altar was erected on such occasions. Before fully interrogating their responses and actions, however, I would like to pause briefly to consider where they stand in relation to the existing literature on "culturalism" and "ethnicism" in Sarawak—and in particular, one of the few anthropological analyses of the development of Bidayuh cultural consciousness.

Scholarly Perspectives on the "Culturalization" and "Politicization" of Ritual

As Chapter 1 mentioned, the "culturalization" and "politicization" of indigenous rituals such as *adat gawai* is an issue that has concerned anthropologists, historians, and other social scientists since at least the early-1980s. Within Sarawakian scholarship, such developments have largely been analyzed through political frameworks; recent examples include John Postill's book on Iban engagements with media in the context of nation-building (2008), Clare Boulanger's study of Dayak ethnicity in urban circles (2009), and Paulette Dellios's (2002) and Craig Latrell's (2008) descriptions of the rhetorical and material construction of multiculturalist ideals in the Sarawak Cultural Village. The study most germane to the present chapter, however, is a thought-provoking article by Robert Winzeler (1997), which traces the evolution of the *baruk* (headhouse) into a Bidayuh ethnic emblem—a process that we examined in Chapter 1.

Drawing on the works of Bernard Cohn (1987) and Richard Handler (1984, 1988), Winzeler describes this sequence as the "objectification" of Bidayuh culture; the conscious transformation of "previously implicit customs and designs for living...into a public ethnic heritage or 'traditions,' or in some instances into economic commodities" (1997: 202). For Winzeler, such objectifying measures reflect how Bidayuhs, like many "formerly tribal as well as other peoples[, have] become ethnically engaged in new ways" (ibid.: 224), and have thus learned to deploy officially sanctioned "cultural" or "ethnic" artifacts for political ends. He suggests that, given their marginal position within Malaysia, such measures may be seen as a "form of political participation in the state, or...a means of influencing government short of violence and other acts of disobedience" (ibid.: 225). While rightly pointing out that "the development of externalized conceptual categories," such as *adat*, is not new to Southeast Asia, he argues that such objectifications became "far more important and pervasive under European colonial rule and still more so during the postcolonial period" (1997: 224–225). In Winzeler's book, Sarawak's political milieu thus provides the primary impetus for Bidayuhs to engage in cultural objectification, as well as the main framework through which to do so. Here, entities such as the revived *baruk*—and, presumably, the paraphernalia of *adat gawai*—serve as examples of culture and religion politicized; they become objects detached from their original contexts, wielded as instruments in a struggle for recognition and progress within an ethnically skewed system (ibid.: 227).

Winzeler's piece excites and frustrates me in equal measure, for while it strikes a chord with my own fieldwork, it also reaches a conclusion that I find curiously hollow. In part, I suspect, this is due to our differing experiences in Sarawak: Although Winzeler generally refers to "the Bidayuh" as a single entity (1997: 202, 211, 212, 216, 227), most of his informants appear to be urban leaders closely linked to ongoing state-level formulations of cultural policy and practice (ibid.: 203, 206, 222, 226, 227; see also Winzeler 1996). While they retain various kin- and land-based connections in their respective villages, they also tend to define themselves as members of a pan-ethnic, modern, educated elite who have transcended the rural poverty and backwardness in which many of their compatriots still wallow (see Chapter 1). From this position, they hold very specific views on "culture," development, and rural progress that may not always dovetail with those of people in Benuk and other villages. While my acquaintances are certainly not *un*aware of or detached from the "cultural" goings-on in Kuching that Winzeler describes, it would be a stretch to suggest that their views are adequately captured by their urban representatives.

My unease, however, stems less from the idea that we might be talking about different (if overlapping) sections of the population than from the analytical framework and conclusion of Winzeler's analysis. As chapters 1 and 4 have shown, ethnic politics is indeed a crucial backdrop and motivating factor in Bidayuh engagements with the Malaysian state. However, Winzeler's argument essentially stops there, without delving further into how his very subjects—particularly those in villages where *baruk*s still exist (ibid.: 215)—construe the situation. Apart from briefly intimating that "older concerns about spiritual potency, danger, and decline may play some role in the revival of the head-house" (ibid.), his article remains couched in political terms (ibid.: 216). Yet, I wonder if those "older concerns" are as unworthy of attention as they may seem. In this framework there is no room, for example, for the young man who knew enough to murmur invocations to the skulls in Benuk's *pangah* when his friends began photographing them on their mobile phones. Nor is there space for the staunchly Catholic civil servant, mentioned in Chapter 1, who felt patently uncomfortable at a "Bidayuh cultural performance" staged by actual *gawai* practitioners because of the spirits that would materialize. The analyst may see culture and religion being commodified, touristified, politicized—but do Bidayuhs see the same thing?

This was the question with which the present volume began, and which this chapter addresses. My argument is that in order to gain a full understanding of both "culturalism" and religiosity in contemporary Bidayuh communities, we need to look not only at the politics of multiculturalism, ethnicity, and religion but also at how those very rituals that have apparently been objectified are understood to tick. Doing so, I suggest, reveals a set of concepts, principles, and mechanisms at the heart of *adat gawai* that offer an alternative means of construing Bidayuhs' "culture"-making exercises. This is the task to which the next section turns.

How to do Things with *Adat*: Change, Transformation, and Causality

The maxim that humans are in large part responsible for shaping their own fate is embedded in numerous old Bidayuh stories. In keeping with a pan-Bornean theme, for example, several tales concern the origin of prominent or unusual rock formations, relating how they were once people or villages that were turned to stone as punishment for transgressing certain norms, such as laughing at animals (e.g., Brooke 2005: 270–271; Geddes 1961: xxviii; Howes 1952: 77–89; Roth 1980, I: 305–306; Rousseau 1998: 105). Similarly, a variation of an origin story found across Sarawak tells of how the ancestor of today's Bidayuhs lost the skill of literacy—the instrument of governance and power—by either getting his *surat* (letter/written document) wet during a great flood or being tricked or bullied into giving it to the European or the Malay (e.g., Harris 2001: 29–30; Roth 1980, I: 302–303). This resulted in Europeans, then Malays, going on to govern Sarawak, with Bidayuhs having only themselves to blame for their lowly status up to the present. (The Chinese, as always, hover somewhere in the middle—a reflection, perhaps, of their long-standing commercial success but lack of political clout.)

As exercises in causal attribution, these stories contain a clear message with which contemporary Bidayuhs are widely familiar. This is the understanding, also alluded to at various points in this book, that humans are instrumental in shaping their own lives and the world around them; their fate, whether in farming, leadership, or ritual life, is neither inherited nor inherent, but achieved through their own actions. Indeed, even if an occurrence can be attributed to divine intervention, natural phenomena, or other proximate causes lying beyond one's immediate control, its underlying trigger is frequently human. The pervasiveness—and persuasiveness—of this assumption was revealed in two incidents that occurred within days of each other in December 2004. Shortly before Christmas, a boy aged six died suddenly of an asthma attack when out caroling in the village. While deaths of the elderly were accepted with stoic fatalism, those of young people often disturbed the villagers, who would ruminate for days over what might have caused or contributed to it. Speculation began seeping through the village grapevine: Had his rotundity exacerbated his condition, making it harder for him to breathe? Had the cool night air in the middle of the rainy season damaged his lungs? Did the ice cream he ate before setting off cause the attack?

Soon afterwards, however, another more compelling explanation emerged. The boy's grandmother, who had lived with him and his parents, had died in September after an illness. Villagers now recalled that the boy's parents had decided to throw a birthday party for him in October, prior to the end of the customary mourning period for the deceased lady. In Anglican and Catholic practice, bereaved households generally observe a 40-day *patang* (prohibition period) after a death, during which nothing celebratory, such as parties or weddings, should take place. The pieces were beginning to fit. By choosing to hold a birthday party for him before the end of the *patang*, in the very house where his grandmother had died, the boy's parents had committed a grievous error. His traumatic death was, some of my acquaintances reasoned, punishment for his parents' failure to observe postmortem *adat*. The "primary" agent (Gell 1998) behind this event was not asthma, nor his grandmother's vengeful soul, God, Satan, or spirits, but his parents themselves, whose misstep cost them dearly.

Several days later, large areas of Indonesia, Thailand, Sri Lanka, and India were devastated by the Boxing Day tsunami. Since everybody was celebrating Christmas with their televisions and radios on full blast, news of the event spread through the village like wildfire. Particular attention was focused on the Indonesian province of Aceh, the worst-hit region. Over the next few days, conversations in the houses I visited began dwelling on the fact that Aceh had a large, dominant Muslim population. While most of my acquaintances were undeniably shocked by the tragedy and were sympathetic toward its victims, I was struck by the emerging theory, which circulated for months afterward, that one reason Aceh was so badly hit was that it was Muslim.[3] Some people suggested that the Acehnese were being punished by God for the wrongs they had committed, while others attributed it to the ongoing civil strife between different Muslim groups in the province. Playing devil's advocate, I pointed out at one point that many Christian tourists in places such as Thailand had also been killed when the waves struck the beaches. After a brief pause, someone replied, "Well, if they were Christians they should really have been at church that day [Sunday], not holidaying on the beach. Maybe that was why they died."

What underpins these different sequences of causal inference is the widespread and axiomatic awareness that doing makes it so. It is an axiom that, I suggest, forms the basis of many Bidayuhs' conceptualizations and practice of *adat* in general, whether it relates to the responsibilities of being part of a Christian *rawang* and the need to elicit God's mercy and benevolence (Chapter 6) or to the establishment of exchange relations with *gawai* spirits and government officials (Chapter 2). Here, persons and their actions are assigned a causal primacy in relation to the other parties with which they are engaging: God, spirits, illnesses, tsunamis, and so on. These all have their role to play and are often responsible for generating effects that humans could not ordinarily accomplish—but the onus often remains on humans to initiate and influence the agentive sequences leading up to them.

As Chapter 6 revealed, the notion of God's omnipotence rather limits the extent and scope of human agency in the practice of Christianity. In *adat gawai*, however, the stakes for spirit entities are a lot higher, because their very fate and presence are understood to be contingent on what people do. As the story of the white crocodile (Chapter 2) suggests, one of the most contentious, if seldom discussed, ambiguities for Christians in my adoptive village is the reality of the old spirits. While admitting that they should not pay heed to them, my informants are far coyer about whether they think they actually exist. The vague consensus that seems to have emerged, however, is that such spirits are indeed real but that ideally, their presence should not be felt by or relevant to Christians. This is underpinned, moreover, by the pervasive understanding that as long as there are *gawai* practitioners around to engage with the spirits—to maintain relations with them by inviting them to the longhouse, giving them offerings, and feeding and entertaining them—those spirits will continue to exist and act in the world (Chua 2009b: 337).

This principle was first explained to me by a civil servant in her forties during 2005's Gawai Dayak/*gawai sawa* celebrations in Kampung Benuk. Like other villagers, she would occasionally wander over to the longhouse to watch the *gawai* proceedings and would even follow the same food- and movement-related *patang*s as the elderly practitioners to show her solidarity with them. These rituals would conventionally end with the practitioners spending the night near the *sangar* (bamboo altar), joined by a rotating handful of Christian friends and relatives and the odd intoxicated hanger-on, pleased to have found a hospitable spot at which to pass the night. My interlocutor, however, always refused to join in the sleepover, because by then the area would be filled with old spirits who might "disturb" Christians in the vicinity for not praying to them. This was why, she reflected, she would feel completely safe as a Christian in the village only when all the *nyamba gawai* had died and there was no one left to engage with the *gawai* spirits, for then they would all disappear and Benuk would become "pure Christian."[4]

Not everybody, however, shared this woman's anxieties about resentful spirits. Among the non*gawai* practitioners who attended these postritual sleepovers, some protected themselves with Christian prayers, while others seemed blithely unconcerned about their invisible visitors' reactions. Yet, beneath these varied responses lay a deep-seated understanding about the relationship between persons and spirits. The fact that most Christians in the village no longer pray to the old spirits does not render them nonexistent, because there are still other people doing so through *adat gawai*. In other words, it is the continued performance of *adat gawai* by its practitioners that *engenders* and maintains the presence of its spirits.[5] Later, I had a similar conversation with Sumuk Nyangŭ, the most senior *gawai* practitioner. Her answer resonated with what I had already heard: When the *nyamba gawai* had all passed on, there would be no *adat gawai* left. The old spirits, however, were flexible, and would probably learn to listen to Christian prayers. Maybe, she mused, they would even become Christian too; after all, they already knew bits of this new *adat* since so many people were now practicing it. Like the Malay spirits studied by Endicott, these entities seemed to possess an "infinite flexibility"; the "potential to be structured and restructured" (1970: 86) by what people did.

In contrast to that of God and other Christian personages, then, the fate of the old spirits is, in a fundamental existential sense, determined by what people do. In this regard, *gawai* and Christian spirits may be described as causal outcomes of the same order as unfortunate deaths and tsunamis: as consequences of how well or how badly *adat* has been followed by people. Although the agency of spirits, natural phenomena, and other immediate causes is thus not lacking—and is indeed often harnessed—it is ultimately often contingent on the whims, efforts, and failings of persons. This recognition, however, brings us to another related point. More than a theory of agency, the exegeses that we have just examined effectively constitute a theory of change and transformation, for they raise the possibility that even the ontological furniture of the world (such as spirits) can change through human intervention.

After my conversation with Sumuk Nyangŭ, I began asking other villagers what they thought would happen to the old spirits in a "pure" Christian world. Most responses were variants of those already recounted—they would vanish, return to their own villages, stay in the area without making their presence felt, or perhaps become Christian—and many were riddled with the same uncertainty that crept into Sumuk Nyangŭ's voice when she broached the possibility of their conversion. To an extent, of course, their "maybe"s and "I don't know"s reflected the awkwardness of my question, as they could hardly be said to fret about the old spirits on a daily basis. Yet, it is worth noting that what they were disclaiming was not just their knowledge of the correct answer but the very idea that a single, inevitable outcome could even be prescribed in advance. This, I suggest, betrayed the widespread awareness that *adat*—and humans' knowledge of it—is inevitably incomplete. For many Bidayuhs, there are always unknown and unrealized *possibilities* that they accept that they have not encountered or will ever encounter. The old spirits may become Christian when all the *gawai* elders have stopped practicing, or they may not. There is no definite answer, and will not be until after the event.

This awareness of the sheer unpredictability of the future, I suggest, has influenced the way many Bidayuhs deal with the new and the unknown. It appears to generate the conviction that the world is fundamentally one big unfinished project: however much one knows, sees, or experiences, there are always unknown and unfulfilled possibilities lurking out there, beyond immediate human comprehension and perception. Such possibilities may sometimes appear out of nowhere—as Christianity and its personages arguably did when European missionaries first introduced them in the nineteenth century—but they are also commonly brought about by what humans do. Although people often perform *adat* with certain hoped-for or expected outcomes in mind, then, they are always cognizant of the "infinite possibility" (Bellah 1964: 370) nature of their world, as well as their agentive complicity in (re)shaping it.

The upshot of all this is that my acquaintances have developed a distinct willingness to be surprised by the appearance of phenomena about which they never knew or anticipated (see also Strathern 1990). Such surprise, however, is not laced with unease but an almost casual acceptance of the self-evident realness and validity of the new addition. A glance at the rituals of *adat gawai*—which itself came from the sky (Chapter 2)—offers ample proof of this principle at work. The material world of *adat gawai* routinely includes blue-and-white Chinese bowls, cotton textiles made by Iban or other groups, glass necklaces and ceramic beads from Europe, China, and the Middle East, small Chinese brass bells, as well as coins minted by the VOC (Dutch East India Company), Brooke Raj, and Malaysian state that are fastened to the hems of women's hats and skirts so as to jangle when they dance. While food offerings to the spirits consist of a core of preserved fish, cooked chicken, turmeric, rice, betel quid, and *sireh* leaf, it is not uncommon for multicolored Iced Gem biscuits, cans of Stella Artois or Tiger Beer, Marlboro cigarettes and, on at least one occasion during my fieldwork, red table wine ("white people's *arak*") to join them at the *sangar*. Moreover, *adat gawai* practitioners have long been known to incorporate into their chants chunks of speech from languages that they do not understand, including

French, archaic Malay dialects (Aichner 1955: 589; Rubenstein 1991: 63–64; St John 1974, I: 199–200), and even Christian glossolalia (Rubenstein 1991: 64).

Cumulatively, these examples paint a portrait of *adat gawai* as an inherently changeable and adaptable entity. In an apposite replay of its origin myth, the efficacy of its components derives not from their genealogy or origin but from the way they are combined in tandem with other components to produce specific effects. In this respect, Chinese bowls, Tiger Beer, and glossolalia were not objects of suspicion prior to their incorporation into *gawai* rituals but were accepted from the outset as *potentially* valid additions to *adat*. And as long as nothing went horribly wrong as a result of their deployment in ritual, there was no reason not to carry on using them. In the process, they helped to reshape the very content and nature of *adat gawai*, transforming it just as they were transformed into ritual components.

With this in mind, we can now turn back to the question of "culture." How might the ideas about human agency and transformation that we have just explored shed light on the way my Bidayuh acquaintances construe "cultural" phenomena such as the *Khidmat Negara* dance performance? To address this question, I would like to think through an example that foregrounds the relationship between *adat gawai* and "culture": Paka's mini-museum in Kampung Benuk. As the Introduction explained, I was originally drawn to this eccentric collection because it seemed to embody the transformation of religious paraphernalia into reified, politicized objects of culture. During the course of fieldwork, however, a rather different story unraveled, revealing at its core the key to understanding the apparent paradox of "Bidayuh culture."

The "Objectification of Culture"? Objects, Agency, and Transformation in Paka's Mini-Museum

In early 2005, Benuk's mini-museum was in a painfully liminal state. Its owner and curator, Paka anak Otor, had died suddenly, leaving his widow and children in charge of what had been his personal domain for over 40 years. Convinced that Paka would have wanted them to carry on his work, the family stoically spruced up the place, reacquainted themselves with the objects, and grappled with the interpretive challenge of communicating with outsiders who spoke neither Bidayuh nor Malay. Years of interaction with visiting British soldiers, missionaries, and government officials had given Paka a rudimentary grasp of English, which he exploited when civilian tourists and culture-seeking researchers later arrived on his doorstep. His wife and children, however, enjoyed no such advantage, and only awkward smiles, vague gestures, and a deeply uncharacteristic silence passed between them and French backpackers, Singaporean schoolchildren, ex-British servicemen, and other visitors.

When Paka died, I had been in Kampung Benuk for just over a month, spending much of this time learning about "Bidayuh culture" from him. After his death, his widow Sumuk Meroi adopted his role as pedagogue, endeavoring to tell me everything she knew about the objects in the mini-museum. As my visits to the house increased, I was also called upon more frequently to act as the family's translator whenever English-speaking tourists arrived. Soon afterwards, I acceded to Sumuk Meroi's request to produce some sheets of English text that she could hand out to visitors in my absence. In late January, we began working on them, on the understanding that I would write in English what she told me about those objects that she deemed particularly important.

As I explain in detail elsewhere (Chua 2006a), the challenges of this project became rapidly apparent. Some, of course, involved the ethical qualms with which anthropologists are familiar: Did I have the authority to speak for my informants? Would I create a reified, inauthentic set of "cultural objects" for the benefit of tourists? Was I meddling in a situation that should be left to work itself out? These initial misgivings were assuaged by the realization that, as Sumuk Meroi put it, I had been "given" knowledge and therefore ought to give something back by helping the museum. In any case, they paled in comparison to the task of creating the text panels. At times, it felt like the family's descriptions of the collection— consisting mainly of *adat gawai* paraphernalia, domestic artifacts such as baskets, machetes, and water carriers, and heirlooms such as earthenware "dragon" jars and porcelain—stood at cross-purposes with the expectations of the imaginary tourist for whom I was writing. Visitors, I found, often wanted to know the provenance of objects, their place in the broader Bidayuh context, and the meaning or significance of certain patterns and motifs. Such considerations, however, were of only partial interest to Sumuk Meroi. As we circled the room during our first session, she declared that we should focus on *hentik* (antiques) that had acquired *pangkat* (rank, status) through their age and usage and objects that were "*asar* Bidayuh"—that is, "authentically" or "originally" Bidayuh (figure 7.1). Her final selection was a motley assemblage, which included the following:

A collection of nineteenth-century blue-and-white trade porcelain and earthenware jars manufactured in China and acquired by Bidayuhs through trade over several centuries. Such items were used to store rice, liquor, and preserved foods and are valued across Borneo as precious heirlooms. Blue-and-white bowls are also important holders of offerings in *adat gawai* rituals; when tapped with a metal blade, they produce a specific sound that summons spirits in the vicinity to the ritual site.

A number of ritual hats worn by *gawai* practitioners for different occasions, including the distinctive red, black, and white *sepiya* (now a centerpiece of female "cultural" dress), a conical rattan, bead, and shell *tukua*, worn by girls when they were initiated into *gawai*, and the intricately beaded *gubak*, worn by old men and women with a high level of *gawai* knowledge.

A thin wooden swing (*ayun*) on which female *gawai* practitioners (*dayung băris*) rock back and forth for hours after a ritual, chanting and singing.

A wooden *gawai* ritual staff (*sikud*) with incised designs, ending in a clump of feathers and colorful strips of cloth. Such staffs can be used only by the most senior, knowledgeable practitioners to summon spirits and bless the ritual proceedings.

A warp-*ikat* skirt, made by Iban weavers and probably bought in Kuching, which Paka's daughters wore during *adat gawai* rituals and dances.

While some of these objects were clearly Bidayuh from start to finish, many others might be described as distinctly foreign. Yet, Sumuk Meroi designated them all *asar*, a concept that, I soon realized, had little to do with their geographical or cultural origins. In contrast to the Western museological notion of provenance, an object's claim to being *asar* in the mini-museum did not rest on its claim to an exclusive, unbroken link with a single source. If the museum had a taxonomy, it was not determined by the "genealogical thinking" that, as Mary Bouquet argues, has historically informed Euro-American museum collections (2000: 172; see also Thomas 1991: 4–5). Instead, it was not at all contradictory for Sumuk Meroi to explain that a blue-and-white porcelain bowl was *asar Cina* (from China; Chinese) at the same time that it was *asar* Bidayuh: The two identities could be collapsed simultaneously into a single artifact. Put differently, this was

Figure 7.1 Heirloom jars and other artifacts at Paka's mini-museum, Kampung Benuk, 2008.

not a Chinese bowl that had been transplanted into a Bidayuh frame-work; it simply *was* a Bidayuh bowl whose Chinese-ness was equally self-evident. Beholden as I was at the time to the provenance-seeking tourist of my mind's eye, I did not pursue this potentially awkward theme in the text panels, settling on a straightforward expository formula that stated both the origins and the uses of particular artifacts in the village (Chua 2006a: 30–35; see also Kreps 2003: 41–43).

This text panel project raised critical questions about the notions of provenance and authenticity, which I would now like to pursue further. Chief among them, of course, was the very issue of what made something real, legitimate, *asar*. In retrospect, this question was entrenched not only in my attempts to understand why Sumuk Meroi chose the objects that she did but also in the nagging disquiet I initially felt about undertaking the project—the sense that I, as a non-Bidayuh, should not really be " 'speaking for,' translating the reality of others" (Clifford 1986: 7). Both these concerns, I suggest, reflected the primacy that anthropologists since Malinowski have accorded the notion of context (Dilley 1999; Strathern 1987, 1995): the deeply-ingrained conviction that ethnographic data must be explicated by reference to the distinctive, holistic frameworks in which they are deemed to exist (Dilley 1999: 4).[6] By this logic, good anthropology analyzes things "in context"—participant observation being its most effective strategy to date for "grasp[ing] the native's point of view, his relation to life...*his* vision of *his* world" (Malinowski 1972: 25).

This analytical reliance on context is, I suggest, homologous with what Robbins identifies as the problem of continuity thinking (2007; Introduction), for both tend to gauge the realness and viability of persons and things by their fidelity—or lack thereof—to a distinctive local whole. Contextualizing, however, is never neutral (Dilley 1999: xi), for if context elucidates, it also excludes (ibid.; Strathern 1987: 259–260). Viewed through this lens, persons and things in context are the real stuff by virtue of their genealogical connection with their elucidating framework: They are the forms that context takes (Strathern 1990: 28). By contrast, elements from outside that context—Chinese bowls, perhaps, or Iban skirts—are often more suspect, their presence treated as incursions, their alienness as axiomatic. Consequently, such external impingements, it is assumed, have at the very least to be accounted for, if not incorporated, "syncretized," or even expelled (Sahlins 1985). Yet, my experiences at the mini-museum and elsewhere during fieldwork seemed only to undermine the encompassing explanatory power of context in anthropological analysis. For an entity to be "really," *asar* Bidayuh, it did not have to be genealogically Bidayuh.

If this was the case, what then made it *asar?* When I asked Sumuk Meroi this question, she was mildly affronted and rather exasperated, muttering several times that these objects were "*memang asar*"—naturally, obviously *asar*, no questions needed. As I spent more time discussing these matters with her and others, however, an answer began to emerge. Its roots, I suggest, may be found in our earlier exploration of the agentive capacity of persons and their actions to bring realities into being, as well as the model of human "translatability" examined in Chapter 4. Put simply, the blue-and-white porcelain and the Iban skirt were both *asar* Bidayuh by virtue of performance; the fact that they had been used to *do* recognizably Bidayuh things—in this case, *adat gawai* rituals. In the process, they became Bidayuh themselves. Like intermarried spouses, nobody forgot their origins, but the important point was that their "foreignness" was not incommensurate with their "Bidayuh-ness"; they just *were* Bidayuh things.

To complicate the story, however, it became clear that like those spouses, the objects were not stuck in a single guise but could effectively become and un-become other things when the situation required. When Paka opened his mini-museum in the 1960s, *adat gawai* was still being practiced by the vast majority of the village population. The fact that most of his household's *gawai* paraphernalia were put on display had little bearing on their use in rituals, when they were taken off the shelves and returned following the proceedings. In this way, the artifacts constantly shuttled between being museum pieces that were nice to look at, as Paka once described them, and being *gawai* objects: fully agentive components of potent constitutive sequences dedicated to keeping the crops healthy, the skulls in the *pangah* content, healing illnesses, and so on. Their potency, however, was confined to the ritual; put back on display, they once again became display pieces and could be handled and worn freely by tourists, who often took photographs with them. Villagers who recalled these occasions told me that this was safe because the latter did not know how to use the objects and accessories properly and were therefore unlikely to cause anything to happen with them.

As more of the family converted to Christianity, their *gawai* collection became increasingly stationary, remaining on display more often than it was used. Eventually, when Paka and his wife became Catholic in the 1990s, the objects ceased being active *gawai* components, and, partly in response to the growing touristic discourse of "multiculturalism" in Sarawak, became objects of "Bidayuh culture" (*budaya* Bidayuh) attracting schoolchildren, university students, journalists, and researchers. Today, such items would be depicted in *gawai* terms only when their history is being recounted; the rest of the time, they are simply spoken of as *asar* Bidayuh objects. Their *gawai*ness, however, is self-evident, and it would be perfectly acceptable for them to be redeployed in a contemporary ritual.

Such objects thus remain translatable, maintaining their freedom to "become" (*jadi*) different things. Indeed, examples of this abound beyond the mini-museum, with various "old" entities being given new, Christian identities and functions as a result of "inculturation" (Chapter 5). Many village chapels, for example, have now installed the same blue-and-white bowls that were once used in *gawai* rituals at their entrances as holy water holders, in which the congregation dip their fingers in order to cross themselves. While these are said to have become Christian bowls, their Chineseness and *gawai*ness are never fully elided. Instead, they are able to "evoke past and future simultaneously" (Strathern 1990: 29), with the knowledge of their earlier manifestations serving as reminders of their capacity for further transformation.

Continuity, Transformation, and the "Objectification" of "Culture"?

The shifting fate of Paka's mini-museum collection offers some important insights into the nature of both *adat gawai* and its off-shoot, "Bidayuh culture." First, these examples reveal the existence of a combinatory logic that underpins notions of ritual efficacy: one that locates the capacity to make things happen at the *confluence* of human intention, action, and material elements. Here, ritual potency is not innate or inherited but elicited through specific assemblages and permutations. Tourists can thus freely handle *adat gawai* objects in the space of the mini-museum because they are protected by their ignorance of how to use them; it is only when they are combined correctly that they make things happen. This does not mean that such assemblages are always fixed and unchanging—far from it, as earlier examples reveal—but it does highlight the pervasive awareness that what matters is how things come together and the effects they produce. Put differently, the components of *adat gawai*—whether material artifacts or actions, chants, and sounds—are seldom deemed to be potent in and of themselves but acquire their agentive capacity and effects mainly in combination with other elements.

As I suggest elsewhere (Chua n.d.), this constitutive mechanism may also be said to underlie a great deal of Christian religiosity—the "thingy" and performative nature of which we examined in Chapter 3. In this regard, both *gawai* and Christian practice are underpinned to different extents by the axiom that the capacity to make things happen lies predominantly at the level of human action. Within this framework, exegetical and causal primacy is assigned to performance and effect, rather than provenance or origin. Consequently, the identity of a set of actions, objects, and effects stems less from their individual essences or genealogies than it does from the ways in which they are brought together and deployed. Taken together, these understandings stack up to an *adat gawai*-based model of transformation that obviates the problem of context described earlier. Here, things do not act as fragments of their "original context" but *create their own context anew* every time they are brought together in one assemblage or another. In this way, multiple elements, regardless of their provenance, can be folded into a single transformative process, untroubled by any apparent context-based mismatches in the present. Linguistically and conceptually, this folding in is often sealed by the term (used by Sumuk Meroi) "*memang*," which in both Bidayuh and Malay means "naturally," "of course," "surely," or "actually."[7] It is a notion that brooks no debate or dissent; its truth is self-referential and self-evident, even if it is simultaneously accepted to be "unverifiable" (Rousseau 1998: 113; see also Metcalf 1991: 5; Tsing 1993: 128). *Memang* thus masks the heterogeneous origins of the components of *adat* at any one time, lending it a just-so quality—"a transcendent 'timelessness' that *defies* historical change but does not deny it" (Toren 1988: 713; italics in original).

To illustrate this point, let us think through the fate of the blue-and-white porcelain bowl. As we have seen, such bowls have undergone several transformative stages: made in China and exported to Southeast Asian markets; acquired by Bidayuh households through coastal and riverine trade networks; turned into intrinsic components of *gawai* rituals; left on a shelf in a mini-museum as *"asar Bidayuh"* or "cultural" objects; placed at the entrance of a village chapel as holy water holders. Throughout this sequence, the material object—the blue-and-white bowl itself—stays the same, retaining its physical consistency. However, rather than entering a different phase of its "social life" (Appadurai 1986) or "cultural biography" (Kopytoff 1986) with each transformation, I would argue that the bowl-as-object becomes *part of a different thing:* a Chinese bowl, an heirloom, a *gawai* bowl, an object of "Bidayuh culture," a Christian bowl.

Each of these things is an irreducible combination of the elements that go into making it; it is not a decontextualized fragment of the past, but simply (*memang*) is what it is. A *gawai* bowl is thus not merely the material artifact held by a *dayung băris* as she taps its rim with a small metal knife while chanting invitations to the spirits in the vicinity. It is all those things at once: the bowl, the knife, the tapping motion, the (appropriately garbed) woman, the tune, and the words of the chant. Cumulatively, these different elements produce an anticipated effect: the attraction of spirits to the *sangar* where their offerings await. Similarly, a Christian bowl consists not only of the physical object but also of the holy water that fills it (itself a combination of sanctification and liquid), the fingers that dip into it, and the sign of the cross that those fingers make on human bodies—a gesture that, my Anglican and Catholic acquaintances say, is intrinsic to the proper performance of Christianity. Finally, a "cultural" bowl is not simply some ritual item wrenched from its original context but a thing that is constituted by and constitutes a specific set of relations with tourists, politicians, and other visitors, the contemporary multiculturalist milieu, and the cameras, guest-books, and gift exchanges that often accompany such interactions (Chua 2009a).

Viewed through this constitutive, combinatory lens, a rather different picture of objectification to those painted by the scholarly analysts
of cultural consciousness mentioned earlier and in the Introduction
begins to emerge. For Winzeler, as for his influences, Cohn (1987)
and Handler (1984, 1988), "cultural objectification" entails plucking
things out of the processual, unreflexive flow of "native lifeways"
(Winzeler 1997: 204) and turning them into stereotypical Cartesian
objects: static, bounded, passive entities to be "scrutinised, identified,
revitalised, and consumed" (Handler 1988: 12) by human subjects.
Within this framework, officially sanctioned versions of "culture,"
"ethnicity," and so on are never quite the real (contextual) thing but
merely "deracinated" (Dellios 2002: 13) approximations of it (see
also, e.g., Handler and Linnekin 1984; Hanson 1989; Keesing 1989,
1996; Linnekin 1983). Taken to its conclusion, this argument posits
that entities such as the *baruk*, or "cultural" performances such as the
Khidmat Negara dance, can only be analyzed as fundamentally alien
constructs that Bidayuhs have somehow absorbed or are manipulating for political ends (Winzeler 1997: 225). To a certain extent, as
Chapter 1 has shown, this is indeed what my acquaintances are doing.
However, what these explorations reveal is that the terms on which
they are engaging with Malaysian multiculturalism are not only those
of the state, or of some external, reified notion of "culture," but also,
crucially, those of *adat gawai* itself.

My argument, then, is that the transformation of *adat gawai*
into "Bidayuh culture" is not a deadening process by which the real
stuff—some original "context"—is irreversibly turned into a thoroughly politicized, reduced, object-like version of it. Instead, it may
be seen as another twist in what my acquaintances themselves view as
an inherently transformative process, in which effects and identities
are generated through what people do and the combinatory packages that they deploy. This process may be viewed as an alternative
model of cultural objectification, in which physical objects such as
blue-and-white bowls are not passive, unchanging, bounded entities,
but components of larger agentive assemblages in which their material properties merge with various other factors. Here, objectification
may be described as a process of giving recognizable form (Strathern
1988) to a multiplicity of elements by holding them in momentary
suspension as a single, apparently discrete, conceptual unit—a "*gawai*
bowl," a "Christian bowl," an object of "culture." In this regard, the
fact that *adat gawai* was originally a ritual complex does not make
its "cultural" manifestations any less valid or (if the correct elements
are used) less potent than the "real" stuff. Even though everybody

knows that "culture" is based on *adat gawai*, they do not necessarily see it as a diminished or simplified version of the real thing, but—like the *gawai* bowl that becomes a Christian bowl—as a whole different thing, implying a different set of relations, practices, and effects.

With this, we can finally return to the puzzles set out by the *Khidmat Negara* performance. Through their responses, I suggest, my interlocutors in the audience were also enunciating their own understandings of the constitutive, combinatory logic that I have just outlined. By depicting the dance performance as *budaya* (culture) rather than *adat*, they were thus not undertaking the same sort of bifurcation that Winzeler does when he distinguishes between "objectifications" and "native lifeways." Instead, they were acknowledging that far from being a pale imitation of the real stuff (*adat gawai*), *budaya* was in fact a different thing altogether. This distinction, I suggest, was what inspired the elderly Catholic man to remark that the girls were chasing away wind. Rather than denouncing the performance as fakery, his comments reflected the widespread understanding that the existence of the old spirits is generated and maintained through the performance of *adat gawai*. Because the girls were not "doing" (*nai*) *adat gawai* but "culture," their actions were unlikely to attract the old spirits, whose presence was vastly diminished in this Christian day and age anyway. In other words, there were probably no spirits around to be chased away that day—just wind.

I say "probably" because, as the provision of the altar showed, there was still no guarantee that the performance would be devoid of potential effects. This was not because it was based on *adat gawai* rituals, but because the sound of gongs might travel far beyond the performance site and draw the attention of spirits in the jungles, mountains, and rivers. Because those spirits would only hear the noise, detached from its combinatory package, they might not realize until they arrived at the village hall that there wasn't in fact a proper ritual for them. The altar was thus a recognition of the agentive properties of a certain component of the dance that could easily spill beyond humans' immediate control. Even *budaya*, it seemed, could sometimes engender *adat*-based effects. The crucial point is that these concerns stemmed not from the context-based considerations over which anthropologists can tie themselves into knots but from the combinatory, constitutive logic that underpins *adat gawai*. The idea that *adat gawai* and "culture" could be both different and the same may have seemed contradictory to a context-seeking anthropologist, but for my acquaintances, this was just the way things were.

If *budaya* is not explicitly directed toward ritual effects, what then does it accomplish? The answer, I suggest, is that it establishes relations not with spirits, but with the Malaysian state and representatives of the *moden* world, whose actions and decisions can have a significant impact in their lives. In many ways, the villagers participating in the *Khidmat Negara* visit were less interested in the teenage recruits than in the letter from the District Office (which turned out to be a brief speech by a government official) and the fact that this was going to be a governmental affair: an occasion on which ties between the village and the state would be established and reinforced. On that day, the key mediator of that relationship—indeed, the thing that consummated it—was "culture." Everyone knew that this was what the contingent (like tourists) had come for, for it was what set Bidayuhs apart from Malaysia's other ethnic groups. And Benuk, I was often told, was in an especially strong position in this respect, because it was the only village in the immediate vicinity to still have a longhouse and a practicing *gawai* population. In this way, the cultural dance performances generated a certain relationship between villagers and visitors, constituting in that moment their respective identities as Bidayuhs and fellow Malaysian citizens. Put differently, "Bidayuh" as a discernible ethnic identity arose within this sphere as a consequence of the relations generated between the village and the wider multiculturalist milieu. And it was this particular relational configuration that made the *adat gawai*-based objects, actions, and tunes what they were: "culture."

While the *effect* of the dance performance was undeniably political, then, the point I wish to make here is that the mechanism and framework through which this occurred was determined not only by the state but also, crucially, by understandings of *adat gawai* and ritual efficacy. While analysts may be tempted to only see ritual politicized in this situation (as it indubitably was), native exegesis on *adat gawai* and "culture" reveals how this was also a case of *politics being ritualized*. As we saw in Chapter 2, *gawai* ritual ceremonies have been part and parcel of Bidayuh villages' relations with the state and other outsiders since at least the mid-nineteenth century, well before the development of any ethnic or cultural consciousness among these populations. In this regard, the staging of modified *adat gawai* dances may be seen as a variation on a long-standing convention of collapsing religious practices and political relations into a concerted "technical" effort (Gell 1999) to bring about beneficial effects. As with regular spirit-oriented rituals, it is their performance, and not their innateness, which is "efficacy's very engine" (Kendall 2006: 213).

Conclusion

The model of a-contextual—or contextually regenerative—transformation that I have just outlined not only challenges conventional anthropological frameworks of analysis but also stands in marked contrast to the debates over continuity and rupture examined in chapters 5 and 6. In many ways, these are premised on Bidayuhs' own context-based concerns: about the power of the old rituals and spirits in the contemporary world, the pertinence of *adat gawai* in the present, and social and moral relations with *gawai* practitioners in a "not yet pure" Christian village. Many of these concerns were precipitated and defined by missionaries, catechists, and institutional churches from the 1960s, all of whom engaged in projects of boundary-drawing in trying to determine which aspects of the past—and indeed the present—were commensurate with Christian practices and understandings. Over time, they enrolled their Bidayuh flocks into these efforts, thereby generating among them a consciousness of the temporal, social, and moral questions—not to mention problems—that came with conversion.

However, what I have tried to argue in this chapter is that conversion and Christianity have not been the only influences on my acquaintances' attitudes toward the *adat gawai* question, for their understandings of the old ways and "culture" continue to be informed by the very concepts, mechanisms, and practices that we have just examined. The result, I suggest, is that many Christians have acquired a double perspective on *adat gawai*, viewing it not only from the outside as the old rituals and fragments of a problematic past but also from the inside as an entity in constant transformation, whose reality, identity, and effect are constantly being recreated through human performance. From this latter perspective, the past is not problematic, and indeed isn't particularly relevant, because what matters are the *potentialities* of things, the *moments* in which they are brought together, and the *effects* that they produce. Moreover, this does not amount to a denial of—a complete rupture from—what came before, but an acknowledgment of the constant possibility of recreating it, unhindered by context-based concerns.

Consequently, despite struggling to reconcile the persistence of the old ways, their practitioners, and other elements of the past with their contemporary lives as Christians, my acquaintances nonetheless remain relatively untroubled by the evolution and fate of *adat gawai itself*—for, like the elderly practitioners, they see it not as an entity shackled to its "context" but as a perennially transformative phenomenon that transcends questions of origins, genealogies, and essences. Such concerns cannot be "explained away" (Henare, Holbraad, and Wastell 2007: 1) through predominantly political means, or as the detritus of older spiritual beliefs (Winzeler 1997: 215), but must be engaged with on their own terms, for it is only through such careful interrogation that we may begin to do justice to the sheer complexity of the *adat gawai* question.

Conclusion

Two days before I left Kampung Benuk at the end of my main stint of doctoral fieldwork in 2005, I went to see Sumuk Meroi in the mini-museum. By this time, we had come to share the easy familiarity and protective closeness that one might find between a grandmother and a granddaughter. We didn't know when we would meet again: I was going back to England to continue with my "big schooling," and she—well, who knew when the end might come? She reflected ruefully, remembering all too well the raw, sudden grief precipitated by her husband's unexpected demise. Today, she was going to give me a goodbye present: a precious possession that she had dusted and cleaned thoroughly once I had told her of my departure. As we sat amid the jars, gongs, necklaces, and television sets, she produced a blue-and-white porcelain bowl that the family had used for many years in *gawai* spirit-summoning rituals, which had then become part of the mini-museum's displays. The soot and grime had been painstakingly removed, and the bowl gleamed beneath the fluorescent ceiling light.

"This is an *asar* bowl," she said solemnly, "It's what *Babai* [grandfather, i.e., Paka] and his father used when they did *gawai*. Take it home with you, and take very good care of it. Show it to your mother and your friends. When you look at it, you will remember (*natŭng*) me, and when I look at this"—fingering the simple gold chain I had given her—"I will think of you. Even after I've died, you will think of me when you look at this bowl. I will pray to God to keep you healthy, give you good work, many children, and keep you cool (*madud*)." Like the woven rattan baskets presented to me by other villagers before I left, this gift embodied the connection between us: a connection that, the givers explained in similar words, would transcend space and the unforgiving passage of time. Unlike the baskets, however, the bowl had an unusually long and varied pedigree: it was a Chinese bowl obtained through trade, which became a *gawai* bowl, then a family heirloom, then a museum display and object of "culture," before becoming my parting gift. The bowl now takes pride of place on my shelf at home in England and is occasionally brought into classes and presentations to demonstrate the agentive and transformative nature of materiality in Bidayuh religious practices.

In those moments, my informants might perhaps say that it has become a teaching bowl: an object formed by the confluence of teacher, students, university setting, and lessons about their *budaya*, which they remember me as having come to study back in 2004. Half a world away from its place of origin, it is continuing to shift and transform as it has throughout the last century. At the same time, however, it is an instantiation of my relationship with my adoptive grandmother, and a fragment of the coeval space (Fabian 1983) I shared—and still share, through regular visits to Sarawak—with my Bidayuh acquaintances. And it is precisely this coevalness that I have tried to capture in this book.

The object of my efforts has been a problem that concerns both anthropologists and Bidayuhs: the ambiguous status of indigenous religion as both an efficacious ritual complex and "culture" in a "not yet pure" Christian community. Rather than attempting to provide an exhaustive account of Bidayuh sociality or Bidayuh Christianity, the preceding chapters have focused on a specific ethnographic puzzle: Why have the majority of Christians in Kampung Benuk sought to maintain, and indeed establish, a relationship of continuity and contiguity with *adat gawai*? This puzzle was, and is, the product of a peculiar historical moment in my fieldsite: a muddy, and in some ways unexpected, pause in what might otherwise have been an inexorable process of conversion. Indeed, had I arrived in Kampung Benuk ten years later, they would probably have passed me by, for by then, the old rituals may well have died out completely. However, during my doctoral fieldwork and in the years since, the very tangible presence and persistence of *adat gawai*—in the form of its rituals, its practitioners, and "culture"—has consistently thrown such issues into problematic relief, thus provoking contemplation, compromise, and even dispute among Christians and *gawai* practitioners.

As the Introduction explains, the extent to which conversion can be analyzed in terms of continuity and discontinuity remains controversial in the study of religion, having most recently been resurrected by Joel Robbins (2007) and other contributors to the embryonic anthropology of Christianity. While this literature has persuasively cast the anthropological spotlight onto our subjects' discourses and models of *dis*continuity, however, it has often left their discourses and models of continuity in the shadows—a consequence, perhaps, of its eagerness to evade the *analytical* problem of "continuity thinking." Yet what I have tried to show in this book is that Christians' own tropes, practices, and experiences of continuity are not merely anthropological (mis)imaginings but are both real and important. The task for anthropologists is not to discard them or treat them as self-evident and unproblematic but to subject them to the same analytical scrutiny as they have recently accorded discourses and experiences of rupture (see also, e.g., Broz 2009; McDonald 2001; Scott 2007; Schwarz and Dussart 2010).

By thinking through Bidayuhs' models and practices of continuity and discontinuity, this book has sought to shed light on both the complexities of Bidayuh Christianity and the ways in which it is implicated in Malaysian multicultural politics and the fate of the old rituals, *adat gawai*. Such entanglements are most clearly manifested in the analytical chapters that comprise Part II. In Chapter 4, I outlined a peculiarly Bidayuh notion of social and ethnic continuity, in which constant maneuverability and translatability—encapsulated in the trope of "becoming"—are valued over rupture and fixity. I further suggested that in the intensely politicized ethnic and religious framework of contemporary Malaysia, Christianity has become an important means of preserving that freedom of movement in the face of Malay-Muslim hegemony, while simultaneously enabling Bidayuhs to stake their claim to *moden*-ity and equality in the national milieu. However, political instrumentality is only one facet of Bidayuh Christianity, which also has far-reaching moral, social, and material influences in its adherents' lives. This point was broached in Chapter 5, which examined how the Anglican and Catholic churches' long-standing policies of vernacularization and "inculturation" have shaped Bidayuhs' relationships with and understandings of the old rituals, resulting in the establishment of a conceptual niche for *adat gawai* as "Bidayuh culture."

The question of how far Christians should break away from the old rituals as they are currently practiced, however, remains contentious and consistently divides the two older churches and the Sidang Injil Borneo. Moreover, as Chapter 6 revealed, things are complicated by the different moral and relational frameworks at play in Bidayuh Christianity. While these usually merge into a vague "love thy neighbor" template, the fissures between them can sometimes be problematically highlighted at *adat gawai* rituals. In these moments, I suggest, the differences between Anglican and Catholic modes of religiosity and those of the Sidang Injil Borneo also become visible, with one embodying a collective, deeply social model of Christianity and the other an individualist, dyadic model. The moral dilemmas that arise from these brief conflicts are as significant as cultural, ethnic, and religious politics, as well as notions of rupture and continuity, in determining how Christians respond to the old ways. Finally, Chapter 7 rounded off the exploration by revealing how *adat gawai* itself can shape Christians' perspectives on its recent evolution and redefinition as "Bidayuh culture." Working through its ritual objects, mechanisms, and principles, I outlined a model of constitutive agency and transformation that revealed how "culture" is not merely a poor imitation or "objectification" of *adat gawai* but a distinctive entity in its own right, with its own contexts, combinations, and effects.

Cumulatively, these explorations paint a portrait of conversion as a simultaneously political, social, cultural, and material process that encompasses both "subjective experience" and "collective existence" (Comaroff and Comaroff 1991: 251) in a complex, and not always unproblematic, relationship. In this regard, the present volume may be seen as an ethnographic contribution to the sizeable—and still growing—anthropological literature on the peculiar forms and trajectories that religious change and transformation can take. Rather than attempting to define conversion or presuming its universality, I have thus used it here as what Mathijs Pelkmans calls a "sensitizing concept" (2009: 12)—as a "strategic theme for understanding wider transformations of social and religious life" (ibid.: 13). However, it is important to reiterate that anthropologists are not the only ones who might deploy "conversion" in this way. As we have seen, my Bidayuh acquaintances have their own understandings, anxieties, and experiences of what "entering Christianity" (*mŭrŭt Kristen*) involves. These may not map directly onto the stereotypical Euro-American idea of conversion that the Comaroffs were so keen to ditch (1991: 250–251), but—like conversion as an analytical category—they serve as important mooring points through which they, and we, can think about and act in the world in which they live.

What such actions and ruminations reveal is that Bidayuh Christianity is neither a bounded "culture" nor a hopelessly fragmented, localized mess, but a complex, relational entity with both monolithic and plural characteristics. It is characterized not only by rupture and individualist modes of religiosity but also by experiences and discourses of contiguity and communality—features that derive as much from its theological content, organizational modes, and institutional policies as from specific local conditions and historical processes. To grapple with these complex, interlocking attributes, however, anthropologists need to move beyond the analytical polemics of essentialism and antiessentialism (Introduction), and to reassert a commitment to ethnographic "thickness" (Ortner 1995): to engaging seriously with Christianity's substantive content and transformative capacity, while never losing sight of its ethnographic particularity, and the ways in which it is experienced, discussed, and reshaped by its adherents. Doing so, I suggest, pushes us toward an ever more nuanced appreciation of the multifarious, yet distinctive and recognizable, forms that Christianity itself can take.

Central to my efforts has been an attempt to think *with*, rather than just about, my acquaintances: to attain exegetical congruence by aligning anthropological analysis with native exegesis rather than holding them apart. This does not entail collapsing them or encompassing one with the other but allowing them to engage productively with each other. Accordingly, I have tried to draw both into a "single language of analysis" (Strathern 1988: 19), with Bidayuh tropes such as *"adat," "budaya,"* and *"jadi"* informing analytical concepts such as "religion," "culture," and "conversion," and vice versa. This is not to suggest, of course, that divergences and contradictions do not exist; indeed, in another incarnation, this study could just as easily have been about urban-rural tensions, changing modes of village leadership (Chua 2009a), or different forms of religiosity (Chua n.d.). In this particular project, however, I have tried to highlight the common epistemological and ontological strands that run through my acquaintances' varied exegeses and experiences: the axiom that humans are ultimately responsible for shaping their own fate, for example, or the shared but not unproblematic sense that conversion to Christianity entails both freedom from and ongoing connectedness with the old ways.

By bringing these strands into the same sphere as anthropological tropes and concerns, I have tried to hold steady an analytical framework that addresses an issue of interest to both me and my Bidayuh acquaintances, albeit for different reasons. In this process, I hope to have edged closer to what Eduardo Viveiros de Castro defined as "the art of anthropology": "the art of determining the problems posed by each culture, not the art of finding solutions to those posed by our own" (2003). *The Christianity of Culture* began with two problems posed by a certain anthropological culture, so to speak: how to deal with the apparent politicization and objectification of indigenous rituals around the world and what to make of its entanglement in Bidayuh communities with recent processes of conversion to Christianity. Over the last several chapters, however, it would have become clear that such analytical problems can only be refractions of the many social, political, moral, and religious challenges faced by Bidayuhs in this *moden*, multicultural, "not yet pure Christian" world. For them, as for anthropologists, there are simply no easy solutions to the *adat gawai* question. All they, and we, can do is think, talk, and act through specific themes, artifacts, and relations—and wait for the answers that only time will bring.

Glossary

B = Bidayuh (Biatah); M = Malay; E = English/derived from English

Adat:	customary law; way of life (B, M)
Adat gawai:	Literally, the customs and laws of *gawai* (see below). Used here to encompass the rituals, principles, practices, and other features of Bidayuhs' pre-Christian lifeworld. Frequently abbreviated to *gawai*. (B)
Agama/Ugama:	Religion. (M)
Anak:	Child. (B, M)
Bangsa:	Race; ethnicity. (M)
Băris:	Chants and songs associated with *adat gawai*. See also *dayung băris*. (B)
Baruk:	See *pangah*. (B—Bau-Jagoi)
Bi- (prefix):	An element or part of the suffix, for example, "people of..."
Bidayuh:	Literally, people of the interior/the land (*dayŭh*)
Bimadis:	Relation; siblings. (B)
Birăjang:	Dance or procession usually performed at *adat gawai* rituals. (B)
Biya:	Free or release from a prohibition or taboo (*patang*). (B)
Branda:	A generic term for white people, deriving from the widespread Malay term *belanda*, which referred to all Dutch people (Hollander). (B)
Budaya:	Culture. (M)
Bumiputera:	Literally, "sons of the soil/land." A Sanskritic term used in Malaysia to refer to all indigenous groups. (M)
Dayak:	(1) Person; (2) The endonym prevalent in most Bidayuh communities; (3) A pan-ethnic label

used by governments and observers throughout Borneo's history to refer to its (usually non-Muslim) indigenous groups. (B)

Dayung băris: Literally, "chanting woman." Female *adat gawai* practitioners whose chants and songs are instrumental to rituals. (B)

Dosa: Sin. (B, M, deriving from Sanskrit)

Dunia jah: Literally, "the old world." Often used to denote the pre-Christian, distant past (B).

Dunia moden: The modern world. (B, M, E)

Gawai: Feast; festival; celebration; ritual. Often used as shorthand for the old ritual complex, *adat gawai* but can simply refer to a large party for humans or nonhumans. (B)

I.C.: Shorthand for the Malaysian identity card (officially known as MyKad). (M)

Jadi: Become; come into being; happen (B, M)

Jah: The distant past. (B)

Kampung: Village; an official unit of governance in Malaysia. (M)

Ketua Kaum: Literally, "community head." The official, salaried position of the village chief. (M)

Kirieng: Malay. (B)

Kristen: Christian (E)

Madud: Cold, coolness; implies an ideal state of health, safety, and social and cosmological equilibrium. (B)

Mangŭh: Shame; embarrassment. (B)

Masi: Mercy; pity; compassion. (E)

Memang: Of course; naturally. (B, M)

Moden: Modern. (E)

Mŭrŭt: Enter; be admitted into. (B)

Nawar: To heal, soothe, or relieve pain and sickness. (B)

Ngyen: Give. (B)

Nyamba: Old; mature; elderly person; also used as a term of respect. (B)

Nyamba gawai: The *gawai*-practicing elders. (B)

Padi: Rice (unhusked); paddy. (B, M)

Pangah: A standalone structure customarily used for as a meeting hall, sleeping area for guests and unmarried males, and store for the village's collection of heads. See also *baruk.* (B)

Păras: Hot; heatiness; implies a state of danger, illness, and instability. (B)

Păris:	See *patang*. (B)
Patang:	Taboo or prohibition on specific actions, areas, and other realms of life. Associated with both *adat gawai* rituals and Christianity. See also *păris*. (B, M)
Patut:	Proper; correct; appropriate. (B, M)
Rais:	Place of residence, for example, a village or country. (B)
Rami:	Raucous; crowded; fun-filled; enjoyable. (B)
Rawang:	Household. (B)
Rindu:	Love; fondness; to miss someone. (B, M)
Sănang:	Easy; calm. (B, M)
Sangar:	Bamboo "altar" used in *adat gawai* rituals. (B)
Simangi:	(1) Life force, soul-stuff, potency; (2) Individual soul or spirit. Cognate of the Malay *semangat*. (B)
Simayang:	Pray. From the Malay and Sanskrit *sembhayang:*. (B)
Susah:	Difficulty; hardship; sadness. (B, M)
Tăpa:	The supreme creator-being in *adat gawai*; the Christian God. (B)
Tăru:	Fear. (B)
Tong:	Way of speaking. (B)
Tua gawai:	Male ritual chief in *adat gawai*. (Abbreviated from *Ketua*.) (B)
Umot:	Demon. (B)
Wayang:	Performance; stage-play; film show. (M)

Notes

Introduction

1. The story of Paka's mini-museum and my involvement in it are recounted in Chapter 7 and Chua (2006a, 2009a).

2. *Adat gawai* has in fact taken longer than two to three years to die out; at the time of writing (2011), its practitioners are still alive, although they are less able and willing to undertake rituals on a regular basis. This remark, however, captured the pervasive sense of *gawai*'s impending demise among most villagers, which, in turn, colors their characterizations of it.

3. Strathern (1995).

4. Like Chris Hann (2007: 404), however, I would suggest that Robbins and others have somewhat overstated this point. While there is truth to the contention that anthropologists have treated Christian populations as "repugnant cultural others" (Harding 1991) or as "disappointing subalterns" (Maxwell 2006: 10), one need only look at the works of major scholars such as Douglas (2002), Leach (2001; Leach and Aycock 1983), and Turner (Turner and Turner 1978) to realize how "virtually every new paradigm in the anthropology of religion [over the last half-century] has been applied to Christianity" (Hann 2007: 404). Indeed, it is striking that a full decade before calls for an anthropology of Christianity, John Barker was already exhorting anthropologists to "take Melanesian Christianity seriously as an ethnographic subject" (1992: 145). Within Southeast Asian studies alone, works such as Vincente Rafael's study of translation in sixteenth-century Tagalog Catholicism (1993) and Lorraine Aragon's exploration of "the distinctive theology and 'culture of Protestantism'" in Central Sulawesi (2000: 14) offer further proof that earlier anthropological engagements with Christianity were often more subtle and rigorous than they have been given retrospective credit for.

5. A small selection of examples includes Aragon (1996, 2000), Barker (1993, 2003), Buckser and Glazier (2003), Comaroff and Comaroff (1991), Hefner (1993b), James and Johnson (1988), Kammerer

(1990, 1996), Keyes (1993, 1996), Schneider and Lindenbaum (1987), Rafael (1993), Stewart and Shaw (1994), van der Veer (1996), and Vilaça (1997).

6. It is important to note, however, that each approach is not as simplistic as this cursory genealogical sketch implies: many "cultural particularists" do acknowledge the distinctiveness and "striking continuities over time and space" (Hefner 1993a: 5) of world religions, while many anthropologists of Christianity do situate their expositions on Christian cultures in their political and historical contexts.

7. Among these are the millenarian Urapmin studied by Robbins (2004), the Ghanaian pentecostalists studied by Birgit Meyer (1999), and the "Friday apostolics" in Zimbabwe studied by Matthew Engelke (2007; see also Harding 1991; Keane 2007; Tomlinson 2009).

8. For a striking example of such slippage, see Bialecki, Haynes, and Robbins (2008).

9. Anthropologists who have recently dealt explicitly with this theme include Amster (2009), Broz (2009), McDonald (2001), and Scott (2007) and articles in Schwarz and Dussart (2010).

10. During my doctoral fieldwork, Benuk had 473 registered households and an estimated population of 2,500. In practice, this figure was smaller and constantly shifting, particularly since many people lived elsewhere but maintained village links through home and land ownership and kin connections.

11. At the fourth Bidayuh Cultural Symposium in 2003 (Chapter 1), for example, it was estimated that about 20 percent of working-age Bidayuhs were illiterate, while more than 68 percent aged 15 to 24 were unemployed (Ridu 2003: 18). The latter statistics, however, may not have taken into account the seasonal and irregular labor in which many people engage.

12. While Benuk's dialect is both syntactically and phonetically distinctive, it nonetheless shares enough family resemblances with other local dialects to be classified as Biatah. See Rensch et al. (2006) for further information.

13. In the Bau-Jagoi, Siburan, Penrissen, and Padawan areas, this has been abetted by the fact that their dialects share a significant proportion of their lexicons, even though accents and intonations vary significantly. Bukar-Sadong and Selako do, however, pose genuine linguistic challenges, although it is not uncommon for Bidayuhs from elsewhere to simply pick them up through exposure to them.

14. "Sindŭ" (mother) is frequently abbreviated to "Ndŭ," just as names such as Crispin (her eldest daughter) are usually shortened to just their last syllable ("Pin"). Teknonyms are discussed in Chapter 4.

15. In 2007, the family made the village their main home, with Ndŭ Pin commuting to work everyday, and her husband growing vegetables, pepper, and other small cash crops on their land after he retired.

16. As Chapter 1 explains, "Dayak" remains the preferred endonym among most villagers. The subtle differences between it and "Bidayuh" are explored in Chapter 4.
17. Unfortunately, a discussion of gender relations is beyond the scope of the present monograph. However, it is worth clarifying that, as in much of island Southeast Asia (Errington 1990: 5), women do not occupy a structurally inferior position to men but are seen as playing distinct but complementary roles to them.

1 Looking Like a Culture: *Moden*-ity and Multiculturalism in a Malaysian Village

1. Unless otherwise stated, all demographic statistics are taken from the 2000 Malaysian census (Jabatan Perangkaan Malaysia 2001).
2. As happened in the past (e.g., Howes 1952: 64–73), villages in Sarawak and West Kalimantan that share genealogical or regional links take part in occasional exchange visits, which often involve large rituals and/or communal meals, also known as *gawai*.
3. For broader overviews of Borneo's populations at different times in history, see Avé and King (1986), Hose and McDougall (1993), King (1993), Leach (1950), Roth (1980), and Rousseau (1990).
4. Histories of the Brooke Raj can be found in Baring-Gould and Bampfylde (1909), Criswell (1994), Payne (2004), Reece (1982, 2004), Runciman (1960), and Walker (2002).
5. For details of this eventful period, see Boulanger (2009), Reece (1982, 1998), and Runciman (1960).
6. See Leach (1950). His recommendations resulted in anthropological surveys of the Iban, Land Dayaks (Bidayuh), Melanau, and Chinese by Derek Freeman (1970), William Geddes (1954), Stephen Morris (1953), and T'ien Ju-Kang (1950) respectively; these studies "greatly contributed to the establishment of these ethnic groups as scientific objects" (Boulanger 2009: 41).
7. While widely used officially and unofficially, "Orang Ulu" remains a controversial category because of its perceived connotations of isolation and backwardness. Since the 1960s and 1970s, there have been occasional attempts to reframe it, but none have yet prevailed.
8. "Malay," like "Land Dayak," also conceals a taxonomical jumble. Once a loose appellation for all Muslims in the region, it was redefined by colonial rulers in the nineteenth century as a distinctive race or nation, with its own language, customs, and religion (Harrisson 1970; Milner 1995: Chapter 4; Reid 2001).
9. Also translated as Malay rule, supremacy, or lordship. This slogan has been criticized by both non-Malay political parties and the Malay left, and its "Malayizing" effect on Malaysia has been widely debated in political and scholarly publications (e.g., Jawan 1991; Jawan and King 1994; Kahn 2006; Loh 1992; Loh and Kahn 1992; Mahathir

1970; Mandal 2001; Milner 1998; Muhammad 1992; Reid 2001; Siddique and Suryadinata 1981; Shamsul 1998, 2004). In October 2008, however, then-Deputy Prime Minister (and now Prime Minister) Najib Razak hinted in an interview with Bloomberg that it might be time to dispense with the system (Whitley and Haslinda Amin 2008). As of 2011, this has not happened, and the slogan continues to fan controversy.

10. Details of the plan can be found at the Web site of the Institut Integriti Malaysia (http://www.iim.com.my/index.php). Accessed November 25, 2009.

11. *Bumi* is a Sanskrit loan-word meaning "soil" or "earth," while *putera* refers to "son." In Malaysia and Indonesia (where the term *pribumi* is more commonly used), it generally refers to indigenes (Siddique and Suryadinata 1981: 662–663; Watson 1996: 10).

12. This does not suggest that Sarawakians—or indeed other Malaysians—adhere unquestioningly to these categories. As various scholars (e.g., Barnard and Maier 2004; Boulanger 2009; Kahn 2006; Nagata 1974) have shown, however compelling its institutional manifestations, ethnicity remains a fluid affair in Malaysia that can be manipulated, defied, or evaded as well as being absorbed.

13. In 2007, Prime Minister Abdullah Ahmad Badawi set out a new slogan, *Misi 2057* ("Mission 2057"), designed to guide Malaysia's development in the next 50 years. As this was meant to complement and extend *Wawasan 2020*, I discuss these two plans in the same breath.

14. SCV Web site (http://www.scv.com.my).

15. Interestingly, although a large proportion of Sarawak's Chinese population are economically dominant urban dwellers, they are represented in the SCV by a farmhouse. The nearby Malay house, by contrast, stands out for its opulence and prosperity (Winzeler 1997: 206; cf. Dellios 2002).

16. As the then-Director of the Sarawak Museum asked at the second Sarawak Cultural Symposium (1993), "What kind of society do we wish to have as we approach the industrialized goals we set ourselves to? What are the cultural elements we wish to maintain when we have reached the target of an industrialized nation? What type of country model should we attempt to emulate—the Western Euro-American model, or the Japanese modern society?" (Kedit 1994: 5).

17. All the Bidayuh papers were compiled in Chin and Kedit (1989).

18. Like many Bornean groups, the Bidayuh historically took heads during enemy raids and conflicts, and for specific ritual purposes. This part of their history, however, does not feature very prominently in their contemporary lives and identities (but see chapters 5 and 6); consequently, I do not devote much time and space to it here.

19. http://www.bidayuh.com, a community Web site and forum, describes itself as "Bidayuh's Internet Baruk." Accessed November 25, 2009.

20. "Annah Rais Longhouse Adventure," http://longhouseadventure .com.
21. "Homestay operators urged to link up with Tourism Ministry," *The Star*, May 26, 2009.
22. Peter Nansian Ngusie, President's Message, REDEEMS Web site, http://www.redeems.my/web/?page_id=68. Accessed November 25, 2009.

2 Following the Rice Year: *Adat Gawai,* Past and Present

1. Non*gawai* people often "sponsor" (English) aspects of *gawai* rituals as a gesture of support for elderly practitioners, by contributing cash, food, or drink.
2. Strikingly, cars bearing Malay tourists were not stopped, probably for the reasons examined in Chapter 4.
3. Much scholarly ink has been spilled on contemporary political mani-festations of *adat* in Indonesia; recent examples include Avonius (2003), Burns (2004), Davidson and Henley (2007), and McWilliam (2006).
4. Of course, pharmaceuticals contain their own element of "technical virtuosity," in that most people cannot explain what they contain and how they work. In this regard, they can be more opaque than the healing substances used in *gawai* and Christian rites!
5. "*[A]dat adi dog ndai nga rami-pawun*" (Adat Bidayuh 1994: 25).
6. Nonetheless, there are differentiable areas of expertise, responsi-bilities, and activities; for details and examples, see Geddes (1954), Lindell (2000), and Nuek (2002).
7. The conversion was that of a middle-aged woman whose *gawai*-practicing mother, with whom she lived, had just died. After the event, she was persuaded by her daughter in Kuala Lumpur to become Christian so that she could be better taken care of. See also Chapter 3.
8. My fact-finding efforts, however, were sometimes thwarted by my acquaintances' refusal to explain things in detail—a strategy that, I suggest elsewhere (Chua 2009b) was actually one way of protecting me from potentially dangerous knowledge.
9. These are complementary tasks carried out by men and women on hill slopes: the men move ahead dibbling holes in the ground, fol-lowed by the women, who sprinkle seeds in them.
10. In popular and official Malaysian parlance, *semangat* can also mean vitality, zest, and spiritedness. For detailed descriptions, see Endicott (1970), Skeat (1900), and Walker (2002).
11. In Singai, such souls become *ieng* (Lindell 2000: 125), which in the Penrissen area is another generic name for spirit beings. *Ieng* prob-ably derives from the Sanskrit *yang*—divinity/divine aspect.
12. Also known as *ieng podi* in Singai (Lindell 2000: 129).

13. All sources assume that Tăpa is male, although the term 'ayŭh' (he/she/it) is not gender specific.

14. Geddes (1954: 25) and Harris (2001: 171) note that the term for the supreme being also commonly designates all spirit entities.

15. Omen animals play an important role in most Bornean societies; see Amster (1998: 289–290), Chua (2009b), Geddes (1954: 23–24, 74), Harris (2001: 89–92), Hose and McDougall (1993: 51–60), Lindell (2000: 110–117), Nuek (2002: 142–145, 192), Roth (1980, I: 221–231), Rousseau (1998: 67–72), and Sidaway (1969: 145–148).

16. This could be related to the story recounted in Roth (1980, I: 70).

3   The Making of a "Not Yet Pure Christian" Village

1. For surveys of Christianity in Sarawak, see Archdiocese of Kuching (1981), Kedit et al. (1998), Lees (1979), Ooi (1991), Rooney (1981), and Saunders (1992).

2. This was an annex of the new Batu Lintang Teacher Training College, set up on the site of a Second World War Prisoner of War camp.

3. Denis wanted me to record the names of the first group of Anglican converts, which he had carefully documented: Michael Toda Sanub, Edmund Kosri Nugi, Goben, Ninja Sare, Herbert Nanyau Simam, Edward Dandu Sokim, Henry Nessem Sanub, William Barui Kareh, and Tassan Mijad.

4. One of Fiona Harris's informants explained that he became Christian primarily because he hated killing chickens for *gawai* rituals (2001: 158–159)!

5. As we shall see, however, Christianity is not devoid of *patang*s—the concept of which has been applied to various practices, such as the ban on sociable or celebratory events during Lent and postmortem mourning periods.

6. Indeed, Sidaway noted in his 1969 article that Christian converts in Benuk were stepping in to fill the role of the village undertaker because they were willing to handle dead bodies without payment (1969: 144).

7. By this, I am not suggesting that Bidayuhs had previously lived in a bounded, self-contained "microcosm" (as Horton's argument implies) but that developments in the rest of Sarawak and Malaysia were not inconsequential to their switching of *adat*s.

8. As Lindell (2000) has shown, and as I have found in other villages, however, relations between the majority and the new Christians were not always civil. In some cases, this led to Christians establishing separate villages or building houses in other parts of the village. Such maneuvers may have reflected an overarching keenness to keep the peace (see Chapter 6), whether through mutual accommodation or through avoidance of conflict.

9. For detailed descriptions of the SIB, see Amster (1998) and Lees (1979).
10. A Malay term meaning "mutual help" or "cooperation," *gotong-royong* refers to an officially sanctioned collective activity that builds community coherence and improves the surroundings. The term has achieved ideological significance in Malaysian and Indonesian politics as a metaphor for togetherness and unity (Bowen 1986).
11. However, it is not uncommon for a single household to contain members of different churches, in which case they receive a visit from each.
12. Conversely, in the *gawai* past, the body would be disposed of within a day or two after death, and no further rites were held to commemorate the deceased.
13. I was not able to discover why these markers were used, as they are simply accepted unquestioningly as *adat Kristen*. However, the 40-day marker—which may be a nod toward the time Jesus spent in the wilderness and the period of Lent—is significant, because it brings to an end a sort of *patang* period for the bereaved household, during which time they are not meant to do anything festive or celebratory (see also Aragon 1996).
14. There are exceptions to this tendency, which run roughly parallel to the main divisions between the denominations. Anglicans and Catholics, for example, do not consume Communion at each other's services, and only Catholics recite the rosary (although some Anglicans collect rosary beads as part of a larger cornucopia of Christian paraphernalia).
15. Although many women are involved in church administration, from heading chapel councils to running interest groups, priests and prayer leaders are all male—a legacy of the gendered conventions prevalent during the height of conversion in the 1970s.

4   Why Bidayuhs Don't Want to Become Muslim: Ethnicity, Christianity, and the Politics of Religion

1. This did not mean that intermarriage was a novel phenomenon, but simply that it was happening more frequently in the *moden* world.
2. The tendency to characterize Islam by reference to its dietary laws is common among indigenous minorities throughout Southeast Asia (e.g., Aragon 1996: 359; Atkinson 1983: 690; Connolly 2009: 499; Harrisson 1970: 20; Lenhart 2003: 306).
3. Bidayuh teknonyms are often, but not always, derived from the name of one's firstborn child or grandchild. Meanwhile, persons who remain single or childless for a long time might be given a teknonym that may not be replaced even if they later have children. It is also possible to change one's teknonym if the person after whom one is named dies prematurely. See also Geddes (1961: 36).

4. I had similar experiences in 2007, when I began working in the Padawan region, where other variants of Biatah are spoken. Many people quickly surmised from my accent that I had learned to speak the language in Benuk, and instinctively adopted its intonation and idioms when conversing with me.

5. Interestingly, studies of religious conversion among other Southeast Asian minorities have revealed similar concerns about freedom of movement and entrapment. Yet, the religion that does the trapping is not always Islam: Christianity is often as much of a culprit in this respect (Atkinson 1983: 690; Hefner 1993b: 118; Keyes 1993: 268–269).

6. This definition derived, in turn, from a peculiar colonial model of Malay-ness (Benjamin 2003: 43–44). Up to the early twentieth century, non-Muslim and non-Malay-speaking groups were sometimes subsumed under the category of "Malays and other natives of the Archipelago," while other Muslims, such as Arabs, were classified separately (Hirschman 1987: 567, 571). See Hefner (1997), Hooker (2004), and Shamsul (1997) for overviews of how Islam became an inalienable, state-sanctioned aspect of mainstream Malay-ness.

7. "Syariah Court Decides Nyonya Tahir Not A Muslim," Bernama. com, January 23, 2006; "Nyonya Tahir a Non-Muslim," *The Star*, January 24, 2006; "Syariah High Court Lets Muslim Renounce Islam and Return to Buddhism," *The Star*, May 9, 2008.

8. This is a compulsory identification document that must be carried by all Malaysian citizens. Its current incarnation, "MyKad," was among the world's first biometric identity cards when it was introduced in 2001. It carries a microchip that stores personal, health, employment, and financial data, and acts as a driving license, internal passport, cash card, and public transport pass. The identity card must be produced in virtually every state-related transaction, including opening bank accounts, registering at clinics, and enrolling at education institutions.

9. The requirement to state one's religion on one's identity card is applicable solely to Muslims (Kortteinen 2008: 230); others have their religious affiliation recorded but not displayed. This amendment to the National Registration Act was brought into effect by gazette notification in 2000.

10. For further details, see Kortteinen (2008); "Once a Muslim, Always a Muslim in Malaysia," *Asian Sentinel*, May 30, 2007; "Malaysia Rejects Christian Appeal," BBC News, May 30, 2007; "Rayuan Lina Joy ditolak—Mahkamah Persekutuan putuskan perkataan Islam kekal dalam Mykad," *Utusan Malaysia*, May 31, 2007.

11. "Lina Joy v Majlis Agama Islam Wilayah Persekutuan & 2 Ors 2005 [CA]." http://www.malaysianbar.org.my/selected_judgements/lina_joy_v_majlis_agama_islam_wilayah_persekutuan_2_ors_2005_ca.html.

12. "Steady" is one of several English words that have been incorporated into everyday village lingo. Other things that might be described as "steady" include a good party, a new job, or one's performance in a competition.

13. A fuller version of this argument can be found in Chua (2007b).

14. By this, Cathy did not mean one of her parents' brothers—both her parents were Bidayuh—but a more distant relation.

15. During fieldwork, I found that several other people also highlighted the retention of converts' original names on their identity cards as proof that they were still Bidayuh and not fully Malay.

16. This man told me that he had converted for two reasons: first, because *adat gawai* was in decline and he wanted to follow a religion with a large and dedicated base of followers (see Chapter 3), and second, that Islam was a generous religion that took care of the poor and the needy, by setting up schools and giving out financial aid. Conversely, some Christians in the same area characterized him as a "parasite" who was only after the handouts and other perks that the government reserved specifically for Muslim converts. Whatever the case, it was obvious that his conversion had caused some controversy in the area.

17. Confucianism has had a checkered history in Indonesia. Originally listed by President Sukarno as one of the independent republic's six official religions (along with Islam, Hinduism, Buddhism, Catholicism, and Protestantism), it was dropped from the list during President Suharto's reign in the 1970s, but it was reinstated following the fall of his regime in 1998 (see Ong 2008 and Yang 2005).

18. At the time, the Sarawak Electricity Supply Company was in the process of being fully privatized (July 2005). Most people, however, continue to associate the electricity supply and other infrastructural features with the state.

5 Speaking of (Dis)Continuity: Cultures of Christianity and the Christianization of "Culture"

1. In the past, the *nyamba gawai* would traverse the whole village site. In recent years, however, the elderly women have visited only as many houses as they can manage in the vicinity of the longhouse.

2. Up to 2008, gambling stalls set up by Chinese from Kota Padawan were a regular feature of Benuk's Gawai celebrations. These would mushroom along the communal veranda of the longhouse (*tanju*), for which each household would be paid rent of a few hundred Malaysian Ringgit. However, this has ceased in the last few years—a development that some of my acquaintances have attributed to the new village head, a strict SIB member who disapproves of such activities.

3. In Singai and some other areas, they could also be cremated (Aichner 1955: 223; Lindell 2000: 185–188; Nuek 2002: 87).

4. While the inhabitants of Singai were well known to European observers and their neighbors for their belligerence (Chang 2002: 173; Lindell 2000: 224; Roth 1980, I: 70; Nuek 2002: 119), other groups in the First Division did their share of fighting—as evidenced by both oral histories and the collections of skulls that can still be found in various *pangah*s and even households.

5. These usually included rice farms, the jungle, and the river; urban and other *moden* settings appear to have been exempt from this ruling, which meant that schoolchildren and workers could move about in keeping with their schedules.

6. Indeed, Geddes (1954: 45) notes that "*kaper*" in Bukar-Sadong also referred to the repugnant stench of a corpse.

7. Dreams were and are seen by many Bidayuhs as significant events through which they can view omens, receive messages from spirits or God, meet deceased spirits and other tutelary entities, and get inspiration of various sorts, ranging from the solution to a problem to the winning lottery ticket number.

8. *Pinyawa'a* is the endonym for members of the 13 villages originating from Kampung Gayu in Padawan, as well as their version of the Biatah dialect (Harris 2001; Mashman and Nayoi 2000: 226).

6 "We Are One in Jesus"? Sociality, Salvation, and Moral Dilemmas

1. In His Christian manifestation, *Tăpa* is sometimes called *Tuhan Tăpa*. *Tuhan* is the Malay term for "God" and is used in Malay-language material and services throughout Malaysia and Indonesia.

2. Not all my acquaintances can identify the people responsible for Jesus's death; these are often described as "*dayak arap*," or just "bad people."

3. *Rindu* can also mean "longing for," "feeling fond of," or "being well inclined towards" (Nais 1988: 500), and it is this affective mixture to which my acquaintances refer to their relationship with God and Jesus.

4. The Arabic equivalent of Satan, "Shaitan," may have been known to Bidayuhs and other Borneans through their historical interactions with Muslims, long before they converted. As far as I can discern, however, "Satan" as it is presently is was probably introduced with Christianity.

5. Set out as a national slogan and political program by Prime Minister Najib Razak in 2010, "One Malaysia" advocates national cohesion, ethnic harmony, and unity of purpose as Malaysia strives to become a fully developed nation by 2020. For further details, see http://www.1malaysia.com.my.

6. Parents are responsible for parceling out their property among their offspring in a manner of their choosing. The household and the

property within it will ultimately be passed on to the child or the member who takes care of it or its head (Adat Bidayuh 1994:108).

7. Priests and prayer leaders occupy positions of relative but not exceptional seniority within this set of relations as mediators (to greater or lesser degrees) between humans and God.

8. Because many Bidayuh villages are—or were, up to relatively recently—dependent on generators for their electricity, this image would have struck a strong chord with his listeners.

9. This may also account for their lack of interest in or even knowledge of Hell and other affiliated concepts, such as original sin and the Catholic notion of Purgatory.

10. I should clarify that SIBs, like other pentecostalists, do talk about deliverance in the context of being freed from the past (Chapter 5; see also Meyer 1998, 1999); however, this is not the sense in which I am using the term here.

7 Thinking through *Adat Gawai*: "Culture," Transformation, and the Matter of Religiosity

1. For further details, see http://www.khidmatnegara.gov.my.

2. Competitions in which model longhouses replete with "traditional" paraphernalia are constructed and displayed are occasionally held in Benuk and elsewhere. These are usually part of wider "cultural" celebrations, such as Gawai Dayak-related events (Chapter 1).

3. See Chapter 4 for an exploration of some reasons for Bidayuhs' mistrust of Malays.

4. In a similar vein, Lindell's Bidayuh informant suggested that the spirits would "return to the heavens and...no longer visit us here on Earth" (2000: 105).

5. Koepping recounts a similar instance in a Kadazan village in Sabah, whereby a Christian woman feared an attack on her house by some ancestral spirits, because the latter "*knew her mother*, staying in that house, *recognized their existence and rights*...[and] armed with that knowledge...would be able to attack any person in the house, each representing all" (2006: 70; italics added).

6. Although this "powerful modernist frame" of comparison between "us" and "them" was destabilized by postmodernist movements in the 1980s (Strathern 1987: 264), the underlying impulse to deal with ethnographic phenomena on their own terms persists unabated in contemporary anthropology.

7. A similar Biatah word, which is used less often in daily conversation, is *taŭn*.

Bibliography

Abbott, Walter, ed. 1966. *The Documents of Vatican II.* London: Geoffrey Chapman.

Abdullah Ahmad Badawi. 2006. "Building a Civilisation to Elevate the Nation's Dignity." Speech tabling the Ninth Malaysia Plan, 31 March 2006. Prime Minister's Office of Malaysia. http://www3.pmo.gov.my/RancanganWeb/Rancangan1.nsf/ucapanPMEng?openForm. Accessed June 26, 2009.

Abdul Rahman Embong. 2001. "The Culture and Practice of Pluralism in Postcolonial Malaysia." In *The Politics of Multiculturalism: Pluralism and Citizenship in Malaysia, Singapore, and Indonesia,* edited by Robert W. Hefner, 59–85. Honolulu: University of Hawaii Press.

Abu-Lughod, Lila. 1999. "Preface." In *Veiled Sentiments: Honor and Poetry in a Bedouin Society,* 2d ed., xi–xxvii. Berkeley: University of California Press.

Ackerman, Susan, and Raymond L. M. Lee. 1988. *Heaven in Transition: Non-Muslim Religious Innovation and Ethnic Identity in Malaysia.* Honolulu: University of Hawaii Press.

Adams, Kathleen. 1997. "Ethnic Tourism and the Re-negotiation of Tradition in Tana Toraja (Sulawesi, Indonesia)." *Ethnology* 36: 309–320.

———. 1998. "More than an Ethnic Marker: Toraja Art as Identity Negotiator." *American Ethnologist* 25: 327–351.

Adat Bidayuh. 1994. *Adat Bidayuh 1994 (Piminyu Biatah).* Kuching, Malaysia: Percetakan Nasional Malaysia.

Aichner, Peter. 1955. "Adat Begawai Among the Land-Dayaks." *Sarawak Museum Journal* 6 (6): 588–589.

Amster, Matthew. 1998. "Community, Ethnicity, and Modes of Association among the Kelabit of Sarawak, East Malaysia." PhD diss., Brandeis University.

———. 2009. "Portable Potency: Christianity, Mobility and Spiritual Landscapes among the Kelabit." *Anthropological Forum* 19 (3): 307–322.

Anderson, Benedict R. O. G. 1991. *Imagined Communities: Reflections on the Origin and Spread of Nationalism,* rev. and ext. ed. New York, NY: Verso.

Ang, Edmund. 2005. *Sarawak and Brunei Diocesan News*, Third Quarter 2005. http://kuching.anglican.org/third_quarter_2005.pdf. Accessed November 13, 2009.

Angrosino, Michael V. 1994. "The Culture Concept and the Mission of the Roman Catholic Church." *American Anthropologist* (n.s.) 96 (4): 824–832.

Appadurai, Arjun. 1986. "Introduction." In *The Social Life of Things: Commodities in Cultural Perspective*, edited by Arjun Appadurai, 3–63. Cambridge: Cambridge University Press.

Aragon, Lorraine. 1996. "Reorganizing the Cosmology: The Reinterpretation of Deities and Religious Practice by Protestants in Central Sulawesi, Indonesia." *Journal of Southeast Asian Studies* 27 (2): 350–373.

———. 2000. *Fields of the Lord: Animism, Christian Minorities, and State Development in Indonesia*. Honolulu: University of Hawaii Press.

Archdiocese of Kuching. 1981. *100 years in Sarawak: Centenary Celebrations of the Archdiocese of Kuching*. Kuching, Malaysia: Archdiocese of Kuching.

Asad, Talal. 1993. "The Construction of Religion as an Anthropological Category." In *Genealogies of Religion: Discipline and Reasons of Power in Christianity and Islam* 27–54. Baltimore: Johns Hopkins University Press.

Atkinson, Jane M. 1983. "Religions in Dialogue: The Construction of an Indonesian Minority Religion." *American Ethnologist* 10 (4): 684–696.

Avé, Jan B., and Victor T. King. 1986. *People of the Weeping Forest: Tradition and Change in Borneo*. Leiden, the Netherlands: National Museum of Ethnology.

Avonius, Leena. 2003. "Reforming *ADAT*: Indonesian Indigenous People in the Era of Reformasi." *The Asia Pacific Journal of Anthropology* 4 (1&2): 123–142.

Babadzan, Alain. 2000. "Anthropology, Nationalism and 'the Invention of Tradition.'" *Anthropological Forum* 10 (2): 131–155.

Babcock, Tim. 1974. "Indigenous Ethnicity in Sarawak." *Sarawak Museum Journal* 12 (43): 191–202.

Bala, Poline. 2002. *Changing Borders and Identities in the Kelabit Highlands: Anthropological Reflections on Growing up in a Kelabit Village Near the International Border*. Dayak Studies Contemporary Society Series No. 1. Kota Samarahan, Malaysia: Universiti Malaysia Sarawak.

Banks, Marcus. 1996. *Ethnicity: Anthropological Constructions*. London: Routledge.

Baring-Gould, Sabine, and C. A. Bampfylde. 1909. *A History of Sarawak Under its Two White Rajahs 1839-1908*. London: H. Sotheran and Co.

Barker, John. 1992. "Christianity in Western Melanesian Ethnography." In *History and Tradition in Melanesia Anthropology*, edited by James G. Carrier, 144–173, Berkeley: University of California Press.

———. 1993. " 'We are Ekelesia': Conversion in Uiaku, Papua New Guinea." In *Christian Conversion: Historical and Anthropological Perspectives on a*

Great Transformation, edited by Robert W. Hefner, 199–230. Berkeley: University of California Press. http://faculty.arts.ubc.ca/barker /PDF/1993 We Are Ekelesia %28full%29.pdf

———. 2003. "Christian Bodies: Dialectics of Sickness and Salvation Among the Maisin of Papua New Guinea." *Journal of Religious History* 27 (3): 272–292.

———. 2008. "Toward an Anthropology of Christianity." *American Anthropologist* 110 (3): 377–381.

Barnard, Timothy P., ed. 2004. *Contesting Malayness: Malay Identity Across Boundaries*. Singapore: Singapore University Press.

Barnard, Timothy P., and Hendrik M. J. Maier. 2004. "Melayu, Malay, Maleis: Journeys Through the Identity of a Collection." In *Contesting Malayness: Malay Identity Across Boundaries*, edited by Timothy P. Barnard, ix–xiii. Singapore: Singapore University Press.

Barth, Frederik. 1969. "Introduction." In *Ethnic Groups and Boundaries: The Social Organisation of Cultural Difference*, edited by Frederik Barth, 9–38. Oslo, Norway: Universitetsforlaget.

Baxstrom, Richard. Forthcoming. "Living on the Horizon of the Everlasting Present: Power, Planning, and the Emergence of Baroque Forms of Life in Urban Malaysia." In *Southeast Asian Perspectives on Power*, edited by Liana Chua, Joanna Cook, Nicholas Long, and Lee Wilson. London: Routledge.

Baumann, Gerd. 1996. *Contesting Culture: Discourses of Identity in Multi-Ethnic London*. Cambridge: Cambridge University Press.

Beccari, Odoardo. 1986 [1904]. *Wanderings in the Great Forests of Borneo*. Singapore: Oxford University Press.

Bellah, Robert N. 1964. "Religious Evolution." *American Sociological Review* 29 (3): 358–374.

Benjamin, Geoffrey. 2003. "On Being Tribal in the Malay World." In *Tribal Communities in the Malay World: Historical, Cultural and Social Perspectives*, edited by Geoffrey Benjamin and Cynthia Chou, 7–76. Singapore: Institute of East Asian Studies, and Leiden: International Institute for Asian Studies.

Bialecki, Jon, Naomi Haynes, and Joel Robbins. 2008. "The Anthropology of Christianity." *Religion Compass* 2 (6): 1139–1158.

Bloch, Maurice. 1986. *From Blessing to Violence: History and Ideology in the Circumcision Ritual of the Merina of Madagascar*. Cambridge: Cambridge University Press.

Boulanger, Clare L. 2000. "On Dayak, Orang Ulu, Bidayuh, and other Imperfect Ethnic Categories in Sarawak." In *Borneo 2000: Proceedings of the Sixth Biennial Borneo Research Conference. Ethnicity, Culture and Society*, edited by Michael Leigh, 44–65. Kota Samarahan: Institute of East Asian Studies, Universiti Malaysia Sarawak.

———. 2009. *A Sleeping Tiger: Ethnicity, Class, and New Dayak Dreams in Urban Sarawak*. Lanham, MD: University Press of America.

Bouquet, Mary. 2000. "Figures of Relations: Re-Connecting Kinship Studies and Museum Collections." In *Cultures of Relatedness: New Approaches to the Study of Kinship*, edited by Janet Carsten, 167–190. Cambridge: Cambridge University Press.

Bowen, John. 1986. "On the Political Construction of Tradition: Gotong Royong in Indonesia." *Journal of Asian Studies* 45 (3): 545–561.

Brooke, Charles. 1990 [1866]. *Ten Years in Sarawak*. Singapore: Oxford University Press.

Brooke, Margaret. 2005 [1913]. *My Life in Sarawak*. Shah Alam: Oxford University Press.

Brosius, Christiane, and Karin M. Polit. 2011. "Introduction: Ritual, Heritage and Identity in a Globalised World." In *Ritual, Heritage and Identity: The Politics of Culture and Performance in a Globalised World*, edited by Christiane Brosius and Karin M. Polit, 1–16. New Delhi, India: Routledge.

Brosius, Peter. 2003. "The Forest and the Nation: Negotiating Citizenship in Sarawak, East Malaysia." In *Cultural Citizenship in Island Southeast Asia: Nation and Belonging in the Hinterlands*, edited by Renato Rosaldo, 76–133. Berkeley: University of California Press.

Broz, Ludek. 2009. "Conversion to Religion?: Negotiating Continuity and Discontinuity in Contemporary Altai." In *Conversion after Socialism: Disruptions, Modernisms and Technologies of Faith in the Former Soviet Union*, edited by Mathijs Pelkmans, 17–37. Oxford: Berghahn.

Bruton, Roy. 1993. *Farewell to Democracy in Sarawak: Theoretical Exploration of Socio-cultural Transmissions, with Reference to Change, Conflict and Contradiction*. Braunton, Devon: Merlin Books.

Buckser, Andrew, and Stephen D. Glazier, eds. 2003. *The Anthropology of Religious Conversion*. Lanham, MD: Rowman and Littlefield.

Burns, Peter. 2004. *The Leiden Legacy: Concepts of Law in Indonesia*. Leiden: KTLV.

Candea, Matei. 2007. "Arbitrary Locations: In Defence of the Bounded Field-site." *Journal of the Royal Anthropological Institute* 13 (1): 167–184.

Cannell, Fenella. 1999. *Power and Intimacy in the Christian Philippines*. Cambridge: Cambridge University Press.

———. 2005. "The Christianity of Anthropology." *Journal of the Royal Anthropological Institute* 11 (2): 335–356.

———. 2006. "Introduction." In *The Anthropology of Christianity*, edited by Fenella Cannell, 1–50. Durham: Duke University Press.

Carrithers, Michael. 1985. "An Alternative Social History of the Self." In *The Category of the Person*, edited by Michael Carrithers, Steven Collins, and Steven Lukes, 234–256. Cambridge: Cambridge University Press.

Carsten, Janet. 1997. *The Heat of the Hearth: The Process of Kinship in a Malay Fishing Community*. Oxford: Clarendon Press.

Chang Pat Foh. 2002. *History of Bidayuh in Kuching Division Sarawak*. Kuching, Malaysia: Sarawak Press.

————. 2004. *History of Serian Bidayuh in Samarahan Division Sarawak.* Kuching, Malaysia: Sarawak Press.

Chin, Lucas. 1980. *Cultural Heritage of Sarawak.* Kuching, Malaysia: Sarawak Museum.

Chin, Lucas, and Peter M. Kedit. 1989. "Introduction." In *Sarawak Cultural Heritage Symposium Held in Conjunction with 25th Anniversary of Independence.* Special Issue of the *Sarawak Museum Journal* 40 (61) Part I: xi–xiii.

Christian, William A. 1989. *Person and God in a Spanish Valley.* Princeton: Princeton University Press.

Chou, Cynthia. 1997. "Orang Suku Laut Identity." In *Images of Malay-Indonesian Identity,* edited by Michael Hitchcock and Victor T. King, 148–160. Kuala Lumpur, Malaysia: Oxford University Press.

Chua, Liana. 2006a. *Antiques and Adat: The Changing Face of Paka's Mini-museum, Kampung Benuk, Penrissen, Kuching.* Institute of East Asian Studies Working Paper Series No. 11. Kota Samarahan, Malaysia: Universiti Malaysia Sarawak.

————. 2006b. "Looking for the *Tambok*: Some Ethnographic Notes on Bidayuh Basketry." *Sarawak Museum Journal* 62 (83): 1–32.

————. 2007a. "Objects of Culture: Constituting Bidayuh-ness in Sarawak, East Malaysia." PhD diss., University of Cambridge.

————. 2007b. "Fixity and Flux: Bidayuh (Dis)engagements with the Malaysian Ethnic System." *Ethnos* 72 (2): 262–288.

————. 2009a. "What's in a (Big) Name? The Art and Agency of a Bornean Photographic Collection." *Anthropological Forum* 19 (1): 33–52.

————. 2009b. "To Know or not to Know? Practices of Knowledge and Ignorance among Bidayuhs in an 'Impurely' Christian World." *Journal of the Royal Anthropological Institute* 15: 332–348.

————. 2010. "Eating One's Way through Fieldwork: Reflections on Food and (Malaysian) Sociality." In *The Malaysian Way of Life,* edited by Julian C. H. Lee, 73–77. Shah Alam: Marshall Cavendish.

————. n.d. "The Problem with 'Empty Crosses': Thinking Through Materiality in Bidayuh Religious Practices." In *Spirit of Things: Materiality in an Age of Religious Pluralism in Southeast Asia,* edited by Julius Bautista. Cornell: Cornell Southeast Asia Program Publications.

Chupungco, Anscar J. 1992. *Liturgical Inculturation: Sacramentals, Religiosity and Catechesis.* Collegeville, MN: Liturgical Press.

Clifford, James. 1986. "Introduction: Partial Truths." In *Writing Culture: The Poetics and Politics of Ethnography,* edited by James Clifford and George Marcus, 1–26. Berkeley: University of California Press.

Cohen, Ronald. 1978. "Ethnicity: Problem and Focus in Anthropology." *Annual Review of Anthropology* 7: 379–403.

Cohn, Bernard. 1987. "The Census, Social Structure and Objectification in South Asia." In *An Anthropologist Among the Historians,* 224–254. New Delhi, India: Oxford University Press.

Coleman, Simon. 2000. *The Globalisation of Charismatic Christianity: Spreading the Gospel of Prosperity.* Cambridge: Cambridge University Press.

———. 2007. "When Silence isn't Golden: Charismatic Speech and the Limits of Literalism." In *The Limits of Meaning: Case Studies in the Anthropology of Christianity*, edited by Matthew Engelke and Matt Tomlinson, 39–61. New York, NY: Berghahn.

———. 2010. "An Anthropological Apologetics." *Global Christianity, Global Critique*, edited by Matthew Engelke and Joel Robbins. Special Issue of *South Atlantic Quarterly* 109 (4): 791–810.

Comaroff, John L., and Jean Comaroff. 1991. *Of Revelation and Revolution, Vol I. Christianity, Colonialism, and Consciousness in South Africa.* Chicago: University of Chicago Press.

———. 2009. *Ethnicity, Inc.* Chicago: University of Chicago Press.

Connolly, Jennifer. 2009. "Forbidden Intimacies: Christian-Muslim Intermarriage in East Kalimantan, Indonesia." *American Ethnologist* 36 (3): 492–506.

Cramb, Robert A., and Robert H. W. Reece, eds. 1988. *Development in Sarawak: Historical and Contemporary Perspectives.* Clayton, Victoria: Monash University Centre for Southeast Asian Studies.

Criswell, Colin. 1994. *The End of the Brooke Raj in Sarawak.* Stirling: Kiscadale.

Davidson, Jamie, and Peter Henley, eds. 2007. *The Revival of Tradition in Indonesian Politics: The Deployment of* Adat *from Colonialism to Indigenism.* London: Routledge.

Dellios, Paulette. 2002. The museumification of the village: Cultural subversion in the 21st century. *The Culture Mandala: Bulletin of the Centre for East-West Cultural and Economic Studies* 5 (1): 1–16.

Dilley, Roy. 1999. "Introduction." *In The Problem of Context*, edited by Roy Dilley, 1–46. New York and Oxford: Berghahn.

Diocese of Kuching. 2009. *Atur Simayang Liturgy Bauh Ngga Atur Simayang Roh, Darŭm Pinminyu Biatah.* Kuching, Malaysia: Diocese of Kuching.

Douglas, Mary. 2002. *Purity and Danger.* London: Routledge.

Dumont, Louis. 1986. *Essays on Individualism: Modern Ideology in Anthropological Perspective.* Chicago: University of Chicago Press.

Durkheim, Émile. 2001. [1912] *The Elementary Forms of Religious Life*, translated by Carol Cosman. Oxford: Oxford University Press.

Endicott, Kirk. 1970. *An Analysis of Malay Magic.* Oxford: Clarendon Press.

Engelke, Matthew. 2002. "The Problem of *Belief*: Evans-Pritchard and Victor Turner on 'the Inner Life'." *Anthropology Today* 18 (6): 3–8.

———. 2004. "Discontinuity and the Discourse of Conversion." *Journal of Religion in Africa.* 34 (1&2): 82–109.

———. 2007. *A Problem of Presence: Beyond Scripture in an African Church.* Berkeley: University of California Press.

———. 2010. "Past Pentecostalism: Notes on Rupture, Realignment, and Everyday Life in Pentecostal and African Independent Churches." *Africa* 80 (2): 177–199.

Engelke, Matthew, and Matt Tomlinson, eds. 2006. *The Limits of Meaning: Case Studies in the Anthropology of Christianity.* New York, NY: Berghahn Books.

Englund, Harri. 2007. "Pentecostalism Beyond Belief: Trust and Democracy in a Malawian Township." *Africa* 77 (4): 477–499.

Errington, Shelly. 1990. "Recasting Sex, Gender and Power: A Theoretical and Regional Overview." In *Power and Difference: Gender in Island Southeast Asia,* edited by Jane M. Atkinson and Shelly Errington, 1–58. Stanford: Stanford University Press.

Fabian, Johannes. 1983. *Time and the Other: How Anthropology Makes its Object.* New York, NY: Columbia University Press.

Foucault, Michel. 1978. *The History of Sexuality, Vol. I: An Introduction,* translated by Robert Hurley. New York, NY: Pantheon.

Frazer, James. 1922. *The Golden Bough.* London: Macmillan.

Freeman, Derek. 1970 [1955]. *Report on the Iban.* London: Athlone Press.

Furnivall, John S. 1944. *Netherlands India: A Study of Plural Economy.* Cambridge: Cambridge University Press.

Geddes, William. 1954. *The Land Dayaks of Sarawak: A Report on a Social Economic Survey of the Land Dayaks of Sarawak Presented to the Colonial Social Science Research Council.* London: HM Stationery Office for the Colonial Office.

——— 1961 [1957]. *Nine Dayak Nights.* London: Oxford University Press.

Geertz, Clifford. 1993a [1973]. "Thick Description: Toward an Interpretive Theory of Culture." In *The Interpretation of Cultures,* 3–30. London: Fontana Press.

———. 1993b [1973]. "Religion as a Cultural System. In *The Interpretation of Cultures,* 87–125. London: Fontana Press.

———. 1993c [1973]. "'Internal Conversion' in Contemporary Bali." In *The Interpretation of Cultures,* 170–189. London: Fontana Press.

———. 1993d. [1973] "The Integrative Revolution: Primordial Sentiments and Civil Politics in the New States, 255–310. In *The Interpretation of Cultures.* London: Fontana Press.

Geertz, Hildred, and Clifford Geertz. 1964. "Teknonymy in Bali: Parenthood, Age-grading and Genealogical Amnesia." *Journal of the Royal Anthropological Institute* 94: 94–108.

Gell, Alfred. 1998. *Art and Agency: An Anthropological Theory.* Oxford: Clarendon Press.

———. 1999 [1992]. "The Technology of Enchantment and the Enchantment of Technology." In *The Art of Anthropology,* edited by Eric Hirsch, 159–186. London: Athlone Press.

Gereja Katolik St Ann. 2004. *Aran Tuhan: Buk Katekisem Darum Piminyu Bidayuh Biatah.* Kota Padawan, Malaysia: Gereja Katolik St Ann.

Grijpstra, Bouwes G. 1976. *Common Efforts in the Development of Rural Sarawak, Malaysia.* Amsterdam, the Netherlands: Van Gorcum.

Guyer, Jane I. 2007. "Prophecy and the Near Future: Thoughts on Macroeconomic, Evangelical, and Punctuated Time." *American Ethnologist* 34 (3): 409–421.

Haddon, Alfred C. 1901. *Head-Hunters: Black, White and Brown.* London: Methuen.

Handler, Richard. 1984. "On Sociocultural Discontinuity: Nationalism and Cultural Objectification in Quebec." *Current Anthropology* 25 (1): 55–71.

———. 1985. "On Dialogue and Destructive Analysis: Problems in Narrating Nationalism and Ethnicity." *Journal of Anthropological Research* 41 (2): 171–182.

———. 1988. *Nationalism and the Politics of Culture in Quebec.* London: University of Wisconsin Press.

———. 2011. "The 'Ritualisation of Ritual' in the Construction of Heritage." In *Ritual, Heritage and Identity: The Politics of Culture and Performance in a Globalised World,* edited by Christiane Brosius and Karin M. Polit, 39–54. New Delhi, India: Routledge.

Handler, Richard, and Jocelyn Linnekin. 1984. Tradition, genuine or spurious. *Journal of American Folklore* 97 (385): 273–290.

Hann, Chris. 2007. "The Anthropology of Christianity *Per Se.*" *Archives Européennes de Sociologie* 48 (3): 391–418.

Hann, Chris, and Hermann Goltz. 2010. "Introduction: The Other Christianity?" In *Eastern Christians in Anthropological Perspective,* edited by Chris Hann and Hermann Goltz, 1–29. Berkeley: University of California Press.

Hanson, Alan. 1989. "The Making of the Maori: Culture Invention and its Logic." *American Anthropologist* 91 (4): 890–902.

Harding, Susan. 1991. "Representing Fundamentalism: The Problem of the Repugnant Cultural Other." *Social Research* 58 (2): 373–393.

Harris, Fiona. 2001. "Growing Gods: Processes of Religious Change in Sarawak, Malaysia." PhD diss., University of Edinburgh.

Harris, Olivia. 2006. "The Eternal Return of Conversion: Christianity as Contested Domain in Highland Bolivia." In *The Anthropology of Christianity,* edited by Fenella Cannell, 51–76. Durham: Duke University Press.

Harrisson, Barbara. 1990. *Pusaka: Heirloom Jars of Borneo.* Oxford: Oxford University Press.

Harrisson, Tom. 1970. *The Malays of South-West Sarawak before Malaysia: A Socio-Ecological Survey.* London: Macmillan.

Hefner, Robert. 1993a. "Introduction: World Building and the Rationality of Conversion." In *Conversion to Christianity: Historical and Anthropological Perspectives on a Great Transformation,* edited by Robert Hefner, 3–44. Berkeley: University of California Press.

———. 1993b. "Of Faith and Commitment: Christian Conversion in Muslim Java." In *Conversion to Christianity: Historical and Anthropological Perspectives on a Great Transformation,* edited by Robert Hefner, 99–125. Berkeley: University of California Press.

———. 1997. "Introduction." In *Islam in an Era of Nation-States: Politics and Religious Revival in Muslim Southeast Asia*, edited by Robert W. Hefner and Patricia Horvatich, 3–40. Honolulu: University of Hawaii Press.

———. 2001. "Introduction: Multiculturalism and Citizenship in Malaysia, Singapore and Indonesia." In *The Politics of Multiculturalism: Pluralism and Citizenship in Malaysia, Singapore and Indonesia*, edited by Robert W. Hefner, 1–58. Honolulu: University of Hawaii Press.

Henare, Amiria, Martin Holbraad, and Sari Wastell. 2007. "Introduction." In *Thinking Through Things: Theorizing Artefacts Ethnographically*, edited by Amiria Henare, Martin Holbraad, and Sari Wastell, 1–31. London: Routledge.

Hirsch, Eric. 2007. "Looking Like a Culture." *Anthropological Forum* 17 (3): 225–238.

———. 2008. "God or *Tidibe*? Melanesian Christianity and the Problem of Wholes." *Ethnos* 73 (2): 141–162.

Hirschkind, Charles. 2001. "The Ethics of Listening: Cassette-Sermon Audition in Contemporary Egypt." *American Ethnologist* 28 (3): 623–649.

Hirschman, Charles. 1987. "The Meaning and Measurement of Ethnicity in Malaysia: An Analysis of Census Classifications." *The Journal of Asian Studies* 46 (3): 555–582.

Hobsbawm, Eric. 1983. "Introduction: Inventing Traditions." In *The Invention of Tradition*, edited by Eric Hobsbawm and Terence Ranger, 1–14. Cambridge: Cambridge University Press.

Hobsbawm, Eric, and Terence Ranger, eds. 1983. *The Invention of Tradition*. Cambridge: Cambridge University Press.

Hoffstaedter, Gerhard. 2008. "Representing Culture in Malaysian Cultural Theme Parks: Tensions and Contradictions." *Anthropological Forum* 18 (2): 139–160.

Hooker, M. B. 1972. *Adat Laws in Modern Malaya*. Kuala Lumpur, Malaysia: Oxford University Press.

———. 1974. "Adat and Islam in Malaya." *Bijdragen tot de Taal-, Land- en Volkenkunde* 130 (1): 69–90.

Hooker, Virginia M. 2004. "Refiguring Malay and Islam in Contemporary Malaysia." In *Contesting Malayness: Malay Identity Across Boundaries*, edited by Timothy P. Barnard, 149–167. Singapore: Singapore University Press.

Horton, Robin. 1971. "African Conversion." *Africa* XLI (2): 85–108.

Hose, Charles, 1994 [1927]. *Fifty Years of Romance and Research in Borneo*, with an Introduction by Brian Durrans. Kuala Lumpur, Malaysia: Oxford University Press.

Hose, Charles, and William McDougall. 1993 [1912]. *The Pagan Tribes of Borneo*, with an Introduction by Brian Durrans. 2 vols. Singapore: Oxford University Press.

Howe, Leo. 2004. "Late Medieval Christianity, Balinese Hinduism, and the Doctrinal Mode of Religiosity." In *Ritual and Meaning: Toward a Comparative Anthropology of Religion*, edited by Harvey Whitehouse and James Laidlaw, 134–154. Walnut Creek: Altamira Press.

Howell, Brian M. 2003. "Practical Belief and the Localization of Christianity: Pentecostal and Denominational Christianity in Global/Local Perspective." *Religion* 33: 233–248.

————. 2007. "The Repugnant Cultural Other Speaks Back." *Anthropological Theory* 7 (4): 371–391.

————. 2008. *Christianity in the Local Context: Southern Baptists in the Philippines*. New York, NY: Palgrave Macmillan.

Howes, Peter H. H. 1952. *Shǔn Nyamba Nang (A Collection of Land Dayak Stories)*. London: Macmillan & Co.

————. 1956. "The Padawan Community Development Scheme." *The Chronicle: A Quarterly Report of the Borneo Mission Association* 34 (4): 46.

————. 1960. "Why Some of the Best People aren't Christian." *Sarawak Museum Journal* 9 (15): 488–495.

James, Wendy, and Douglas H. Johnson, eds. 1988. *Vernacular Christianity: Essays in the Social Anthropology of Religion Presented to Godfrey Lienhardt*. New York, NY: Lilian Barber Press.

Jawan, Jayum. 1991. *The Ethnic Factor in Modern Politics: The Case of Sarawak*. Occasional Paper No. 20. Hull: Centre for Southeast Asian Studies, University of Hull.

Jawan, Jayum, and Victor King. 1994. *Ethnicity and Electoral Politics in Sarawak*. Selangor: Penerbit Universiti Kebangsaan Malaysia.

Jebens, Holger. 2005. *Pathways to Heaven: Contesting Mainline and Fundamentalist Christianity in Pairundu (Southern Highlands Province, Papua New Guinea)*. Oxford: Berghahn.

————. 2011. "Beyond Globalisation and Localisation: Denominational Pluralism in a Papua New Guinean Village." *The Asia Pacific Journal of Anthropology* 12 (1): 91–110.

Jenkins, Richard. 1997. *Rethinking Ethnicity: Arguments and Explorations*. London: Sage.

Jenkins, Timothy. 1999. *Religion in English Everyday Life: An Ethnographic Approach*. Oxford: Berghahn.

John Paul II, Pope. 1990. "Redemptoris Missio: On the Permanent Validity of the Church's Missionary Mandate." http://www.vatican.va/holy _father/john_paul_ii/encyclicals/documents/hf_jp-ii_enc_07121990 _redemptoris-missio_en.html. Accessed November 11, 2009.

Kahn, Joel S. 1992. "Class, Ethnicity and Diversity: Some Remarks on Malay Culture in Malaysia." In *Fragmented Vision: Culture and Politics in Contemporary Malaysia*, edited by Joel S. Kahn and Francis K. W. Loh, 158–178. Honolulu: University of Hawaii Press.

————. 1993. *Constituting the Minangkabau: Peasants, Culture and Modernity in Colonial Indonesia*. Providence: Berg.

———. 1998. "Introduction." In *Southeast Asian Identities: Culture and the Politics of Representation in Indonesia, Malaysia, Singapore and Thailand*, edited by Joel S. Kahn, 1–27. Singapore: Institute of East Asian Studies, and London: I.B. Tauris.

———. 2006. *Other Malays: Nationalism and Cosmopolitanism in the Modern Malay World*. Honolulu: University of Hawaii Press.

Kammerer, Cornelia A. 1990. "Customs and Christian Conversion among Akha Highlanders of Burma and Thailand." *American Ethnologist* 17 (2): 277–291.

———. 1996. "Discarding the Basket: The Reinterpretation of Tradition by Akha Christians of Northern Thailand." *Journal of Southeast Asian Studies* 27 (2): 320–333.

Keane, Webb. 1997. *Signs of Recognition: Power and Hazards of Representation in an Indonesian Society*. Berkeley: University of California Press.

———. 2007. *Christian Moderns: Freedom and Fetish in the Mission Encounter*. Berkeley: University of California Press.

———. 2008. "The Evidence of the Senses and the Materiality of Religion." In *The Objects of Evidence: Anthropological Approaches to the Production of Knowledge*, edited by M. Engelke, S110–S127. Special issue of the *Journal of the Royal Anthropological Institute*.

Kedit, Peter M. 1994. "Cultural Symposium II: An Agenda for Cultural Readaptation." Special Issue of the *Sarawak Museum Journal* 47 (68, Pt. I): 1–6.

Kedit, Peter, Aeries S. Jingan, D. Tsen, T. Chung, Heidi Munan, and Y. John. 1998. *150 Years of the Anglican Church in Borneo 1848-1998*. Kuching, Malaysia: Bishop of Kuching.

Keesing, Roger. 1989. "Creating the Past: Custom and Identity in the Contemporary Pacific." *The Contemporary Pacific* 1 (1&2): 19–42.

———. 1996. "Class, Culture, Custom." In *Melanesian Modernities*, edited by Jonathan Friedman and James G. Carrier, 162–182. Lund, Sweden: Lund University Press.

Keller, Eva. 2005. *The Road to Clarity: Seventh-Day Adventism in Madagascar*. New York, NY: Palgrave Macmillan.

Kempton, Wayne. 2008. Transcription of *Four Nurses in Borneo*. (n.d.) Tape recording. London: Society for the Propagation of the Gospel. http://anglicanhistory.org/asia/sarawak/four_nurses.

Kendall, Laurel. 2006. "When a Shaman Becomes a Cultural Icon, What Happens to Efficacy? Some Observations from Korea." In *Ritual and Identity: Performative Practices as Effective Transformations of Social Reality*, edited by Klaus-Peter Köpping, Bernhard Leistle, and Michael Rudolph, 195–218. Hamburg, Germany: LIT.

Keppel, Henry. 1846. *The Expedition to Borneo of H.M.S. Dido for the Suppression of Piracy. With Extracts from the Journal of James Brooke, Esq. of Sarawak*. London: Chapman and Hall.

Kessler, Clive. 1992. "Archaism and Modernity: Contemporary Malay Political Culture." In *Fragmented Vision: Culture and Politics in Contemporary Malaysia*, edited by Joel S. Kahn and Francis K. W. Loh, 133–157. Honolulu: University of Hawaii Press.

Keyes, Charles. 1993. "Why the Thai are Not Christians: Buddhist and Christian Conversion in Thailand." In *Conversion to Christianity: Historical and Anthropological Perspectives on a Great Transformation*, edited by Robert Hefner, 259–283. Berkeley: University of California Press.

———. 1996. "Being Protestant Christians in Southeast Asian Worlds." *Protestants and Tradition in Southeast Asia*, edited by Charles Keyes. Special Issue of the *Journal of Southeast Asian Studies* 27 (2): 280–292.

King, Victor T. 1988. "Models and Realities: Malaysian National Planning and East Malaysian Development Problems." *Modern Asian Studies* 22 (2): 263–298.

———. 1993. *The Peoples of Borneo*. Oxford: Blackwell.

King, Victor T., and William D. Wilder. 2003. *The Modern Anthropology of Southeast Asia: An Introduction*. London: RoutledgeCurzon.

Kiong, Frank. 2003. "Culture and Education." In *Creating a New Bidayuh Identity*, edited by James D. Mamit, Ahi A. Sarok, and Nicholas Amin, 55–62. Kuching, Malaysia: Dayak Bidayuh National Association.

Kipp, Rita S. 1993. *Disassociated Identities: Ethnicity, Religion, and Class in an Indonesian Society*. Ann Arbor: University of Michigan Press.

Kipp, Rita S., and Rodgers. 1987. "Introduction: Indonesian Religions in Society." In *Indonesian Religions in Transition*, edited by Rita S. Kipp and Susan Rodgers, 1–29. Tucson: University of Arizona Press.

Kirsch, Thomas G. 2004. "Restaging the Will to Believe: Religious Pluralism, Anti-Syncretism, and the Problem of Belief. *American Anthropologist* 106 (4): 699–709.

Koepping, Elizabeth. 2006. "Hunting with the Head: Borneo Villagers Negotiating Exclusivist Religion. *Studies in World Christianity* 12 (1): 59–78.

Kopytoff, Igor. 1986. "The Cultural Biography of Things: Commoditization as Process." In *The Social Life of Things: Commodities in Cultural Perspective*, edited by Arjun Appadurai, 64–91. Cambridge: Cambridge University Press.

Kortteinen, Timo. 2008. "Islamic Resurgence and the Ethnicization of the Malaysian State: The Case of Lina Joy." *Sojourn: Journal of Social Issues in Southeast Asia* 23 (2): 216–233.

Kreps, Christina. 2003. *Liberating Culture: Cross-Cultural Perspectives on Museums, Curation and Heritage Preservation*. London: Routledge.

Laidlaw, James. 2002. "For an Anthropology of Ethics and Freedom." *Journal of the Royal Anthropological Institute* 8 (2): 311–332.

Lampe, Frederick P. 2010. "The Anthropology of Christianity: Context, Contestation, Rupture, and Continuity." *Reviews in Anthropology* 39: 66–88.

Langub, Jayl. 1994. "The Role of the Majlis Adat Istiadat in the Preservation of the Adat of the Natives of Sarawak." *Sarawak Museum Journal* 47 (68): 7–16.

Latour, Bruno. 1993. *We Have Never Been Modern*, translated by Catherine Porter. London: Harvester Wheatsheaf.

Latrell, Craig T. 2008. "Exotic Dancing: Performing Tribal and Regional Identities in East Malaysia's Cultural Villages." *TDR: The Drama Review* 52 (4): 41–63.

Leach, Edmund. 1950. *Social Science Research in Sarawak*. London: H.M. Stationery Office.

———. 2001 [1966]. "Virgin Birth." In *The Essential Edmund Leach*, Vol. 2, edited by Stephen Hugh-Jones and James Laidlaw, 102–119. Yale: Yale University Press.

Leach, Edmund, and D. Alan Aycock. 1983. *Structuralist Interpretations of Biblical Myth*. Cambridge: Cambridge University Press.

Lees, Shirley. 1979. *Drunk Before Dawn*. Sevenoaks: OMF Books.

Leigh, Michael. 1974. *The Rising Moon: Political Change in Sarawak*. Sydney: Sydney University Press.

Lenhart, Lioba. 2003. "Orang Suku Laut Identity: The Construction of Ethnic Realities." In *Tribal Communities in the Malay World: Historical, Cultural and Social Perspectives*, edited by Geoffrey Benjamin and Cynthia Chou, 293–317. Singapore: Institute of East Asian Studies and Leiden: International Institute for Asian Studies.

Lindell, Pamela N. 2000. "The Longhouse and the Legacy of History: Religion, Architecture, and Change Among the Bisingai of Sarawak (Malaysia)." PhD diss., University of Nevada, Reno.

Lindstrom, Lamont. 1982. "Leftamap Kastom: The Political History of Tradition on Tanna, Vanuatu." In *Reinventing Traditional Culture: The Politics of Kastom in Island Melanesia*, edited by Roger Keesing and Robert Tonkinson. Special Issue of *Mankind* 13 (4): 316–329.

Linnekin, Jocelyn. 1983. "Defining Tradition: Variations on the Hawaiian Identity." *American Ethnologist* 10: 241–252.

———. 1991. "Cultural Invention and the Dilemma of Authenticity." *American Anthropologist* 93: 446–449.

———. 1992. "On the Theory and Politics of Cultural Construction in the Pacific." *Oceania* 62 (4): 249–263.

———. 1997. "Consuming Cultures: Tourism and the Commoditization of Cultural Identity in the Island Pacific." In *Tourism, Ethnicity and the State in Asian and Pacific Societies*, edited by Michel Picard and Robert E. Wood, 215–250. Honolulu: University of Hawaii Press.

Loh, Francis K. W. 1992. "Modernisation, Cultural Revival and Counter-Hegemony: The Kadazans of Sabah in the 1980s." In *Fragmented Vision: Culture and Politics in Contemporary Malaysia*, edited by Joel S. Kahn and Francis K. W. Loh, 225–253. Honolulu: University of Hawaii Press.

———. 2001. "Where Has (Ethnic) Politics Gone? The Case of the BN Non-Malay Politicians and Political Parties." In *The Politics of*

Multiculturalism: Pluralism and Citizenship in Malaysia, Singapore, and Indonesia, edited by Robert W. Hefner, 165–182. Honolulu: University of Hawaii Press.

Loh, Francis K. W., and Joel S. Kahn. 1992. "Introduction." In *Fragmented Vision: Culture and Politics in Contemporary Malaysia*, edited by Joel S. Kahn and Francis K. W. Loh, 1–17. Honolulu: University of Hawaii Press.

Luhrmann, Tanya. 2004. "Metakinesis: How God Becomes Intimate in Contemporary U.S. Christianity." *American Anthropologist* 106 (3): 518–528.

Mahathir bin Mohamad. 1970. *The Malay Dilemma*. Singapore: Asia Pacific Press.

———. 1991. "The Way Forward." Prime Minister's Office of Malaysia. http://www.pmo.gov.my/?menu=page&page=1904. Accessed June 25, 2009.

Mahmood, Saba. 2001. "Rehearsed Spontaneity and the Conventionality of Ritual: Disciplines of *Salat*." *American Ethnologist* 28 (4): 827–853.

Malinowski, Bronislaw. 1972 [1922]. *Argonauts of the Western Pacific*. London: Routledge and Kegan Paul.

Mamit, James D. 2003. "Cohesiveness Towards a Common Goal—A Knowledgeable and Progressive Community." In *Creating a New Bidayuh Identity*, edited by James D. Mamit, Ahi A. Sarok, and Nicholas Amin, 25–34. Kuching, Malaysia: Dayak Bidayuh National Association.

Mamit, James D., Ahi A. Sarok, and Nicholas Amin, eds. 2003. *Creating a New Bidayuh Identity*. Kuching, Malaysia: Dayak Bidayuh National Association.

Mandal, Sumit K. 2001. "Boundaries and Beyond: Whither the Cultural Bases of Political Community in Malaysia?" In *The Politics of Multiculturalism: Pluralism and Citizenship in Malaysia, Singapore, and Indonesia*, edited by Robert W. Hefner, 141–164. Honolulu: University of Hawaii Press.

Mashman, Valerie, and Patricia Nayoi. 2000. "Emblems for Identity: Ethnic Costume, Catholicism and Continuity: A Pinyawa'a Bidayuh Study at Kampong Gayu." In *Borneo 2000: Proceedings of the Sixth Biennial Borneo Research Conference*, edited by Michael Leigh, 223–249. Kota Samarahan, Malaysia: Institute of East Asian Studies.

Mauss, Marcel. 1985 [1938]. "A Category of the Human Mind: The Notion of Person, the Notion of Self." In *The Category of the Person*, edited by Michael Carrithers, Steven Collins, and Steven Lukes, 1–25. Cambridge: Cambridge University Press.

Maxwell, David. 2006. *African Gifts of the Spirit: Pentecostalism and the Rise of a Zimbabwean Transnational Religious Movement*. Oxford: James Currey.

Metcalf, Peter. 1991 [1982]. *A Borneo Journey into Death: Berawan Eschatology from its Rituals*. Kuala Lumpur, Malaysia: S. Abdul Majeed and Co.

———. 2002. *They Lie, We Lie: Getting on with Anthropology*. London: Routledge.

McDonald, Heather. 2001. *Blood, Bones and Spirit: Aboriginal Christianity in an East Kimberley Town*. New York, NY: Palgrave Macmillan.

McDougall, Debra. 2009. "Christianity, Relationality and the Material Limits of Individualism: Reflections on Robbins' *Becoming Sinners.*" *The Asia Pacific Journal of Anthropology* 10 (1): 1–19.

McWilliam, Andrew. 2006. "Historical Reflections on Customary Land Rights in Indonesia." *The Asia Pacific Journal of Anthropology* 7 (1): 45–64.

Meyer, Birgit. 1998. "'Make a Complete Break with the Past': Memory and Post-Colonial Modernity in Ghanaian Pentecostalist Discourse." *Journal of Religion in Africa* 28 (3): 316–349.

———. 1999. *Translating the Devil: Religion and Modernity Among the Ewe in Ghana.* Trenton, NJ: Africa World Press.

———. 2010. "Aesthetics of Persuasion: Global Christianity and Pentecostalism's Sensational Forms." *South Atlantic Quarterly* 109 (4): 741–763.

Milner, Anthony C. 1986. "Introduction to Malay Local History." *Journal of Southeast Asian Studies* 17 (1): 1–4.

———. 1995. *The Invention of Politics in Colonial Malaysia: Contesting Nationalism and the Expansion of the Public Sphere.* Cambridge: Cambridge University Press.

———. 1998. "Ideological Work in Constructing the Malay Majority." In *Making Majorities: Constituting the Nation in Japan, Korea, China, Malaysia, Fiji, Turkey, and the United States,* edited by Dru C. Gladney, 151–172. Stanford: Stanford University Press.

Minos, Peter. 2000. *The Future of Dayak Bidayuh in Malaysia.* Kuching, Malaysia: Lynch Media Services.

1847. "Mission to the Island of Borneo." *The Colonial Church Chronicle and Missionary Journal* I (1): 26–34. http://anglicanhistory.org/asia/sarawak/mission1847.html. Accessed August 29, 2011.

Mitchell, Jon P., and Hildi J. Mitchell. 2008. "For Belief: Embodiment and Immanence in Catholicism and Mormonism." *Social Analysis* 52 (1): 79–94.

Morgan, David. 2010a. "Introduction: The Matter of Belief." In *Religion and Material Culture: The Matter of Belief,* edited by David Morgan, 1–17. London: Routledge.

———, ed. 2010b. *Religion and Material Culture: The Matter of Belief.* London: Routledge.

Morris, H. Stephen. 1953. *Report on a Melanau Sago Producing Community in Sarawak.* London: H.M. Stationery Office.

Muhammad, Ikmal Said. 1992. "Ethnic Perspectives of the Left in Malaysia." In *Fragmented Vision: Culture and Politics in Contemporary Malaysia,* edited by Joel S. Kahn and Francis K. W. Loh, 254–281. Honolulu: University of Hawaii Press.

Munan, Heidi. 1989. *Sarawak Crafts: Methods, Materials and Motifs.* Singapore: Oxford University Press.

Mundy, Rodney N. 1848. *Narrative of Events in Borneo and Celebes Down to the Occupation of Labuan. From the Journals of James Brooke, Esq.* London: J. Murray.

Nagata, Judith. 1974. "What is a Malay? Situational Selection of Ethnic Identity in a Plural Society." *American Ethnologist* 1 (2): 331–350.

Nais, William. 1988. *Daya Bidayuh-English Dictionary*. Kuching, Malaysia: Persatuan Kesusasteraan Sarawak.

Noakes, J. L. 1950. *Sarawak and Brunei: A Report on the 1947 Population Census*. Kuching, Malaysia: Government Printer.

Noeb, Jonas, and Leo Mario Noeb. n.d. *Gawia Katang in Kupuo Opar 1993*. Unpublished manuscript.

Nuek, Patrick R. 2002. *A Dayak Bidayuh Community: Rituals, Ceremonies and Festivals*. Kuching, Malaysia: Lee Ming Press.

Ong, Susy. 2008. "Ethnic Chinese Religions: Some Recent Developments." In *Ethnic Chinese in Contemporary Indonesia*, edited by Leo Suryadinata, 97--116. Singapore: ISEAS Publications.

Ooi, Keat Gin 1991. "Mission Education in Sarawak During the Period of Brooke Rule 1840-1946." *Sarawak Museum Journal* 42 (63): 282–373.

———. 1997. *Of Free Trade and Native Interests: The Brookes and the Economic Development of Sarawak, 1841-1941*. Kuala Lumpur, Malaysia: Oxford University Press.

Ortner, Sherry B. 1995. "Resistance and the Problem of Ethnographic Refusal." *Comparative Studies in Society and History* 37 (1): 173–193.

Otto, Ton, and Poul Pedersen. 2005. "Disentangling Traditions: Culture, Agency and Power." In *Tradition and Agency: Tracing Cultural Continuity and Invention*, edited by Ton Otto and Poul Pedersen, 11–49. Aarhus, Denmark: Aarhus University Press.

Parmer, J. Norman. 1957. "Constitutional Change in Malaya's Plural Society." *Far Eastern Review* XXVI (10): 145–152.

Paul VI, Pope. 1965. *Pastoral Constitution on the Church in the Modern World. Gaudium et spes*. http://www.vatican.va/archive/hist_councils /ii_vatican_council/documents/vat-ii_cons_19651207_gaudium-et-spes_en.html. Accessed November 11, 2009.

Payne, Robert. 2004 [1960]. *The White Rajahs of Sarawak*. Shah Alam: Oxford University Press.

Peletz, Michael G. 2002. *Islamic Modern: Religious Courts and Cultural Politics in Malaysia*. Princeton: Princeton University Press.

Pelkmans, Mathijs. 2009. "Introduction: Post-Soviet Space and the Unexpected Turns of Religious Life." In *Conversion after Socialism: Disruptions, Modernisms and Technologies of Faith in the Former Soviet Union*, edited by Mathijs Pelkmans, 1–16. Oxford: Berghahn.

Pels, Peter. 1998. "The Spirit of Matter: On Fetish, Rarity, Fact and Fancy." In *Border Fetishisms: Material Objects in Unstable Spaces*, edited by Patricia Spyer, 91–121. London: Routledge.

Pemberton, John. 1994. *On the Subject of "Java"*. Ithaca: Cornell University Press.

Pina-Cabral, João de. 2009. "The All-or-Nothing Syndrome and the Human Condition." *Social Analysis* 53 (2): 163–176.

Postill, John. 2008. *Media and Nation building: How the Iban Became Malaysian.* New York, NY: Berghahn Books.

Pringle, Robert. 1970. *Rajahs and Rebels: The Ibans of Sarawak under Brooke Rule, 1841-1941.* London: Macmillan.

Rafael, Vincente. 1993. *Contracting Colonialism: Translation and Christian Conversion in Tagalog Society Under Early Spanish Rule.* Durham: Duke University Press.

Reece, Robert. 1982. *The Name of Brooke: The End of White Rajah Rule in Sarawak.* Kuala Lumpur, Malaysia: Oxford University Press.

———. 1998. *Masa Jepun: Sarawak under the Japanese 1941-1945.* Kuching, Malaysia: Sarawak Literary Society.

———. 2004. *The White Rajahs of Sarawak: A Borneo Dynasty.* Singapore: Archipelago Press.

Reid, Anthony D. 2001. "Understanding *Melayu* (Malay) as a Source of Diverse Modern Identities." *Journal of Southeast Asian Studies* 32 (3): 295–313.

Rensch, Calvin R., Carolyn M. Rensch, Jonas Noeb, and Robert S. Ridu. 2006. *The Bidayuh Language: Yesterday, Today and Tomorrow.* Kuching, Malaysia: Dayak Bidayuh National Association.

Ridu, Jacob. 2003. "Reflections of the Past and Capacity Building Towards the 21st Century." In *Creating a New Bidayuh Identity*, edited by James D. Mamit, Ahi A. Sarok, and Nicholas Amin, 15–24. Kuching, Malaysia: Dayak Bidayuh National Association.

Robbins, Joel. 2001a. "Introduction: Global Religions, Pacific Island Transformations." In *Charismatic and Pentecostal Christianity in Oceania*, edited by Joel Robbins, Pamela Stewart, and Andrew Strathern. Special issue of the *Journal of Ritual Studies* 15 (2): 7–12.

———. 2001b. "Secrecy and the Sense of an Ending: Narrative, Time, and Everyday Millenarianism in Papua New Guinea and in Christian Fundamentalism." *Comparative Studies in Society and History* 43 (3): 525–551.

———. 2003. "What is a Christian? Notes towards an Anthropology of Christianity." *Religion* 33: 191–199.

———. 2004. *Becoming Sinners: Christianity and Moral Torment in a Papua New Guinea Society.* Berkeley: University of California Press.

———. 2007. "Continuity Thinking and the problem of Christian culture: Belief, time, and the anthropology of Christianity." *Current Anthropology* 48 (1): 5–38.

Robbins, Joel, and Engelke, Matthew. 2010. "Introduction." In *Global Christianity, Global Critique*, edited by Matthew Engelke and Joel Robbins. Special Issue of *South Atlantic Quarterly* 109 (4): 623–631.

Rooney, John. 1981. *Khabar Gembira: A History of the Catholic Church in East Malaysia and Brunei (1880-1976).* London: Burns and Oates Ltd and Mill Hill Missionaries.

Rössler, Martin. 1997. "Islamization and the Reshaping of Identities in Rural South Sulawesi." In *Islam in an Era of Nation-States: Politics and*

Religious Revival in Muslim Southeast Asia, edited by Robert W. Hefner and Patricia Horvatich, 275–306. Honolulu: University of Hawaii Press.

Roth, Henry L. 1980 [1896]. *The Natives of Sarawak and British North Borneo.* 2 vols. Kuala Lumpur, Malaysia: University of Malaya Press.

Rousseau, Jerome. 1990. *Central Borneo: Ethnic Life and Social Life in a Stratified Society.* Oxford: Clarendon Press.

———. 1998. *Kayan Religion. Ritual Life and Religious Reform in Central Borneo.* Leiden: KITLV Press.

Rubenstein, Carol. 1991. "The Flying Silver Message Stick: Update 1985-86 on Long Songs Collected 1971-74." *Sarawak Museum Journal* 42 (63): 61–158.

Runciman, Stephen. 1960. *The White Rajahs: A History of Sarawak from 1841 to 1946.* Cambridge: Cambridge University Press.

Rustam A. Sani. 1994. "Aspirasi Sosio-budaya Bangsa Malaysia dari Perspektif Wawasan 2020." Special issue of the *Sarawak Museum Journal* 47 (68, Pt. I): 165–179.

Sahlins, Marshall. 1985. *Islands of History.* Chicago: University of Chicago Press.

———. 1996. "The Sadness of Sweetness: The Native Anthropology of Western Cosmology." *Current Anthropology* 37 (3): 395–428.

———. 1999. "Two or Three Things that I Know about Culture." *Journal of the Royal Anthropological Institute* 5: 399–421.

Sarok, Ahi A. 2003. "Introduction." In *Creating a New Bidayuh Identity,* edited by James D. Mamit, Ahi A. Sarok, and Nicholas Amin, 1–14. Kuching, Malaysia: Dayak Bidayuh National Association.

Sather, Clifford. 2004. "Adat." In *Southeast Asia: A Historical Encyclopedia, from Angkor Wat to East Timor,* edited by Ooi Keat Gin, 123–124. Santa Barbara: ABC-Clio.

Saunders, Graham. 1992. *Bishops and Brookes: The Anglican Mission and the Brooke Raj in Sarawak 1848-1941.* Singapore: Oxford University Press.

Schieffelin, Edward L. 1985. "Performance and the Cultural Construction of Reality." *American Ethnologist* 12 (4): 707–724.

Schiller, Anne. 1997. *Small Sacrifices: Religious Change and Cultural Identity among the Ngaju of Indonesia.* New York, NY: Oxford University Press.

Schineller, Peter. 1990. *A Handbook on Inculturation.* New York, NY: Paulist Press.

Schneider, Jane, and Shirley Lindenbaum. 1987. "Introduction: Frontiers of Christian Evangelism: Essays in Honor of Joyce Riegelhaupt." In *Frontiers of Christian Evangelism.* Special Issue of the *American Ethnologist* 14 (1): 1–8.

Schrauwers, Albert. 1998. "Returning to the 'origin': Church and State in the Ethnographies of the 'To Pamona'." In *Southeast Asian Identities: Culture and the Politics of Representation in Indonesia, Malaysia, Singapore, and Thailand,* edited by Joel Kahn, 203–226. Singapore: ISEAS, and London: I.B. Tauris.

Schreiter, Robert J. 1985. *Constructing Local Theologies*. London: SCM.

Schwarz, Carolyn, and Françoise Dussart, eds. 2010. *Christianity in Aboriginal Australia Revisited*. Special Issue of *The Australian Journal of Anthropology* 21 (1): 1–128.

Scott, James. 1985. *Weapons of the Weak: Everyday Forms of Peasant Resistance*. New Haven, CT: Yale University Press.

———. 1998. *Seeing Like a State: How Certain Schemes to Improve the Human Condition have Failed*. New Haven, CT: Yale University Press.

Scott, Michael. 2005. "'I was Like Abraham': Notes on the Anthropology of Christianity from the Solomon Islands." *Ethnos* 70 (1): 101–125.

———. 2007. *The Severed Snake: Matrilineages, Making Place, and Melanesian Christianity in Southeast Solomon Islands*. Durham, NC: Carolina Academic Press.

Shamsul Amri Baharuddin. 1997. "Identity Construction, Nation Formation, and Islamic Revivalism in Malaysia." In *Islam in an Era of Nation-States: Politics and Religious Revival in Muslim Southeast Asia*, edited by Robert W. Hefner and Patricia Horvatich, 207–227. Honolulu: University of Hawaii Press.

———. 1998. "Bureaucratic Management of Identity in a Modern State: 'Malayness' in Postwar Malaysia." In *Making Majorities: Constituting the Nation in Japan, Korea, China, Malaysia, Fiji, Turkey, and the United States*, edited by Dru C. Gladney, 135–150. Stanford: Stanford University Press.

———. 2001. "The Redefinition of Politics and the Transformation of Malaysian Pluralism." In *The Politics of Multiculturalism: Pluralism and Citizenship in Malaysia, Singapore, and Indonesia*, edited by Robert W. Hefner, 204–226. Honolulu: University of Hawaii Press.

———. 2004. "A History of an Identity, an Identity of a History: The Idea and Practice of 'Malayness' in Malaysia Reconsidered." In *Contesting Malayness: Malay Identity across Boundaries*, edited by Timothy P. Barnard, 135–148. Singapore: Singapore University Press.

Shorter, Aylward. 1989. *Toward a Theory of Inculturation*. Maryknoll, NY: Orbis Books.

Sidaway, David. 1969. "Influence of Christianity on Biatah-Speaking Land Dayaks." *Sarawak Museum Journal* 17 (34/5): 139–152.

Siddique, Sharon, and Leo Suryadinata. 1981. "Bumiputra and Pribumi: Economic Nationalism (Indiginism) in Malaysia and Indonesia." *Pacific Affairs* 54 (4): 662–687.

Siegel, James. 1986. *Solo in the New Order: Language and Hierarchy in an Indonesian City*. Princeton, NJ: Princeton University Press.

Skeat, Walter W. 1900. *Malay Magic: Being an Introduction to the Folklore and Popular Religion of the Malay Peninsula*. London: Macmillan.

Spencer, Jonathan. 1990. "Writing Within: Anthropology, Nationalism, and Culture in Sri Lanka. *Current Anthropology* 31 (3): 283–300.

Steedly, Mary M. 1999. "The State of Culture Theory in the Anthropology of Southeast Asia." *Annual Review of Anthropology* 28: 431–454.

St John, Spencer. 1974. [1862]. *Life in the Forests of the Far East.* 2 vols. Kuala Lumpur, Malaysia: Oxford University Press.

Strathern, Marilyn. 1987. "Out of Context: The Persuasive Fictions of Anthropology." *Current Anthropology* 28 (3): 251–281.

———. 1988. *The Gender of the Gift.* Berkeley: University of California Press.

———. 1990. "Artefacts of History: Events and the Interpretation of Images." In *Culture and History in the Pacific*, edited by Jukka Siikala, 24–44. Helsinki: The Finnish Anthropological Society, Transactions No. 27.

———. 1995. "Foreword." In *Shifting Contexts: Transformations in Anthropological Knowledge*, edited by Marilyn Strathern, 1–12. London: Routledge.

———. 2008. "Old and New Reflections." In *How Do We Know? Evidence, Ethnography, and the Making of Anthropological Knowledge*, edited by Liana Chua, Casey High, and Timm Lau, 20–35. Newcastle: Cambridge Scholars Publishing.

Stewart, Charles. 1999. "Syncretism and its Synonyms: Reflections on Cultural Mixture." *Diacritics* 29 (3): 40–62.

Stewart, Charles, and Rosalind Shaw, eds. 1994. *Syncretism/Anti-syncretism: The Politics of Religious Synthesis.* London: Routledge.

Swettenham, Frank. 1948. *British Malaya: An Account of the Origin and Progress of British Influence in Malaya.* London: Allen and Unwin.

Thomas, Nicholas. 1991. *Entangled Objects: Exchange, Material Culture and Colonialism in the Pacific.* Cambridge: Harvard University Press.

———. 1992. "The Inversion of Tradition." *American Ethnologist* 19 (2): 213–232.

T'ien Ju-Kang. 1950. *A Report on the Organisation of the Chinese Community in Sarawak.* Kuching, Malaysia: Government Printing Office.

Tobin, Jeffrey. 1994. "Cultural Construction and Native Nationalism: Report from the Hawaiian Front." *boundary 2* 21 (1): 111–133.

Tomlinson, Matt. 2009. *In God's Image: The Metaculture of Fijian Christianity.* Berkeley: University of California Press.

Tomlinson, Matt, and Matthew Engelke. 2006. "Meaning, Anthropology, Christianity." In *The Limits of Meaning: Case Studies in the Anthropology of Christianity*, edited by Matthew Engelke and Matt Tomlinson, 1–37. New York, NY: Berghahn Books.

Toren, Christina. 1988. "Making the Present, Revealing the Past: The Mutability and Continuity of Tradition as Process." *Man* (n.s.) 23: 696–717.

Tovey, Phillip. 2004. *Inculturation of Christian Worship: Exploring the Eucharist.* Aldershot: Ashgate.

Tsing, Anna L. 1993. *In the Realm of the Diamond Queen: Marginality in an Out-of-the-Way Place.* Princeton: Princeton University Press.

Turner, Terence. 1993. "Anthropology and Multiculturalism: What is Anthropology that Multiculturalists Should be Mindful of It?" *Cultural Anthropology* 8 (4): 411–429.

Turner, Victor 1967. *The Forest of Symbols: Aspects of Ndembu Ritual*. Ithaca: Cornell University Press.

Turner, Victor, and Edith Turner. 1978. *Image and Pilgrimage in Christian Culture: Anthropological Perspectives*. New York, NY: Columbia University Press.

Tylor, E. B. 1913 [1871]. *Primitive Culture*. London: Murray.

Van der Veer, Peter, ed. 1996. *Conversion to Modernities: The Globalization of Christianity*, edited by Peter van der Veer. London: Routledge.

Varney, Peter. 1968. "The Methodist Church in Sarawak and its Work Amongst the Iban from 1939 to 1968." Unpublished paper.

Vilaça, Aparecida. 1997. "Christians without Faith: Some Aspects of the Conversion of the Wari' (Pakaa Nova)." *Ethnos* 62 (1&2): 91–115.

Viveiros de Castro, Eduardo. 2003. *AND*. Manchester Papers in Social Anthropology No. 7. Manchester: Manchester University Press.

Volkman, Toby A. 1990. "Visions and Revisions: Toraja Culture and the Tourist Gaze." *American Anthropologist* 17 (1): 91–110.

Wadley, Reed, Angela Pashia, and Craig T. Palmer. 2006. "Religious Scepticism and its Social Context: An Analysis of Iban Shamanism." *Anthropological Forum* 16 (1): 41–54.

Wagner, Roy. 1981. *The Invention of Culture*. Chicago: University of Chicago Press.

Walker, John H. 2002. *Power and Prowess: The Origins of Brooke Kingship in Sarawak*. Crows Nest: Allen and Unwin, and Honolulu: University of Hawaii Press.

Watson, Charles W. 1996. "Reconstructing Malay Identity." *Anthropology Today* 12 (5): 10–14.

Weber, Max. 1956. *The Sociology of Religion*, translated by Ephraim Fischoff. Boston: Beacon Press.

———. 1958. *The Protestant Ethic and the Spirit of Capitalism*, translated by Talcott Parsons. New York, NY: Charles Scribner's Sons.

Westerwoudt, E. v. R. 2002 [1924]. *Felix Westerwoudt: Missioner in Borneo*, translated by T. W. Lefeber. Maryknoll, NY: Catholic Foreign Mission Society of America.

Whitehouse, Harvey. 2006. "Appropriated and Monolithic Christianity in Melanesia." In *The Anthropology of Christianity*, edited by Fenella Cannell, 295–307. Durham: Duke University Press.

Whitley, Angus, and Haslinda Amin. 2008. "Najib Backs Ending Malay Preferences, Adopting Opponent's View." *Bloomberg*, 24 October 2008. http://www.bloomberg.com.au/apps/news?pid=20601110&sid=aVMjn Z8s4vsU. Accessed June 26, 2009.

Winzeler, Robert. 1996. "Bidayuh Architecture: Tradition, Change, Revival." *Sarawak Museum Journal* 50 (71): 1–23.

———. 1997. "Modern Bidayuh Ethnicity and the Politics of Culture in Sarawak." In *Indigenous Peoples and the State*, edited by Robert Winzeler, 201–227. Yale Southeast Asia Monograph 46. New Haven: Yale University Press.

Wood, Peter. 1993. "Afterword: Boundaries and Horizons." In *Conversion to Christianity: Historical and Anthropological Perspectives on a Great Transformation*, edited by Robert Hefner, 305–321. Berkeley: University of California Press.

Yang, Heryanto. 2005. "The History and Legal Position of Confucianism in Postindependence Indonesia." *Marburg Journal of Religion* 10 (1): 1–8.

Zainal Kling. 1997. "*Adat*: Collective Self-image." In *Images of Malay-Indonesian Identity*, edited by Michael Hitchcock and Victor T. King, 45–51. Kuala Lumpur, Malaysia: Oxford University Press.

Index